Skills for RHETORIC

Student

Developing
Persuasive
Communication

James P. Stobaugh

First printing: May 2013
Third printing: May 2016

Master Books®, P.O. Box 726, Green Forest, AR 72638

Master Books® is a division of the New Leaf Publishing Group, Inc.

ISBN: 978-0-89051-710-9
ISBN: 978-1-61458-322-6 (ebook)
Library of Congress Catalog Number: 2013938352

Cover design by Diana Bogardus.
Interior design by Terry White.

Scripture quotations taken from The Holy Bible, New International Version®, Copyright © 1973, 1978, 1984, 2011 by Biblica, Inc.™ Used by permission of Zondervan, All rights reserved worldwide.

Please consider requesting that a copy of this volume be purchased by your local library system.

Printed in the United States of America

Please visit our website for other great titles:
www.masterbooks.com

For information regarding author interviews, please contact the publicity department at (870) 438-5288

Acknowledgments

I thank my four children and my distance learning students, including Chris Lloyd, Nick Concepcion, J.B. Ruutleman, Abigail Miller, Daniel McHenry, Marissa Lin, Hannah Huynh, Sarah Leavitt, Austin Allen, Zach Blackford, Daniel Greenidge, Alouette Greenidge, John Micah Braswell, Jonathan Knudsten, Sean Tracy, Laurel Fish, John Doughtery, Megan Norman, and Julia Pershe, who so graciously allowed me to use their essays. Finally, and most of all, I want to thank my best friend and lifelong editor, my wife, Karen.

"Come, let us glorify the Lord and praise His name forever . . ." (Psalm 34:3)

Master Books®
A Division of New Leaf Publishing Group
www.masterbooks.com

Contents

Using Your Student Textbook 4

Preface 5

1. Writing Task: Overview (Part One) 7
2. Writing Task: Overview (Part Two) 17
3. Writing Task: Eyewitness Account 27
4. Writing Skill: Firsthand Experience 35
5. Writing Skill: The Descriptive Essay 44
6. Writing Skill: Descriptive vs. Coercive Essay 52
7. Writing Skill: Persuasive Advertisement Essay 61
8. Writing Skill: Summary Report 69
9. Writing Skill: Précis 76
10. Writing Skill: The Character Profile 83
11. The General Analysis Essay 92
12. The General Synthesis Essay 101
13. Literary Analysis 111
14. Evaluation Essay 119
15. The Cause/Effect Essay 127
16. The Comparison/Contrast Essay 134
17. The Problem/Solution Essay 142
18. The Definition Essay 151
19. The Explanatory Essay 158
20. Fact, Inference, and Opinion 167
21. Historical Profile 174
22. Writing the Research Paper 183
23. Research Paper: Prewriting 189
24. Research Paper: Thesis Statement 198
25. Research Paper: Preliminary Bibliography and Works Cited Page 207
26. Research Paper: Taking Notes (Part One) 216
27. Research Paper: Taking Notes (Part Two) and Preliminary Outline 225
28. Research Paper: Designing a Working Plan 235
29. Research Paper: The Introduction (Part One) 242
30. Research Paper: The Introduction (Part Two) 251
31. Research Paper: The Body (Part One) 259
32. Research Paper: The Body (Part Two) 267
33. Research Paper: The Conclusion 277
34. Research Paper: Rewriting and Submission 286

Using Your Student Textbook

How this course has been developed:

1. **Chapters:** This course has 34 chapters (representing 34 weeks of study).

2. **Lessons:** Each chapter has four instructive lessons, taking approximately 45 to 60 minutes each, with an exam or writing assignment due on Friday.

3. **Grading:** Depending on the grading option chosen, the parent/educator will grade the daily concept builders, and the weekly tests and essays. Warm-ups are not meant to be evaluated for a grade since the content does not actually relate directly to the lesson.

4. **Course credit:** If a student has satisfactorily completed all assignments for this course, it is equivalent to one credit of writing and one credit of speech.

Throughout this course you will find the following:

1. **Chapter learning objectives:** Always read the "First Thoughts" and "Chapter Learning Objectives" in order to comprehend the scope of the material to be covered in a particular week.

2. **Concept builders:** Students should complete a daily concept builder Monday through Thursday. These activities take 15 minutes or less and emphasize a particular concept that is vital to that particular chapter topic. These will relate to a subject covered in the chapter, though not necessarily in that day's lesson. Answers are available in the teacher guide.

3. **Warm-ups:** Students should write or give oral responses for warm-ups to the parent/educator Monday through Thursday. These are not necessarily meant to be evaluated, but should stimulate discussion.

4. **Weekly essay tests:** Students will write one essay per week. These are available in the teacher guide and online.

5. **Daily prayer journal:** Students are encouraged to write in a prayer journal every day. A parent/educator may include this in the overall grade. If so, it is encouraged that the grade be based on participation rather than on the content, since this is a deeply personal expression of a student's walk with God.

6. **Final project/portfolio:** Students will correct and rewrite their weekly essays for their final portfolio.

7. **Research paper:** Starting in chapter 22, students will begin the process of preparing a research paper. This will be due at the end of the course.

What you will need each day:

1. A notepad or computer for your writing assignments.

2. A pen or pencil for taking notes and for essays.

3. A prayer journal so you can keep a record of your prayers and devotions.

4. Daily concept builders, weekly essays/speeches, and weekly essay tests and are available in the teacher guide.

Preface

The rise of relativism has had disastrous results. British historian Philip Johnson laments "the great vacuum" that has been filled with totalitarian regimes and facile thinking. Rhetoric ferrets out truth. If there is no truth, can there be any sense of authority? And can a society survive if there is no authority? Without a legitimate, honest, well-considered rhetoric, will history be reduced to the pleasure principle? Literary criticism, at least in the area of the written classics, forces us to dance with reality.

In some ways, American evangelical Christianity's loss of rhetorical skills — and I think rhetoric is akin to apologetics — has presaged disaster in many arenas. Without rhetoric, we Christians have no tools to engage modern culture. In some ways, we have lost mainline denominations to neo-orthodoxy, and we have lost universities to liberals. Where is a modern Jonathan Edwards? A modern C.S. Lewis? Good thinking and good talking may redeem the Church from both the overzealous and the skeptic. Rhetorical skills may help us regain the intellectual and spiritual high ground we so grievously surrendered without a fight.[1] George Marsden in *The Soul of the American University* and Leslie Newbigen in *Foolishness to the Greeks* both conclude that we Christians have conceded much of American culture to modernism by our inability to merge thought and communication in a clear thought and inspiration. We fail to persuade modernist culture. Without the main tool to do battle — rhetoric — evangelicals allow orthodoxy to be sacrificed on the altar of relativism.

In conclusion, *Skills for Rhetoric* is more than an English course: it is an attempt to equip you to participate in apologetics.

---

1   Alister McGrath, *Evangelicalism and the Future of Christianity* (Downers Grove, IL: InterVarsity Press, 1995).

Weekly Implementation Schedule — Suggestions

If you follow this schedule, you will get all your work done in a timely way.

1. **Have students write in a prayer journal at least three times/week.** Journal writing is one the best forms of reflection. The prayer journal should be a narrative of their spiritual journey. Encourage the entries to be mechanically correct, but the primary purpose is to pique creativity and spiritual formation. In *Skills for Rhetoric*, students are invited to journal through 1 and 2 Kings.

2. **Have students produce a Final Portfolio for Chapters 1–21;** the research paper will be added last. The Final Portfolio should include corrected essays, speeches, literary reviews, writing journal, vocabulary cards, pictures from field trips, and other pertinent material. In this teacher's edition, teachers will be prompted to engage students in progress discussions.

3. **Guide students through the research paper process in Chapters 22–34.** As students proceed through the process, teachers will be prompted on how to complete all requisite components of the research paper. At the end of each chapter, parent/educators will be prompted to engage students in progress discussions.

4. **Make sure students submit the Final Portfolio and complete the Research Paper.** The final portfolio should include corrected essays, speeches, literary reviews, writing journal, vocabulary cards, pictures from field trips, and other pertinent material. The research paper will include: a cover sheet, outline with thesis statement, the paper itself, a works cited (bibliography) page, and appropriate footnotes. Throughout the research process, you can collect and comment on the preliminary bibliography, preliminary outline with thesis statement, notes, revised outline, first draft with footnotes, rewrites, and works cited page. Working the research in stages tremendously aids the process for students, keeps parents/educators apprised of student progress and/or frustrations, and aids the final evaluation. Learning good strategies and techniques for research is a vital tool for future success in any writing program.

Vocabulary Concerns:

While there is no list of vocabulary words provided for students, each week students are expected to "review their vocabulary words daily." With this guidance, students are simply asked to note words that they do not recognize and to develop a means to expand their vocabularies. This can be as easy as writing out words and their dictionary meanings on 3 x 5 cards. When students meet a strange word for the first time, they should do their best to figure out the word in context, then look up the word in the dictionary.

Chapter 1

Style (Writing and Speaking): Components of Writing and Planning

Public Speaking Task: Types and Purposes of Speeches and The Outline

First Thoughts

The heart of *Skills for Rhetoric* is the notion of rhetoric, which is the ability to communicate effectively through the written and spoken word. Written and spoken are the crucial concepts of understanding rhetoric. Rhetoric is a discipline demanding that the writer dutifully follow rules of grammar, logic, and communication to explain, describe, and clarify.

Quality rhetoric is important and necessary. Greek philosophers proffered that a democracy demands a responsible, well-considered rhetoric. It is absolutely necessary that we participate in legitimate conversation about important issues. Rhetoric will help us do that.

Chapter Learning Objectives

In chapter 1 we examine the basic components of rhetoric: speaking and writing.

Look Ahead for Friday

- Turn in a final copy of essay and speech
- Take Weekly Essay/Test

Write a one or two-page essay of your choice or an essay on the topic "My Many Virtues." Next, underline the thesis statement, *italicize the introduction*, put in **bold letters the transitions**, and, finally, type/write the CONCLUSION IN CAPITAL LETTERS.

Emphasize the following elements of essays: starting point, purpose, form, audience, voice, and point of view.

This essay should include an outline with thesis statement, a rough draft, several revisions, a final copy, and five new (circled) vocabulary words. Your essay must pay particular attention to style (focus, content, organization).

Compose a one-minute speech on the topic "My Many Virtues" and present it in front of an audience like your family. Entice and earn your audience's interest with your introduction, fulfill the promise that you make in the introduction, and then present your audience with a final conclusion(s).

Rhetoric as Heart of Apologetics

Rhetoric is at the heart of apologetics, a systematic argumentative discourse in defense of Christianity. It is my prayer that these courses will ultimately prepare you to think apologetically.

To ignore rhetoric is to invite ourselves on a dangerous search for truth. Our mindless search for relevance and literalness has gotten us pretty lost in the cosmos. When something we seek is easily obtained by computer chip or digital photograph, then we lazily refuse to engage ourselves in the discipline of metaphor. For example, love is not easily photographed. Only the metaphor does it justice. Question: if we lose the written metaphor, will we also lose love? How can we understand 1 Corinthians 13 without first understanding metaphor? Metaphor, or comparison between two ostensibly dissimilar phenomena, is absolutely critical to understanding abstract theological concepts, and, for that matter, it is critical to creative problem solving.

The problems of this age demand a kind of thinking that is promoted and encouraged by rhetoric. The problems of this age will literally remain unsolved. However, rhetoric, through the power of metaphor, will invite this generation to look for more creative solutions. Immorality, for instance, will not be removed unless we look to the written Word, that is, the Bible, for answers. Nothing in our experience offers a solution. We will not understand the Bible unless we can employ metaphorical thinking. How else will we apply the Savior's ethical teachings spoken 2,000 years ago? Metaphor, along with other mysteries, has been victim of 20th-century pretension, pomposity, and obsequious thinking.

Loss of metaphor is only the beginning of the problem. Gertrude Himmelfarb, *On Looking into the Abyss*, laments that great literary works are no longer read — and if they are, there are no rules for interpreting them. In philosophy, indeed in all communication, truth and reality are considered relative. Without rules, the rhetorician is invited to come to any kind of conclusion and is on pretty shaky ground. Gordon Conwell's seminary professor David Wells, in *God in the Wastelands*, argues that evangelical Christians who believe in a personal relationship with God, as well as non-Christians, have both drunk from the trough of modernity. We have both embraced a sort of existential faith instead of a confessional faith. If it feels good, do it and believe it. Unless evangelicals participate in serious apologetics, God will be "weightless."

Daily Assignment

- Warm up: What is your favorite book? Why?
- Students will complete Concept Builder 1-A.
- Prayer journal: Students are encouraged to write in their prayer journal every day.
- Students should systematically review their vocabulary words daily.

Writing style concerns quality and substance, not content. Simple stated, style is the way you write. An effective style includes six components: focus, concreteness, vitality, originality, grace, and commitment.

Pre-writing Phase: The Thinking Game

Often called the brainstorming phase, the pre-writing phase is the time you decide what your topic is. What questions must you answer? You should articulate a thesis (a one-sentence statement of purpose for why you are writing about this topic. The thesis typically has two to four specific points contained within it). You should decide what sort of essay this is — for instance, a definition, an exposition, a persuasive argument — and then design a strategy. The first step is the thinking game. It is a technique to perform an in-depth brainstorm of your topic:

On a separate piece of paper, use this worksheet to begin an essay of your choice:

State issue in five sentences. State issue in two sentences. State issue in one sentence.

Name three or more subtopics of issue.

Name three or more subtopics of the subtopics.

What information must be known to solve the problem or to answer the question?

State the answer to the question/problem.

State issue in five sentences. State issue in two sentences. State issue in one sentence.

Once the question is answered/solved, What one or two new issues/answers may arise?

Style (Writing and Speaking): Overview

Who is the audience? What is the task? How can you bring your reader to a point of enlightenment? Are you trying to entertain? To inform? Both? Answers to these and other stylistic questions will focus your paper and move your reader to a desired conclusion or it will move your reader into a place of confusion. Is the focus clearly stated? To what audience is this essay written? Does it focus the reader or confuse the reader? Are your ideas totally relevant and fully developed? Finally, is your paper logically organized?

'Tis hard to say, if greater Want of Skill

Appear in Writing or in Judging ill,

But, of the two, less dang'rous is th' Offence,

To tire our Patience, than mislead our Sense:

Some few in that, but Numbers err in this,

Ten Censure wrong for one who Writes amiss;

A Fool might once himself alone expose,

Now One in Verse makes many more in Prose.[1]

Writing is indeed a task that requires skill.

---

1   *An Essay On Criticism* by Alexander Pope, With Introductory And Explanatory Notes. Go to www.gutenberg.org. type "Alexander Pope"

Daily Assignment

- Warm-up: Who is your favorite biblical character? Why?
- Students will complete Concept Builder 1-B.
- Prayer journal.
- Students should outline all assigned essays and speech for the week.

Pre-writing Phase: Thesis

A thesis statement:

- tells the reader how you will interpret the significance of the subject matter under discussion.

- tells the reader what to expect from the rest of the paper.

- directly answers the question asked of you. A thesis is an interpretation of a question or subject, not the subject itself.

- is usually a single sentence somewhere in your first paragraph that presents your argument to the reader. The rest of the paper, the body of the essay, gathers and organizes evidence that will persuade the reader of the logic of your interpretation. (www.unc.edu/depts/wcweb/handouts/thesis.html.)

Match the following thesis statement and its description.

b ___a___ The American Civil war was caused by many different reasons.

✗ ___d___ The American Civil War was no doubt the worst war ever fought!

a ___c___ While many antebellum issues like immigration and the reform movement added to the causes of the American Civil War, the main cause was slavery expansion.

c ___b___ You the reader will be surprised when I tell you about the causes of the American Civil War!

A. This is a very good thesis statement. It clearly states the purpose of this essay.

B. This statement merely restates the essay topic. It is too general.

C. The thesis does not invite speculation. It informs.

D. This statement is too general and, some would argue, inaccurate. The author of this essay is probably not credentialed to make such a broad generalization.

Writing Tips

Pre-writing Phase Often called the brainstorming phase, the pre-writing phase is the time you decide on exactly what your topic is. What questions must you answer? You should articulate a thesis (a one-sentence statement of purpose for why you are writing about this topic. The thesis typically has two to four specific points contained within it). You should decide what sort of essay this is—for instance, a definition, an exposition, a persuasive argument—and then design a strategy. For example, a clearly persuasive essay will demand that you state the issue and give your opinion in the opening paragraph.

Next, after a thesis statement, you will write an outline. *No matter what length the essay may be, 20 pages or one paragraph, you should create an outline.*

One of the best ways to organize your thoughts is to spend time in concentrated thinking, what some call brainstorming. Thinking through what you want to write is a way to narrow your topic.

Sample Outline

Persuasive Paper with Three Major Points (Arguments)

I.   Introduction: Thesis statement includes a listing or a summary of the three supportive arguments and introduces the paper.

II. Body

    A.   Argument 1 - Evidence (transition words or phrases or sentences to the next topic)

    B.   Argument 2 - Evidence (transition words or phrases or sentences to the next topic)

    C.   Argument 3 - Evidence (transition words or phrases or sentences to the conclusion)

III. Conclusion: Restatement of arguments and evidence used throughout the paper (do not use the words "in conclusion"—just conclude).

NOTE: For greater detail and explanation of outlining, refer to a composition handbook. Careful attention should be paid to parallel structure with words or phrases, to correct form with headings and subheadings, to punctuation, and to pairing of information. Correct outline structure will greatly enhance the writing of any paper.

Sample Outline

Expository Essay with Four Major Points

I.   Introduction: Thesis statement includes a listing or summary of four examples or supports and introduces the paper.

II. Body

    A.   Example 1 - Application (transition words or phrases or sentences to the next topic)

    B.   Example 2 - Application (transition words or phrases or sentences to the next topic)

    C.   Example 3 - Application (transition words or phrases or sentences to the next topic)

    D.   Example 4 - Application (transition words or phrases or sentences to the conclusion)

III. Conclusion: Restatement of thesis, drawing from the evidence or applications used in the paper (do not use the words "in conclusion"—just conclude).

NOTE: For greater detail and explanation of outlining, refer to a composition handbook. Careful attention should be paid to parallel structure with words or phrases, to correct form with headings and subheadings, to punctuation, and to pairing of information. Correct outline structure will greatly enhance the writing of any paper.

Writing Phase

Every essay has a beginning (introduction), a middle part (body), and an ending (conclusion). The introduction must draw the reader into the topic and usually presents the thesis to the reader. The body organizes the material and expounds on the thesis (a one-sentence statement of purpose) in a cogent and inspiring way. The conclusion generally is a solution to the problem or issue or question or is sometimes a summary. Paragraphs in the body are connected with transitional words or phrases: *furthermore, therefore, in spite of.* Another effective transition technique is to mention in the first sentence of a new paragraph a thought or word that occurs in the last sentence of the previous paragraph. In any event, the body should be intentionally organized to advance the purposes of the paper. A disciplined writer always writes a rough draft. Using the well-thought-out outline composed during the pre-writing phase is an excellent way to begin the actual writing. The paper has already been processed mentally and only lacks the writing.

Rewriting Phase

Despite however many rewrites are necessary, when the writer is satisfied that she has effectively communicated her subject, she is ready to write the final copy.

Daily Assignment

- Warm-up: Describe your favorite meal.
- Students will complete a daily Concept Builder.
- Prayer journal.
- Students should write rough drafts of all assigned essays and speech.

CONCEPT BUILDER 1-C

Building an Outline

Next, after a thesis statement, you will write an outline. No matter what length the essay may be, 20 pages or one paragraph, you should create an outline.

Why create an outline?

- Helps you organize your ideas
- Shows the relationships among ideas in your writing
- Defines the limit and purpose of your essay

How do I create an outline?

- Determine the purpose (thesis) of your paper.
- Determine the audience to whom you are writing.

Then:

- Organize: Group related ideas together. I give you two ways to do that in the following exercises.
- Order: Arrange material in subsections from general to specific or from abstract to concrete.

owl.english.purdue.edu/owl/

Remember: An outline is a critical, necessary step!

Create an outline on the topic "My Many Virtues:"

Public Speaking: Overview
Types and Purposes of Speeches
The Speech Outline

General Types of Speeches:

- Informative (didactic) speech,

- Impromptu (extemporaneous) speech,

- Persuasive speech

Every speech has a beginning, middle, and end. The beginning is called the introduction, the middle is called the body, and the end is called the conclusion. The main purpose of the introduction is to capture the reader's attention. The purpose of the body is to fulfill the promise given in the introduction, and the final thoughts in the speech bring a conclusion to the audience. The theme of the essay is reiterated. The body is normally two-thirds to three-fourths of the entire speech. A speech can include many points, but the speaker usually chooses to make one to three main points. Subordinate points support the main points, which likewise are backed by ample evidence.

In speech writing, as in essay writing, the outline is critical. The introduction normally includes a provocative statement or rhetorical question with supporting statements to propel the listener in the intended direction. As in essay writing, stating the thesis or purpose of the speech in the introduction is a necessity. Next, the body presents the many points with supporting details and argument. Finally, the conclusion restates the arguments, summarizes the points, and brings solution or conclusion.

Sample Speech

Introduction: (The thesis is underlined; the transition to the first body paragraph is also underlined.)

<u>Death and pretense are real entities with which we will all ultimately deal. Jesus really died on the cross.</u> This was not some metaphorical event or pretense or some dramatic hoax. No, He really died. Today, we have as much problem believing that Jesus died as we do that He arose from the grave. Our ever-present media promises us eternal bliss and immortality. Eat your vegetables, drink plenty of water, take these vitamins, exercise daily, and you will live forever. <u>Nowadays, we pretend death will not affect us, but it was not always so.</u>

[This introduction sets the tone, direction, and content for the reader. The reader knows to expect some commentary about death in general, about the death of Jesus, and something about pretense and understandings about death. Next, the body of the speech fulfills the expectations that the introduction has set up. Notice the points from the introduction.]

Body: (The speech's major points are highlighted in bold. The transitional sentences are underlined.)

<u>**Death** was something our parents and grandparents had to face with more finality and frequency, perhaps, than we do.</u> The average life span was lower than it is now. **Medical science** was not as successful as it is now in saving human life. Infant mortality was higher. Since there were fewer hospitals and no nursing homes, sick and dying relatives died at home. It was the custom years ago for the "wake" to be held in the family's living room, followed by the burial of the dead in a local church cemetery. When our grandparents went to

church on Sundays, they were reminded of the reality of death as they passed the marble grave markers of their loved ones. Death was always present in one form or another. <u>There is another death that was significant then, as it is now.</u>

Conclusion: (The final thoughts in this speech excerpt bring the audience a conclusion. The theme of death, with its surrounding attitudes of pretense or reality, is reiterated).

Jesus Christ died on the cross. He was not pretending. There was no magic trick. He was really dead—really dead. He did not die quietly in bed with all His friends surrounding Him. No, He died a humiliating, messy, public death. In other words, until the women visited the tomb, one thing was certain on this first Easter morning: Jesus bar Joseph was very, very dead. That explains why, at first, the disciples did not believe these women who had been sent to them specifically by Jesus. If you had watched the Lord die on a cross two days previously, would you have believed them? In this tangible world, death and dying are not mere pretense. It is into the world of reality, of death and dying, that the early disciples—and you and I—are invited to enter by the Apostle Paul.

Daily Assignment

- Warm-up: Who is your best friend and why?
- Students will complete Concept Builder 1-D.
- Prayer journal.
- Review the assigned text. Keep vocabulary cards.
- This is the day that students should write, and then rewrite, the final drafts of their assigned essay and speech.

CONCEPT
BUILDER
1-D

Top Ten Most Frequent Essay Problems

1. Agreement between the Subject and Verb: Use singular forms of verbs with singular subjects and use plural forms of verbs with plural subjects.

   WRONG: Everyone finished their homework.

   RIGHT: Everyone finished his homework (*Everyone* is an indefinite singular pronoun.)

2. Using the Second-Person Pronoun — "you," "your" should rarely, if ever, be used in a formal essay.

   WRONG: You know what I mean (Too informal).

3. Redundancy: Never use "I think" or "It seems to me"

   WRONG: I think that is true.

   RIGHT: That is true (We know you think it, or you would not write it!)

4. Tense consistency: Use the same tense (usually present) throughout the paper.

   WRONG: I was ready to go, but my friend is tired.

   RIGHT: I am ready to go, but my friend is tired.

5. Misplaced Modifiers: Place the phrase or clause close to its modifier.

   WRONG: The man drove the car with a bright smile into the garage.

   RIGHT: The man with a bright smile drove the car into the garage.

6. Antecedent Pronoun Problems: Make sure pronouns match (agree) in number and gender with their antecedents.

   WRONG: Mary and Susan both enjoyed her dinner.

   RIGHT: Mary and Susan both enjoyed their dinners.

7. Parallelism: Make certain that your list/sentence includes similar phrase types.

   WRONG: I like to take a walk and swimming.

   RIGHT: I like walking and swimming

8. Affect vs. Effect: Affect is a verb; Effect is a noun unless it means to achieve.

   WRONG: His mood effects me negatively.

   RIGHT: His mood affects me negatively.

   RIGHT: The effects of his mood are devastating.

9. Dangling Prepositions: Rarely end a sentence with an unmodified preposition.

   WRONG: Who were you speaking to?

   RIGHT: To whom were you speaking?

10. Transitions: Make certain that paragraphs are connected with transitions (e.g., furthermore, therefore, in spite of).

   RIGHT: Furthermore, Jack London loves to describe animal behavior.

Problem Sentence	Problem #	Correct Sentence
I believe that Nazi Germany started World War II.	3	Nazi Germany started World War II.
Hitler attacked Stalin in 1941; he destroyed most of Russia's military.	10	Hitler attacked Stalin in July, therefore he destroyed most of Russias military
The German army attacked on July 22, 1941, but the Russian army is not ready.	4	The German army attacked on July 22, 1941, but the Russian army was not ready
The German soldier attacked the railroad station with a black SS uniform.	5	The German soldier with the black ss uniform attacked the railroad station
The surprise attack completely affected the outcome of the first year of fighting.	8	The surprise attack completely affected the outcome of the first year of fighting
The German army loved to fight and overwhelming its enemies.	7	The German army loved fighting and overwhelming its enemies
You should know that Germany almost captured Moscow in 1941.	2	Germany almost captured Moscow in 1941
Every soldier finished their tour of duty.	1	Every soldier finished his tour of duty.
Hitler and his generals enjoyed his victories.	6	Hitler and his generals enjoyed their victories
Ultimately the German army won the Kiev campaign because they tried to.	9	Ultimately because they tried to the German army won the Kiev campaign

Writing Task: Overview (Part Two)

Chapter 2

Style (Writing and Speaking): Paragraph - Topic Sentence/Thesis

Public Speaking Task: Selecting your Topic, Researching Your Topic, and Knowing your Audience

First Thoughts

As you write, it is imperative that you know the purpose of your essay and that you have identified your audience. Why are you writing this essay? Who will read what you write? What expectations do you bring to this paper? What expectations do your readers bring?

The purpose of your essay will probably fall into four categories: persuasive, expository, descriptive, and narrative. Persuasive essays argue a point. Descriptive essays describe a person, place, or thing. Expository essays give information and explain. Narratives are stories.

When you think about your audience, ask yourself these questions: What prejudices exist in your audience? What is the age range of your audience? Background? Are they friends? Enemies? Who are they? What terms must you define to prevent misunderstanding and to fully inform the audience of what you mean when you use a particular word or set of words? Will you need to write in a formal or informal style?

Chapter Learning Objectives

In chapter 2 we continue to examine the basic components of rhetoric: speaking and writing.

Look Ahead for Friday

- Turn in a final copy of essay and speech
- Take Weekly Essay/Test

Write two 75-word essays on the topic, "The importance of finishing my chores before I go to soccer/ballet/practice." The first essay is written for your team. The second essay is written for your parents. Write as precisely as possible. This essay should include an outline with thesis, rough draft, final copy containing five new (circled) vocabulary words, and cue cards (index cards). Give a copy to instructor/parent to evaluate.

Prepare and then present one speech for two audiences on the topic, "The importance of finishing my chores before I go to soccer/ballet/practice." The first speech is presented to your team. The second speech is presented to your parents. Speech preparation includes an outline with thesis, rough draft, final copy containing five new (circled) vocabulary words, and cue cards (index cards), oral practice for speech delivery. Give a copy to instructor/parent to evaluate.

Final Project

Correct and rewrite all essays and place them in your Final Portfolio.

Summary

Often you want to write what others have written, actually what you have read. In fact, you will be influenced by whatever you have read about your topic and may even be writing about what you read, but you need to develop your own writing style; you need to write your own stories. As one scholar explains, "The best writers tend to be people with something on their minds that they want to get off, curious people who want to discover things, or think things through, and tell what they have come up with." You choose, or you are given, a subject — soccer. Then, you choose, or you are given, a topic — defensive tactics. The biggest challenge for most writers is in limiting — not broadening — the topic (see the discussion on the Thinking Game from Lesson 1). The thesis and outline help you limit your topic and organize it into a paper. Finally, you must ask yourself, "What tone do I want to exhibit in this paper?" If you are writing a paper discussing your brother's bedroom, you can afford to be whimsical and humorous. On the other hand, if you are writing a paper on the Holocaust, your tone will be somber and serious.

In summary, follow these steps:

1. Choose your subject and topic. Decide on the purpose of your essay.
2. Identify your audience. Adapt your topic to your audience.
3. Read, research, and then create a thesis statement and an outline.
4. Write your essay, carefully following your thesis and outline. Every essay has an introduction, a body, and a conclusion.
5. Use transitions between each paragraph.
6. Revise your essay as many times as necessary.

Daily Assignment

- Warm-up: How do you eat pizza and why?
- Students will complete Concept Builder 2-A.
- Prayer journal: Students are encouraged to write in their prayer journal every day.
- Students should systematically review their vocabulary words daily.

Identifying Paragraphs I

You should organize your sentences into groups of related ideas, or paragraphs. Each paragraph should have a main idea or topic sentence. Next, the body of the paragraph develops the main idea with supporting facts Finally, a new paragraph begins when the scene or topic changes.

In the following essay on George Herbert's poem "The Collar," mark with this symbol ¶ where each new paragraph begins.

The struggle is daily. There are choices we make, people we talk to, and sights that we see. This all is unavoidable, and goes on outside of us but mostly inside. This struggle forces us to choose between the hard way of the cross, or the easy broad path leading to destruction. George Herbert (1593-1633) one of the 17th century poets, wrote a beautiful poem titled, "The Collar." This poem is written in the first person about himself, and not only identifies the struggle between good and evil, but in it he also faces the struggle, and in the end, he wins. The poem begins with the words, "I struck the board, and cried, "no more! I will abroad." Here Herbert is fearfully running away from God and telling him that "no more," and to leave him alone. He knows that he has been given free will, "My lines and life are free; free as the road, loose as the wind, as large as store." But he is not sure he wants to use it, "Shall I still be in suit?" Next, he begins to struggle with what he has lost, "Have I no harvest but a thorn to let me blood, and not restore what I have lost with cordial fruit? Is the year only lost to me? Have I no bays to crown it? No flowers no garlands gay? All blasted? All wasted?" But telling himself that, that cannot be all, "Not so, my heart; but there is fruit, and thou hast hands," he begins to calm down, and see what he has really been given. Then the struggle changes, from being a struggle between running away or staying and becoming having to let go. "Leave thy cold dispute of what is fit and not; forsake thy cage, thy rope of sands, which petty thoughts have made." Here Herbert writes beautiful examples of how we are often tied up in things that we think are important. But in reality if we shake them off, we find that they are of no use to us at all. He goes on to say, "tie up thy fears," which is another example of leaving behind something that we do not need and cannot enter the Kingdom with. The poem ends very simply in submission, "Me thoughts I heard one calling, "Child;" and I replied, "my Lord"" At that point there is no struggle, he is at complete peace. Leaving behind the struggle to immerse oneself in complete submission, is an idea at which some people would laugh. But not George Herbert. When he wrote this poem, he knew that it was a beautiful action. And so it has been captured onto paper, for all of us (Anna).

Style (Writing and Speaking): Paragraphs/Topic Sentence/Thesis Statement

Paragraphs are more than a bunch of connected sentences. They are the building blocks of the prose essay. They are the core of the essay. No matter how effective words and sentences may be, they fail to communicate without the effective creation of paragraphs.

You have already heard about the thesis statement, and you will review this concept when you study the research paper later in this course. The thesis is a one-sentence statement of the overall projection of the paper; it is in the introductory paragraph of the essay and is clearly observable. Similar to a map for a traveler, the thesis statement provides direction for your reader.

Paragraphs in a paper are not merely random thoughts of prose; they are integrated units of thought, all of which hover around the thesis statement. They are rockets aimed toward a target. Every paragraph in the paper can be predicted from a carefully planned thesis statement and a well-constructed outline.

Every paragraph has a topic sentence that is related to the thesis statement. In a sense, the topic sentence of each paragraph can be considered the thesis statement of the paragraph. The thesis statement, however, has a more universal application. It is the one-sentence purpose of the much larger prose piece — the essay — where as the topic sentence is the one-sentence purpose of the paragraph.

Some writers prefer to introduce their essays by having the thesis statement occur at the beginning of the paragraph. Others place it at the end of the introductory paragraph where it can also serve as the transition into the first body paragraph.

The thesis statements or topic sentences of the following paragraphs are underlined.

<u>In "The Pardoner's Tale" Chaucer uses personification and irony to make a point about hypocrisy.</u> He subtly but effectively implies that hypocrisy is the gravest sin. His implication is accomplished through the character of the pardoner, who is the personification of the sins he condemns.

Often a writer will begin a paragraph with a rhetorical question — a question whose answer is obvious or a question whose answer is in the question. Some writers also use a "topic question" to introduce the question they will be exploring in the paper.

<u>How does Chaucer discuss hypocrisy in "The Pardoner's Tale"?</u> He subtly but effectively implies that hypocrisy is the gravest sin. His implication is accomplished through the character of the pardoner, who is the personification of the sins he condemns. In "The Pardoner's Tale" Chaucer uses personification and irony to make a point about hypocrisy.

In any event, every paragraph has a topic sentence and every essay has a thesis statement.

Daily Assignment

- Warm-up: What is gravity?
- Students will complete Concept Builder 2-B.
- Prayer journal.
- Students should outline all assigned essays and speech for the week.

Identifying Topic Sentences

A topic sentence expresses the main idea or purpose of a paragraph. All the other sentences in the paragraph support that main idea. Underline the topic sentences in the following essay.

The Lost Tools of Learning

Dorothy Sayers

That I, whose experience of teaching is extremely limited, should presume to discuss education is a matter, surely, that calls for no apology. It is a kind of behavior to which the present climate of opinion is wholly favorable. Bishops air their opinions about economics; biologists, about metaphysics; inorganic chemists, about theology; the most irrelevant people are appointed to highly technical ministries; and plain, blunt men write to the papers to say that Epstein and Picasso do not know how to draw. Up to a certain point, and provided that the criticisms are made with a reasonable modesty, these activities are commendable. Too much specialization is not a good thing. There is also one excellent reason why the veriest amateur may feel entitled to have an opinion about education. For if we are not all professional teachers, we have all, at some time or another, been taught. Even if we learnt nothing — perhaps in particular if we learnt nothing — our contribution to the discussion may have a potential value.

However, it is in the highest degree improbable that the reforms I propose will ever be carried into effect. Neither the parents, nor the training colleges, nor the examination boards, nor the boards of governors, nor the ministries of education, would countenance them for a moment. For they amount to this: that if we are to produce a society of educated people, fitted to preserve their intellectual freedom amid the complex pressures of our modern society, we must turn back the wheel of progress some four or five hundred years, to the point at which education began to lose sight of its true object, towards the end of the Middle Ages. . .

When we think about the remarkably early age at which the young men went up to university in, let us say, Tudor times, and thereafter were held fit to assume responsibility for the conduct of their own affairs, are we altogether comfortable about that artificial prolongation of intellectual childhood and adolescence into the years of physical maturity which is so marked in our own day? To postpone the acceptance of responsibility to a late date brings with it a number of psychological complications which, while they may interest the psychiatrist, are scarcely beneficial either to the individual or to society. The stock argument in favor of postponing the school-leaving age and prolonging the period of education generally is there is now so much more to learn than there was in the Middle Ages. This is partly true, but not wholly. The modern boy and girl are certainly taught more subjects — but does that always mean that they actually know more?

www.gbt.org/text/sayers.html

Public Speaking: Overview
Selecting and Researching Your Topic
and Knowing Your Audience

The following is the body of a speech presented to a group of young people. The speaker is discussing the importance of taking a stand for Christ in a hostile culture:

There are four key issues that must be settled in your mind:

Identity: Who am I?

Responsibility: What will I do with my life?

Priority: What is really most important to me?

Commitment: How much am I willing to commit?

First, as you begin a new phase of your life, make sure you know who you are and who your God is. "By faith Moses, when he had grown up, refused to be called the son of Pharaoh's daughter" (Hebrews 11:24). He refuses and then chooses. You are a special child. Much loved. You live among a people who do not know who they are. A people without hope. A people who do not know they are loved.

We live in a dysfunctional, dying culture. In *The Aeneid,* Virgil describes our world:

O happy men, thrice happy, four times happy,
Who had the luck to die, with their fathers watching
Below the walls of Troy! (lines 94–96)

But they will look to you to lead them. . . .

Sometimes in a great nation, there are riots,
With the rabble out of hand, and firebrands fly
And cobblestones: whatever they lay their hands on
Is a weapon for their fury, but should they see
One man of noble presence, they fall silent. . . . (lines 148–156)[1]

The Christian teacher Os Guinness encourages Christians with the fact that Americans in the near future will be looking to places of stability and strength for direction. By default, those people whose lives are in reasonably good shape, who have some reason to live beyond the next paycheck, will have almost an inexorable appeal. Like Aeneas in Virgil's *Aeneid,* people will all,

someday after the storm, be thrown on somebody's beach. I hope you will show more discernment than Dido!

Second, Moses accepts responsibility for his life. He "chose to suffer with the people of God rather than to enjoy the short-lived pleasure of sin" (Heb. 11:25). You will be persecuted because you will join the stream of faith that believes Christ is the Way, the Truth, and the Life. This is about responsibility. You will have to be responsible for the call that God places in your life. One of the greatest problems in this generation is confusion about individual responsibility.

Third, you will need to decide fairly soon what is important and valuable in your life, or others will do it for you. You need a cause worth dying for (as well as living for). "For he [Moses] considered the reproach because of the Messiah to be greater wealth than the treasures of Egypt, since his attention was on the reward" (Heb. 11:26). You must exhibit the faith and courage of the three teenagers in Daniel 3:14–18:

Nebuchadnezzar asked them, "Shadrach, Meshach, and Abednego, is it true that you don't serve my gods or worship the gold statue I have set up? Now if you're ready, when you hear the sound of the horn, flute, zither, lyre, harp, drum, and every kind of music, fall down and worship the statue I made. But if you don't worship it, you will immediately be thrown into a furnace of blazing fire — and who is the god who can rescue you from my power?"

Shadrach, Meshach, and Abednego replied to the king, "Nebuchadnezzar, we don't need to give you an answer to this question. If the God we serve exists, then He can rescue us from the furnace of blazing fire, and He can rescue us from the power of you, the king. But even if He does not rescue us, we want you as king to know that we will not serve your gods or worship the gold statue you set up."

---

1   classics.mit.edu/Virgil/aeneid.html.

Finally, you must never take your eyes off the goal. "By faith he left Egypt behind, not being afraid of the king's anger, for Moses persevered, as one who sees Him who is invisible" (Heb. 11:27). How long can you wait? How long can you persevere? The artisans who built the great European cathedrals built them without hope of seeing the completion of the work or, for that matter, without knowing if the work would be completed. However, the artisans were hopeful that technology would be available in the next generation to accomplish the necessary tasks, and that the next generation would have the energy to do the task.

You must have hope. As John Milton in *Paradise Lost* writes:

> A mind not to be chang'd by place or time.
> The mind is its own place, and in itself
> Can make a heaven of hell, a hell of heaven.
> (line 253)

> Here we may reign secure; and in my choice
> To reign is worth ambition, though in hell:
> Better to reign in hell than serve in heaven.
> (line 261)

Daily Assignment

- Warm-up: Why is it cold in Alaska in November?
- Students will complete Concept Builder 2-C.
- Prayer journal.
- Students should write rough drafts of all assigned essays and speech.

CONCEPT BUILDER 2-C

Introduction

The introduction is the broad beginning of the essay that answers three important questions:

1. What is this?
2. Why am I reading it?
3. What argument/position do you want me to accept?

You should answer these questions by doing the following:

1. **Set the context** – provide general information about the main idea, explaining the situation so the reader can make sense of the topic and the claims you make and support. Restate the question and answer it.
2. **State why the main idea is important** – tell the reader why s/he should care and keep reading. Your goal is to create a compelling, clear, and convincing essay the reader will want to read and act upon.
3. **State your thesis/claim** – compose a sentence or two stating the position you will support with logos (sound reasoning: induction, deduction), pathos (balanced emotional appeal), and ethos (author credibility). (owl. english.purdue.edu/owl/)

In summary, all information discussed in the essay is presented in the introduction. No new arguments may be added after the introduction is created. Don't surprise your reader! Presume nothing. Explain everything.

Two Ineffective Introductions

1. The Broad Generalization — When you don't have much to say on a given topic, it is easy to create this kind of introduction. Essentially, this kind of weaker introduction contains several sentences that are vague and don't really say much.
2. The Webster's Dictionary introduction. Dictionary introductions are also ineffective simply because they are so overused.

Choose the best introduction for this essay.

Be Prepared

A Girl Scout learns to swim, not only as an athletic accomplishment, but so that she can save life. She passes her simple tests in child care and home nursing and household efficiency in order to be ready for the big duties when they come. She learns the important facts about her body, so as to keep it the fine machine it was meant to be. And she makes a special point of woodcraft and camp lore, not only for the fun and satisfaction they bring, in themselves, but because they are the best emergency course we have today. A Girl Scout who has passed her First Class test is as ready to help herself, her home and her country as any girl of her age should be expected to prove.

The Slogan: "Do a Good Turn Daily"

This simple recipe for making a very little girl perform every day some slight act of kindness for somebody else is the seed from which grows the larger plant of helping the world along the steady attitude of the older Scout. And this grows later into the great tree of organized, practical community service for the grown Scout — the ideal of every American woman today.

The Pledge:

> "I pledge allegiance to my flag, and to the
> Republic for which it stands; one nation
> indivisible, with liberty and justice for all."

This pledge, though not original with the Girl Scouts, expresses in every phrase their principles and practice. Practical patriotism, in war and peace, is the cornerstone of the organization. A Girl Scout not only knows how to make her flag, and how to fly it; she knows how to respect it and is taught how to spread its great lesson of democracy. Many races, many religions, many classes of society have tested the Girl Scout plan and found that it has something fascinating and helpful in it for every type of young girl.

This broad democracy is American in every sense of the word; and the Patrol System, which is the keynote of the organization, by which eight girls of about the same age and interests elect their Patrol Leader and practice local self-government in every meeting, carries out American ideals in practical detail. (*Official Handbook Of The Girl Scouts*)

A	Colleges are offering training in scouting as a serious course for prospective officers, and prominent citizens in every part of the country are identifying themselves with the Local Councils, in an advisory and helpful capacity.
B	The first National Convention was held in 1915, and each succeeding year has shown a larger and more enthusiastic body of delegates and a public more and more interested in this steadily growing army of girls and young women who are learning in the happiest way how to combine patriotism, outdoor activities of every kind, skill in every branch of domestic science and high standards of community service.
C	At the heart of scouting is character building and patriotism. Scouting prepares young women to be good citizens and productive leaders in the years ahead.

Speech Writing

How do speech writers accomplish their task of speech writing? Speech writing is very similar to essay writing: select the topic, decide on the purpose, identify the audience, read and research, consider the direction of the speech, outline the points to be made, and conclude the points of the speech. The topic is usually dictated by the circumstances or demands of the occasion; it should be sufficiently focused to be manageable but sufficiently broad to be comprehensive. Decide exactly what is to be accomplished with the speech. Since you are not merely giving your speech to an empty room, you must know what kind of people will be hearing what you say, how many there will be, and where you will be presenting the speech. Effective speeches are written on a specific topic to a specific audience in a specific place.

Next, gather material for your speech through reading and researching. A speech is not an essay, but it is a well-constructed, grammatically correct oral presentation based on a written manuscript (unless it is an impromptu/extemporaneous speech).

The topic will power your search for information. If your speech requires technical information, you will need to consult books, periodicals, and perhaps even Internet sources. In some cases, you will need to interview specialists in the field of the topic. Once you find your sources, be very careful to give the source credit in your speech. When you utilize outside sources in your speech, imagine that the authors of these sources are in the audience. Will they know that you are giving them credit?

Finally, quoting a source is only half the battle — you must also understand the source. Often speech writers will present quotes that they really don't understand, thereby giving false impressions or even false information. Be certain that you understand a quote or statement before you present it to an audience; be very careful not to take it out of context and make it mean something that the original author did not mean. If you are confused by what you say, you can be certain that your audience will be doubly confused.

Daily Assignment

- Warm-up: Why is it cool in Australia in July?
- Students will complete Concept Builder 2-D.
- Prayer journal.
- Review the assigned text. Keep vocabulary cards.
- This is the day that students should write, and then rewrite, the final drafts of their assigned essay and speech.

The Conclusion

In a general way, your conclusion will:

- restate your topic and show why it is important
- restate your thesis/claim

Remember that once you accomplish these tasks you are finished. Done. Don't try to bring in new points or end with a sermon. Stay focused! Stay on task! Finish with confident humility.

Choose the best conclusion for this essay.

If there is anything that we all enjoy, it is waking up on a bright spring morning and seeing the sunlight pouring into the room. You all know the poem beginning:

"I remember, I remember
The house where I was born;
The little window where the sun
Came peeping in at morn."

You are feeling fresh and rested and happy after your good night's sleep and you are eager to be up and out among the birds and the flowers. You are perfectly right in being glad to say "Good morning" to the sun, for he is one of the best friends you have. Doesn't he make the flowers blossom, and the trees grow? And he makes the apples redden, too, and the wheat-ears fill out, and the potatoes grow under the ground, and the peas and beans and melons and strawberries and raspberries above it. All these things that feed you and keep you healthy are grown by the heat of the sun. So if it were not for the sunlight we should all starve to death.

A	In conclusion, if you want to be a very productive Christian, you should begin the day with joy in your heart!
B	So you see that Nature is guiding you in the right direction when she makes you love and delight in the bright, warm, golden sunlight; for it is one of the very best friends that you have — indeed, you couldn't possibly live without it.
C	When you are really awake and have had a good look to see what kind of morning it is, you will feel like yawning and stretching, and rubbing your eyes four or five times, before you jump out of bed; and it is a good plan to take plenty of time to do this, unless you are already late for breakfast or school.

Woods Hutchinson, M.D., *The Child's Day* (Boston, MA: Houghton Mifflin Company, 1912

Writing Task: Eyewitness Account

Chapter 3

Style (Writing and Speaking): Paragraph - Introduction

Public Speaking Skill: The Speech Introduction and Converting the Eyewitness Account to a Speech

First Thoughts

An eyewitness account is an essay that attempts to recreate an event as it actually happened. Using powerful imagery and precise language, the eyewitness account recreates an event in precise language. The reader vicariously experiences the described event.

Chapter Learning Objectives

In chapter 3 we learn how to write and then rewrite an eyewitness account.

Look Ahead for Friday

- Turn in a final copy of essay and speech
- Take Weekly Essay/Test

Write a one-page eyewitness account of "How My Family Eats Dinner." Using vivid imagery and precise language, recreate this event in your essay. This essay should include an outline with thesis statement, rough draft, several revisions, and a final copy with five new (circled) vocabulary words. Give a copy to instructor/parent to evaluate.

In front of an audience, present a 3-to 5-minute eyewitness account of how your family eats dinner. The eyewitness speech, like the eyewitness account/essay, requires that you give the reader generous metaphors and imagery to describe your person, place, or event. For this assignment, you don't actually have to be present to be an eyewitness, but you must write as if you were.

There is no argument to defend; there is no story to write. You are merely an eyewitness — a neutral, dispassionate observer of a human event. That does not mean that you cannot search for metaphors or compare to other scenes what is happening in your scene so that your audience can understand what you are observing.

Final Project

Correct and rewrite all essays and place them in your Final Portfolio.

Eyewitness Example

The following is an example of an eyewitness account of an American who has volunteered to fly with the French air force during the World War I battle of Verdun. This American division is called the American Escadrille, an American volunteer force that fought with the Allies.

Beneath the canvas of a huge hangar mechanicians are at work on the motor of an airplane. Outside, on the borders of an aviation field, others loiter awaiting their aërial charge's return from the sky. Near the hangar stands a hut-shaped tent. In front of it several short-winged biplanes are lined up; inside it three or four young men are lolling in wicker chairs.

They wear the uniform of French army aviators. These uniforms, and the grim-looking machine guns mounted on the upper planes of the little aircraft, are the only warlike note in a pleasantly peaceful scene. The war seems very remote. It is hard to believe that the greatest of all battles — Verdun — rages only twenty-five miles to the north, and that the field and hangars and mechanicians and aviators and airplanes are all playing a part therein.

Suddenly there is the distant hum of a motor. One of the pilots emerges from the tent and gazes fixedly up into the blue sky. He points, and one glimpses a black speck against the blue, high overhead. The sound of the motor ceases, and the speck grows larger. It moves earthward in steep dives and circles, and as it swoops closer, takes on the shape of an airplane. Now one can make out the red, white, and blue circles under the wings which mark a French war-plane, and the distinctive insignia of the pilot on its sides.

"Ton patron arrive!" one mechanician cries to another. "Your boss is coming!"

The machine dips sharply over the top of a hangar, straightens out again near the earth at a dizzy speed a few feet above it and, losing momentum in a surprisingly short time, hits the ground with tail and wheels. It bumps along a score of yards and then, its motor whirring again, turns, rolls toward the hangar, and stops. A human form, enveloped in a species of garment for all the world like a diver's suit, and further adorned with goggles and a leather hood, rises unsteadily in the cockpit, clambers awkwardly overboard and slides down to terra firma.

A group of soldiers, enjoying a brief holiday from the trenches in a cantonment near the field, straggle forward and gather timidly about the airplane, listening open-mouthed for what its rider is about to say.

"H--l!" mumbles that gentleman, as he starts divesting himself of his flying garb.

"What's wrong now?" inquires one of the tenants of the tent.

"Everything, or else I've gone nutty," is the indignant reply, delivered while disengaging a leg from its Teddy Bear trousering. "Why, I emptied my whole roller on a Boche this morning, point blank at not fifteen metres off. His machine gun quit firing and his propeller wasn't turning and yet the darn fool just hung up there as if he were tied to a cloud. Say, I was so sure I had him it made me sore — felt like running into him and yelling, 'Now, you fall, you bum!' "

The eyes of the *poilus* register surprise. Not a word of this dialogue, delivered in purest American, is intelligible to them. Why is an aviator in a French uniform speaking a foreign tongue, they mutually ask themselves. Finally one of them, a little chap in a uniform long since bleached of its horizon-blue colour by the mud of the firing line, whisperingly interrogates a mechanician as to the identity of these strange air folk.

"But they are the Americans, my old one," the latter explains with noticeable condescension.

Marvelling afresh, the infantrymen demand further details. They learn that they are witnessing the return of the American Escadrille — composed of Americans who have volunteered to fly for France for the duration of the war — to their station near Bar-le-Duc, twenty-five miles south of Verdun, from a flight over the battle front of the

Meuse. They have barely had time to digest this knowledge when other dots appear in the sky, and one by one turn into airplanes as they wheel downward. Finally all six of the machines that have been aloft are back on the ground and the American Escadrille has one more sortie over the German lines to its credit.[1]

McConnell, using dialogue and colloquial language, effectively offers an eyewitness account of his experiences in World War I.

---

1   James R. McConnell, *Flying for France with the American Escadrille at Verdun* p. 1. www.gutenberg.org/files/6977/6977-h/6977-h.htm

Daily Assignment

- Warm-up: Imagine that you are a dog sleeping in the rain. Describe your dream.
- Students will complete Concept Builder 3-A.
- Prayer journal: Students are encouraged to write in their prayer journal every day.
- Students should systematically review their vocabulary words daily.

CONCEPT BUILDER 3-A

Eyewitness Account

An eyewitness account is an essay that attempts to recreate an event as it actually happened. Using powerful imagery and precise language, the eyewitness account recreates an event in precise language. The reader vicariously experiences the described event. Record an eyewitness account using the following chart.

What happened?	
Who participated?	
When did it happen?	
Where did it happen?	
Why did it happen?	
How did it happen?	
What is the significance of the event?	

Lesson 2

Style (Writing and Speaking): Paragraph Introduction

Every paragraph has a beginning, middle, and ending. Every essay has a beginning (or introductory) paragraph, one or more middle (or main body) paragraphs, and an ending (or conclusion) paragraph. Later in this series, the research paper will be discussed and the introductory paragraph will be discussed in greater depth. However, at this point, suffice it to say that every essay must have an effective introduction. An effective introduction is crucial to the paper. Your reader will read with eagerness a paper introduced with an inspiring introduction and will read with despair a paper with a boring or missing introduction.

The primary goal of the introductory paragraph is to introduce readers to the purpose of the paper. The introduction is one paragraph in the essay. You have one chance to pique your readers' interests. Without actually using the word "purpose" you will give in specific detail the purpose of the paper and then inform readers about what the rest of the paper will reveal or argue. This step is critical to the writing style of your prose creation. Following is an introduction to an essay on themes used in *Anne of Green Gables* by Lucy Maud Montgomery.

Sample Introductory Paragraph

The storyline of *Anne of Green Gables* is the perfect backdrop for its author, Lucy Maud Montgomery, to develop her theme of patient love. In this delightful story of Anne, an orphaned girl who is unexpectedly placed in the care of the elderly Matthew and Marilla Cuthbert readers live with them on their beautiful Prince Edward Island farm, Green Gables. At first, they are horrified to see that they have a girl instead of the requested boy, but, later, as Anne charms them with her poise and winsome personality, they grow to love her dearly.

This introductory paragraph is full of information. Readers meet the protagonist and other main characters. They understand the basic storyline, the setting, and even one of the themes. This introductory paragraph introduces readers to all the main points of the essay. In fact, the introduction makes sure that readers have no unexpected topics as they read the rest of the paper. Later in the essay the points will be expanded, illustrated, and supported more thoroughly, but in the introduction readers know what they will be reading about.

In an interesting way, the introduction sets the stage for the rest of the essay. The props are set on the stage; the characters are introduced; the story is launched. Now, the writing begins. . . .

Daily Assignment

- Warm-up: Imagine that you had one hour to share Jesus Christ with 19 year old Adolf Hitler. What would you say?
- Students will complete Concept Builder 3-B.
- Prayer journal.
- Students should outline all assigned essays and speech for the week.

CONCEPT
BUILDER
3-B

Sequencing

An eyewitness account has a sequence, or logical order. One event leads to another event and so forth. Complete the following sequence chart.

First Event	My soccer team wins its league championship.
Event 2	
Event 3	
Event 4	

Public Speaking: The Engaging-Story Approach And The Eyewitness Speech

By necessity, the speech has to both secure the listener's attention and inform the listener — in some ways mutually exclusive operations. The topic must quickly interest the audience, but it cannot distract the hearer from the main point of the speech.

An engaging, true story is an effective way to earn the listener's attention, but it is only the beginning. You must be sure to move to the next step, stating the points you will make in your speech and lobbying for their significance.

Daily Assignment

- Warm-up: Imagine that you were never born. Who would be affected?

- Students will complete Concept Builder 3-C.

- Prayer journal

- Students should write rough drafts of all assigned essays and speech.

CONCEPT BUILDER 3-C

Sharing Memories

No doubt there are family members who have eyewitness memories of interesting, even historical, events. Use the spider diagram below to create an eyewitness account of an important event in the life of a loved one.

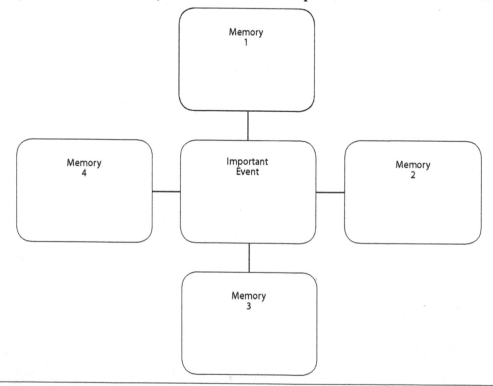

Sample Speech:
The Engaging-Story Approach

A father smiles when he hears that one son will soon graduate from Harvard Business School; another son is busily pursuing a successful career in education; and a final son will soon enter Princeton Theological Seminary. His life in Christ is adequate, but he still feels empty, so this budding saint prays that God will turn his life around.

Later, we see this same 49-year-old husband/father lying in a modern hospital. For four years, he has fought the inhuman ravages of cancer. As the doctors frantically practice their incantations and magic formulas, this broken, gentle man looks up from among the tubes, bandages, and IV bottles, and whispers, "I am not enjoying this, to be sure." A chuckle breaks from his lips. "In fact, this is a horrible way to die. But, you know, in spite of all the pain, I would not change a thing. Oh, I do not want to die. But if I was healed, and it meant that I lost all that I've learned about the Lord, well . . . I would rather die just the way I am now." "Everything," he said with quiet power, "everything I've experienced is worth what I have gained in the knowledge and love in Jesus Christ!" He died two hours later. This unpretentious, unlikely hero was my father, who died one cloudy, miserable Sunday afternoon — on Father's Day, 1983.

Sample Speech

The Introduction Proper To The Speech Presented Above

There is a lesson all Christians will learn at one time or another: inevitably, we must be broken before we will be blessed. We must be broken before we can grow. Have you ever tried to hug a stiff kid? Impossible! It is relatively easy to hug a muddy kid or a sticky kid, but a stiff, wooden, rebellious child is the hardest child to love. God is in the business of breaking us so that we can really love Him and so that He can really bless us. It is easier to love a limp, broken saint than to struggle with a stiff one. Without brokenness, we are ill-prepared to face the violence we see around us.

The final statement "Without brokenness, we are ill-prepared to face the violence we see around us" would be the thesis of the speech.

Daily Assignment

- Warm-up: Imagine that no one came to your birthday party. How would you feel?
- Students will complete Concept Builder 3-D.
- Prayer journal.
- Review the assigned text. Keep vocabulary cards.
- This is the day that students should write, and then rewrite, the final drafts of their assigned essay and speech.

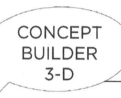

Reliability

Not all eyewitness accounts are reliable, that is the account is not true. It cannot be trusted. What makes an eyewitness account reliable?

1. Participation in the event: Was the participant present?
2. Conflict: If he was, and if there was a conflict, did he participate on one side or the other?
3. Bias: Does he have anything to gain by telling the story in a particular way?
4. Source: Finally, what is the source? Generally speaking, eyewitness accounts that come from diaries are more reliable because the author was not writing it for an audience but merely wanted to record what happened.

Using the criteria above how reliable is the excerpt from a diary by a Spanish explorer, Cabeza de Vaca. Cabeza de Vaca at first was part of but later became the leader of an expedition of about 300 men sent to conquer and colonize Florida. The expedition sailed into Tampa Bay about April 1528, began an overland march to Mexico. During the next two years more than half the men died. He led a small band of survivors to an island, possibly Galveston Island, off the southwestern coast of what is now Texas, where the band was captured by Native Americans. Early in 1535, Cabeza de Vaca and the three other survivors of the expedition escaped and began a trek through what are now the southwestern United States and northern Mexico. In 1536, the four men finally reached Mexico. The following is Vaca's reminiscences of what happened. It is from his diary, but he was asked to write it for the King of Spain.

Passage

It was Our Lord's pleasure, which many a time shows His favor in the hour of greatest distress, that at sunset we turned a point of land and found there shelter and much improvement. Many canoes came and the Indians in them spoke to us, but turned back without waiting. They were tall and well built, and carried neither bows nor arrows. We followed them to their lodges, which were nearly along the inlet, and landed, and in front of the lodges we saw many jars with water, and great quantities of cooked fish. The Chief of that land offered all to the Governor and led him to his abode. The dwellings were of matting and seemed to be permanent. When we entered the home of the chief he gave us plenty of fish, while we gave him of our maize, which they ate in our presence, asking for more. So we gave more to them, and the Governor presented him with some trinkets. While with the chief at his lodge, half an hour after sunset, the Indians suddenly fell upon us and upon our sick people on the beach. They also attacked the house of the chief, where the Governor was, wounding him in the face with a stone. Those who were with him seized the cacique, but as his people were so near he escaped, leaving in our hands a robe of marten-ermine skin, which, I believe, are the finest in the world and give out an odor like amber and musk. A single one can be smelt so far off that it seems as if there were a great many. We saw more of that kind, but none like these. . .

Rate the elements of this excerpt. 1 being the least true. 5 being the most true. Then, rate the overall reliability of the passages by giving the passages a reliability rating.

Criteria of Reliability	Rating
Participation in the event: Was the participant present?	1 2 3 4 5
Conflict: If he was, and if there was a conflict, did he participate on one side or the other?	1 2 3 4 5
Bias: Does he have anything to gain by telling the story in a particular way?	1 2 3 4 5
Source: Finally, what is the source? Generally speaking, eyewitness accounts that come from diaries are more reliable because the author was not writing it for an audience but merely wanted to record what happened.	1 2 3 4 5
Overall Reliability	1 2 3 4 5

Writing Skill: Firsthand Experience

Chapter 4

Style (Writing and Speaking): Paragraph - Main Body

Public Speaking Skill: The Speech Main Body and Converting the Firsthand Experience to a Speech

First Thoughts

A firsthand experience is a detailed description and analysis of a significant event. Unlike the Eyewitness Account, the Firsthand Experience is not merely observation. The opening of the essay must establish the setting of the event. In the rest of the paper the author presents a detailed description of the actual event. The more imagery offered to the reader, the better.

Chapter Learning Objectives

In chapter 4 we will examine how to write a firsthand experience essay.

Look Ahead for Friday

- Turn in a final copy of essay and speech
- Take Weekly Essay/Test

Write a firsthand experience of a life-changing event. This subject essay/oration should be on two pages and include an outline with thesis statement, rough draft, several revisions, and final copy with five new (circled) vocabulary words. Give one copy to teacher/parent.

Present a 2-to-3-minute firsthand experience speech on some experience that changed your life.

Final Project

Correct and rewrite all essays and place them in your Final Portfolio.

Sample Essay:
Firsthand Experience

Setting

A firsthand experience is a detailed description and analysis of a significant event. Unlike the Eyewitness Account, the Firsthand Experience is not merely an observation—it is a candid, first-person impression of an event. The opening of the essay must establish the setting of the event. In the rest of the paper the author presents a detailed description of the actual event. The more imagery offered to the reader, the better.

Read this passage carefully:

I was too late. Forrest Lewis had died twenty minutes earlier. Like wrinkled drapes on a huge bay window, hospital bed sheets lay in an obscene fashion on the shiny tile floor next to an empty hospital bed. Obviously my congregant, Lewis, was not there, but I looked anyway.

Forrest was gone. His sheets were still warm from his body heat, and I could smell his aftershave. But where was Forrest?

My eyes focused on something else in the room—a crumbled piece of paper and cellophane wrap lying next to the trash can like two ominous signals. The cellophane wrap offered no evidence of its genesis, but the paper read: "Turn the corpse over and fold the arms behind its back." Then I knew. Forrest was dead. This was the packaging that held a shroud.

Forrest Lewis had been a member of my church for most of his life. He was a good man. A very good man. Quiet, unpretentious, hard working, he was every pastor's dream parishioner! But now he was dead. .

It is finished. . . .

Two weeks earlier I had traveled to his small but very impressive urban home to give him communion.

"This is my body that is broken for you. . . ."

"How many times, my old friend, have you heard these words?" I thought.

"Take, eat. This is my body that is broken for you . . ."

"What right do I have to serve you communion?" I silently mused. "What do I know about life? About remembering? About death? Teach me, Forrest Lewis, teach me."

With his pallid hands Forrest steadied my shaking.

"Do this in remembrance of me. . . ."

It is finished. . . .

I thought of the future and I shuddered to think how long it would be before it arrived. Forrest thought of the present and shuddered to think how soon it would be over. . . .

It is finished. . . .

I gave him stale crackers, and he filled my afternoon with greatness. I gave him slightly fermented grape juice, and he gave me freshly baked peanut-butter cookies. "Bet You could never guess they were made from margarine," he chuckled.

These were holy cookies. I nervously munched on them all the way home.

It is finished. . . . (James)

Daily Assignment

- Warm-up: Create a dialogue between two children discussing the prospect of attending nursery school.

- Students will complete a daily Concept Builder 4-A.

- Prayer journal: Students are encouraged to write in their prayer journal every day.

- Students should systematically review their vocabulary words daily.

Setting

Use the following chart to determine the setting of the previous passage.

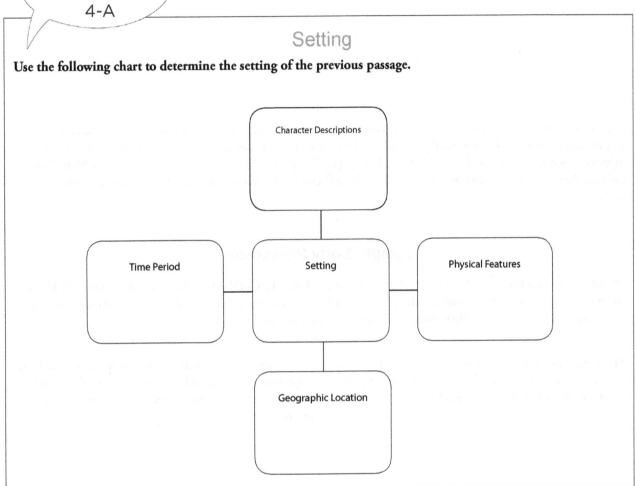

Character Descriptions

Time Period

Setting

Physical Features

Geographic Location

Style (Writing and Speaking): Paragraph Main Body

If the introduction is the bait, so to speak, to attract the attention of the readers, the main body is the hook that actually catches readers. It is the meal provided for the readers. Every paragraph has a topic sentence and several supporting sentences; they make up the body of the paper. Every essay has an introductory paragraph which always presents the purpose statement (or thesis) of the essay, and every essay has several supporting paragraphs (the main body).

Sample Body Paragraph

What seems like a bad turn of events turns into a blessing. While the Cuthberts expected to adopt an orphan boy, by mistake they were sent a young female child. The "mistake" becomes a great blessing to the Cuthberts. Anne also becomes a blessing to others when she saves the life of a neighbor's child.

This paragraph continues the discussion about the theme of love in *Anne of Green Gables*. It states another aspect of the thesis and offers supporting evidence.

In summary, the main body is another exceptionally important part of the whole essay. It is the place where writers give readers the information that the introduction promised.

Daily Assignment

- Warm-up: Create a dialogue between two teens discussing what their pastor preached on Sunday.
- Students will complete Concept Builder 4-B.
- Prayer journal.
- Students should outline all assigned essays and speech for the week.

Style (Writing and Speaking): Paragraph (C) Main Body

How many sentences or paragraphs should be in the main body of this prose unit? Enough to develop thoroughly the thesis statement. That may be 3 paragraphs or it may be 300 paragraphs. However, use as few paragraphs as possible to accomplish your purpose. Writing more to just fill up the page is not indicative of good writing. Every sentence that is included in a paragraph should have a reason for being there. Which paragraphs belong in the body of this essay? Check the ones that belong. Here is the introduction:

Japan is a study of contrasts. On the one hand, it is Asia's first industrialized nation. On the other hand, it is still a very conservative nation.

Body Paragraphs	Does it belong?
The Japanese could be the most cosmopolitan people in Asia, if not the world. They are so dependent on world markets that it imports virtually all of its iron ore, bauxite, oil, copper, and nickel. Japan relies on foreign supplies for over 90 percent of its coal, natural gas, and lead. Over 85 percent of its total energy is imported from abroad. It is perhaps the greatest importer of agricultural goods. Japan is second only to the United States in terms of the total value of its industrial exports. It is the world's greatest exporter of automobiles; it has the greatest number of merchant ships in the world.	Yes or No
Yamato emperors expanded their rule over all of the main islands of Japan except Hokkaido. This ultimately brought great upheaval in Japanese society. Likewise a great smallpox epidemic of 735–737 indelibly changed early Japan. Perhaps one-third of the population perished in those two years.	Yes or No
Yet the Japanese people are more intimately tied to their ancient ancestral roots than they are to events in the rest of the world. Third and fourth-generation Japanese, when asked where they are "from," still name the "old home" of their ancestors. Their lives are tied more closely to the ancient rural agricultural rhythms than to the modern industrial cities where they reside. (Louis G. Perez, *The History of Japan*. Westport, CT. Greenwood Press. 1998. www.questia.com/). How did Japan become a land of so many contrasts?	Yes or No

Public Speaking Task:
The Main Body and the Firsthand Speech

The main body of a speech typically includes two or three points with several sub-points. Each point must be supported by arguments or by illustrations, all of which add credibility to each point. What sort of supporting material should you use? Facts and examples of your argument/illustrations are the best choices. Quotes from authorities, analogies (i.e., comparisons between two different items), and narrative illustrations work well, too. The following is a relatively lengthy body of the speech begun in the previous lesson. By this point, the author has inspired the audience, informed the audience about the purposes of the speech, and is now ready to present the main meal of the speech.

Identify several points the speaker is making.

Daily Assignment

- Warm-up: Create a dialogue between you and the person you will someday marry.
- Students will complete Concept Builder 4-C.
- Prayer journal.
- Students should write rough drafts of all assigned essays and speech.

Drawing Conclusions I

Writers rarely state all the facts. They expect readers to draw conclusions from the facts, from the narrative. By inferring, or figuring out, what is happening, readers become better interpreters of the literary event. What can you infer from the following passage? What conclusions can you draw?

Facts	Inferences
"I have seen God face to face." Genesis 32:30. This is one of the most intense sections of Scripture in the Old Testament. Imagine! Enveloped in eerie darkness, humankind is fighting desperately with Almighty God. There is something of fury, something of evil, in the intense struggling. All of Jacob's ample trickery, all of his pseudospirituality, is struggling with the Perfect God. The wrestlers groan, gasp for breath, and cry as each pushes to even greater efforts. Silhouetted against the rising moon, at times the two figures seem to lose all temporal location. For a moment, generations upon generations of Christians are standing on that hill, struggling, for all they are worth, with Almighty God. Paul, the Pharisee, is struggling alongside Jacob. He snickers as Stephen screams in mortal pain. Peter is pushing against God, even as he denies Him three times. The fire, into which he peers cannot warm his heart, cannot dry the tears that grow out of his betrayal. We see anxious Martin Luther, tired Martin Luther; who has struggled with God all night. We see Luther courageously nailing his 95 theses on the Wittenberg Door. We see Wesley preaching to the prison inmates of 18th-century England; there is brokenness etched on his face. And we take our place on that hill, for we have struggled — we are struggling — we will struggle — with God. The night is not over.	*There is a God.*

Conclusions

Sample Speech:
Main Points

analysis

After we are broken, after we know who is truly in control, we commit ourselves to reality — no matter what the cost, no matter what that reality is.

Jacob was broken and then blessed. Jacob was a conniving, selfish scoundrel. He cheated his brother out of his birthright; he tricked his aging father in order to get the paternal blessing. Then he had no alternative except to flee the inevitable, justifiable wrath of his brother.

But God had other adventures in store for His selfish saint. In Genesis 32, we see Jacob going home. On the way, he received word that his brother, Esau, was planning to meet him with 400 men. Jacob was justifiably scared. Therefore, he divided his party for safety, and then sent most of them ahead with gifts for appeasement. Coward that he was, he even sent his family in front of him so that they, too, might be a part of the buffer be-tween him and his cheated brother.

However, Jacob the *supplanter* was about to run out of tricks. While Jacob waited alone that last night before he was finally to meet Esau, a man came into his campsite and began to wrestle with him. What was said or why the fight began we are not told, but we do know that Jacob's opponent was no ordinary man. Hosea 12:4 indicates that the stranger was an angel of God. In fact, Genesis 32:30 intimates that the visitor may have been an angel or, perhaps, Jesus Christ — assuming the guise of a wrestler.

Jacob was about to learn another very important lesson: a mature person is someone who knows how to accept *necessary* suffering.

Whoever this strange visitor was, he represented God. Therefore, God literally wrestled with Jacob. Jacob had reached the end of his human rope — even though it had taken 20 years or more. He could not take another step in the kingdom until he was broken — broken of his scheming and selfishness.

Sometimes we must experience the death of a vision. Many times in our lives, we seem to have it all together. Our world applauds us as we say all the right things — perhaps even *do* all the right things. But our vision is flawed. It must die. Then it can be replaced by God's vision. We cannot accept the vision, the high calling, unless God has prepared us. (James Stobaugh)

In summary, the main body of a speech develops the heart of the rhetorical experience and justifies the time and energy expended by the audience in the listening process.

Daily Assignment

- Warm-up: Create a dialogue between a homeless man and a Harvard Professor.

- Students will complete Concept Builder 4-D.

- Prayer journal

- Review the assigned text. Keep vocabulary cards.

- This is the day that students should write, and then rewrite, the final drafts of their assigned essay and speech.

Achieving Unity

Every paragraph and every essay will have unity if all its sentences support the main idea. Cross out the sentences that do not belong in this essay.

Samurai Warriors

As the effective influence of the imperial court gradually waned from the 9th century through the 12th century, power moved away from the emperor to local warriors (bushi or samurai). The warriors were typically landholders, many minor landholders, yeoman farmers really. They were not necessarily rich noblemen. They lived in small, fortified compounds, and they offered the surrounding peasant communities succor and protection. Often warriors served as local district officials, judges, even priests. They were, however, quintessential warriors. Much of their time was devoted to the cultivation of warfare. As a result they were very effective administrators and warriors. With their land holdings, military skills, and administrative skills, the warriors were a powerful presence in Japanese society.

At time, samurai families joined together for protection into larger groups based on kinship ties. The emperor, with no standing army, relied on samurai families to maintain local law and order.

By the middle of the 13th century, samurai had become so valuable to the emperor that he appointed a "head samurai" called a shogun. A shogun was a military governor, so to speak, who answered directly to the emperor. He was responsible for maintaining peace in the provinces. He arbitrated differences between rival samurai and other divergent groups.

In the 1870s Japanese leadership sent a group on a diplomatic mission around the world. Under the leadership of Iwakura Tomomi, they were to learn about technologically advanced countries of the West. The Iwakura mission's direct observation of the West left them feeling challenged but hopeful and it seemed possible that Japan could catch up with the Western nations.

In 1232 the shogun promulgated the Joei Code. It clarified the duties of samurai and other officials. The code also restrained unruly samurai by requiring them to respect the rights of the religious temples and shrines.

This era, called the Hojo era, saw the spread of Buddhism. Buddhism stressed personal salvation for ordinary believers. This was in direct contrast to much Japanese thinking that emphasized the needs of the community above the needs of the individual.

There were a series of civil wars that resulted in great turmoil from 1300–1400. Real unity did not occur until a new religious movement emerged, Shintoism.

Japan lost World War II but emerged as one of the premier economic powers of the post-World War II world.

Writing Skill: The Descriptive Essay

Style (Writing and Speaking): Paragraph - Conclusion

Public Speaking Skill: The Speech Conclusion and Converting the Descriptive Essay to a Speech

First Thoughts

The descriptive essay describes a person, place, or thing.

In the age of media mania, good old-fashioned prose description has taken a hit. We would much prefer to take a photograph of a sunset or to record a song by our favorite artist than to describe these things with prose. However, since the whole area of apologetics is at stake, it is critical that we maintain that skill. If we can't describe a sunset, then how do we expect to explain grace to an unsaved person?

Chapter Learning Objectives

In chapter 5 we will write a descriptive essay of someone who helped us mature as a Christian.

Look Ahead for Friday

- Turn in a final copy of essay and speech
- Take Weekly Essay/Test

In a two-page essay, describe a person who had a great impact on your maturation as a Christian. Emphasize the following elements of descriptive essays: starting point, purpose, form, audience, voice, and point of view. This description essay should include an outline with thesis statement, rough draft, several revisions, and final copy with five new (circled) vocabulary words. Your essay must pay particular attention to style (focus, content, organization). Give a copy to instructor/parent to evaluate.

Present a 2- or 3-minute descriptive speech of a person who had a great impact on your maturation as a Christian. A descriptive speech must by definition be full of numerous and well-constructed descriptions. A descriptive speech normally describes its subject *ad nauseum*. You should look for numerous ways, with multiple metaphors, to help your reader grasp what/who you are describing.

Final Project

Correct and rewrite all essays and place them in your Final Portfolio.

Sample Descriptive Essay

East Liberty is a mean, ungenerous place to most folks, but the bag lady fit into a different category. A person has to be strong to survive and Spirit-filled to be victorious. The East Liberty area of Pittsburgh is foreboding. Enterprising entrepreneurs have made drug-dealing a growth industry. Prostitution is a close second but still seasonal industry.

A homeless bag lady visited our inner city, almost ghettoized a corner almost every day. A harbinger of hope, committed to important traditions, she gently laid neatly cut one-inch squares of white bread under the blue and white sign that warned would-be villains that there was a "Neighborhood Watch" ubiquitously guarding our community.

Some said this lady was crazy. We whose stories are so complete and well rehearsed are suspicious of those with stories we do not know, or, if we know them, we cannot comprehend. She had no story. Or at least she was not talking.

We wanted to know who this strange woman was. She offered us very few hints — a frayed L.L. Bean two-sizes-too-big ski jacket with "j" embroidered on the right front pocket. She stuffed her pockets with West Penn Hospital brochures entitled "Cancer — Students Can Survive!"

She came to church once a year. She never said anything, never told us her name. The old woman who wandered the streets of Friendship and Roup remained an anonymous citadel.

She loved to feed the birds. She guarded her pieces of bread from unscrupulous ants, barking blue jays, and mischievous school children. Her face was all seriousness — no hint of a smile. Her work was sacred and important, even if no one else thought so.

I thought her work was important. Even if I didn't know who she was — she accepted my friendly "hellos" with a suspicious frown — I appreciated this solitudinarian who brought bird song to a community muted by hard luck. Standing alone at our corner next to two abandoned buildings ravaged and neglected by time, the homeless bag lady brought magnificence and hope to a community that desperately needed both.

Daily Assignment

- Warm-up: Describe a moment that changed your life.

- Students will complete Concept Builder 5-A.

- Prayer journal: Students are encouraged to write in their prayer journal every day.

- Students should systematically review their vocabulary words daily.

Writing with Sensory Words

Write with words that appeal to the senses.

Write a short essay describing a time when you ate an ice cream cone. Use at least 5 words from the list below.

Sight Words	Audible Words	Sensory/Touch Words	Taste/Smell Words
Ample	Smash	Chilly	Fruity
Drab	Yelp	Oily	Ranchid
Disheveled	Jarring	Slippery	Flowery
Hilarious	Hiss	Frigid	Musty
Scrawny	Clanging	Clammy	Zesty

Lesson 2

Writing Style:
Paragraph — Conclusion

Stopping a paragraph is much like stopping a bicycle: there are many different options — as long as one does not merely jump off the bicycle (abandon the paragraph). The conclusion will be discussed in greater depth later in this curriculum when we discuss the Research Paper. The conclusion is the final opportunity writers have to review a point, to emphasize an argument, or to summarize an issue; the conclusion is not an opportunity to introduce a new, undeveloped point, argument, or issue. The concluding sentence in a paragraph, or the concluding paragraph in a composition, has two important functions: to end the prose construction with grace and to reiterate or bring solution to previously discussed information.

Resist the temptation to use the conclusion to "preach." If you have not already wooed the reader to your position, a final emotional plea is insulting and useless. Stay focused on the purpose of the paper and logically draw a solution or conclusion.

One final personal note: many of us attended or attend schools whose faculty is not Christian. We want to take every opportunity to share the gospel with them. However, in my opinion, the best way to do that is to write well, to argue well, and to show excellence in everything you do. While attending Vanderbilt University eons ago, I wrote a paper for an unbelieving professor entitled "The Mosaic Authorship of the Pentateuch." Nobody in the secular world thinks that Moses wrote the first five books of the Old Testament — in spite of the fact that Jesus Christ claimed that Moses wrote the Pentateuch. However, while the professor did not believe that Moses wrote the Pentateuch, he was so impressed that I wrote a persuasive paper arguing that position that he asked me to share more about my faith. I call that *apologetics*. Write well; argue well; speak well — and let the Holy Spirit take care of the rest.

Daily Assignment

- Warm-up: Describe your best friend.
- Students will complete Concept Builder 5-B.
- Prayer journal.
- Students should outline all assigned essays and speech for the week.

Drawing Conclusions II

What can you infer from this poem by Robert Frost?

Fire and Ice

Some say the world will end in fire,
Some say in ice.
From what I've tasted of desire
I hold with those who favor fire.
But if it had to perish twice,
I think I know enough of hate
To know that for destruction ice
Is also great
And would suffice.

Answer these questions true or false.

True or False. Robert Frost likes to play in the snow.

True or False. Someone must have hurt Frost.

True or False. Frost seems to be unhappy as he writes this poem.

True or False. Frost is writing a poem about fire and ice.

True or False. Frost is writing a poem about love and hatred.

Public Speaking Skill:
The Conclusion

The conclusion of a speech offers more latitude than the conclusion of an essay. While most speeches conclude with some sort of final statement or summary, the persuasive speech (next lesson) usually ends with a call to action. Referencing a previously used image, metaphor, or story is one good way to end a speech. Another is to use a provocative quote from a credible witness. If you can give a personal commitment in the final statement, then you have given the most credible witness that you can. Finally, whatever ending you choose, be sure that your final thoughts are specific, direct, and crystal clear.

Daily Assignment

- Warm-up: Describe the causes of World War I to a two-year-old.

- Students will complete Concept Builder 5-C.

- Prayer journal.

- Students should write rough drafts of all assigned essays and speech.

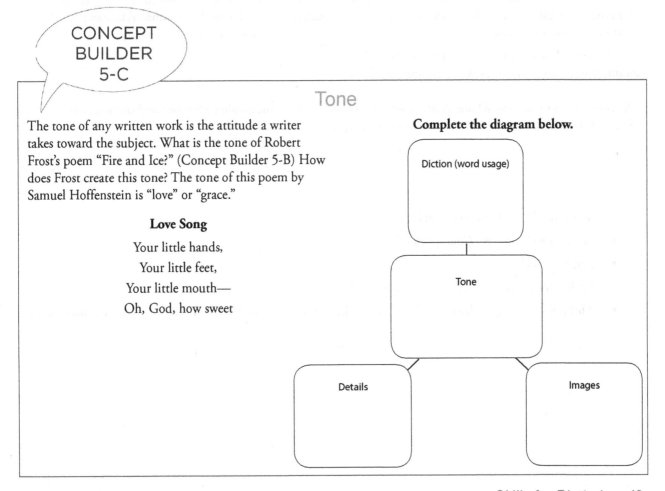

CONCEPT BUILDER 5-C

Tone

The tone of any written work is the attitude a writer takes toward the subject. What is the tone of Robert Frost's poem "Fire and Ice?" (Concept Builder 5-B) How does Frost create this tone? The tone of this poem by Samuel Hoffenstein is "love" or "grace."

Love Song

Your little hands,
Your little feet,
Your little mouth—
Oh, God, how sweet

Complete the diagram below.

Diction (word usage)

Tone

Details

Images

Sample Descriptive Speech

People of all shapes and sizes crowded in rows of bleachers surrounding a homemade canvas ring. The ring was set off by a high-intensity light fastened from the ceiling by army-issue parachute cord. My grandfather and I carefully tiptoed to our seat, avoiding discarded chewing tobacco and snuff juice.

To my seven-year-old eyes it was an amazing sight. Everyone was screaming and shouting and raucously happy. The bad guys were clearly bad and really mean — 350-pound overweight Big Bad Hans with his undersized black trunks and equally small muscle shirt — sported chains and a tattoo on his left arm. And our hero — 225-pound svelte Gorgeous George — blond hair, blue eyed, and wearing a red, white, and blue outfit — was even more impressive.

No one had to tell us that Big Bad Hans was evil incarnate and Gorgeous George was good. Hans walked around the ring growling at us, frowning, showing off. George, on the other hand, was suitably shy, smiling, and waving at the crowd.

The fight began. Big Bad Hans had no intentions of fighting cleanly. And so, before long Gorgeous George was in big trouble. In fact, his head was bleeding profusely, and it appeared that Big Bad Hans had won.

The referee stood over the bloodied and unconscious Gorgeous George and began to count "One, two. . . ."

The crowd was furious. The bad guy was going to win! And he had done it unfairly!

But, before the referee counted "three," George suddenly shook his head and managed to stand. The fight was not over after all! (James Stobaugh)

The writer uses a seven-year-old interpreter to let the reader see and feel the evening when he watched the wrestling match. He used visual, tactile, olfactory, and sensory metaphors to bring the scene alive.

Daily Assignment

- Warm-up: Describe the emotion jealousy.
- Students will complete Concept Builder 5-D.
- Prayer journal.
- Review the assigned text. Keep vocabulary cards.
- This is the day that students should write, and then rewrite, the final drafts of their assigned essay and speech.

Life Application

Descriptive essays draw you into life itself. In the space below, write a poem, draw a picture, or write an essay describing an incident that deeply affected your life.

Incident that Changed My Life

Writing Skill: Descriptive Vs. Coercive Essay

Chapter 6

Style (Writing and Speaking): Paragraph, Unity and Coherence

Public Speaking Skill: Delivery and Converting the Persuasive Essay to a Speech

First Thoughts

A persuasive essay persuades the reader to embrace a particular course of action. Its sole purpose is to persuade. The writer must not digress to write anything that does not advance that sole purpose.

Chapter Learning Objectives

In chapter 6 we learn the difference between coercive and persuasive essay and speech.

Look Ahead for Friday

- Turn in a final copy of essay and speech

- Take Weekly Essay/Test

In American society today there is much discussion about the separation of church and state. The First Amendment to the Constitution of the United States of America reads: "Congress shall make no law respecting an establishment of religion, or prohibiting the free exercise thereof." Some people argue that "under God" in the Pledge of Allegiance is a violation of the First Amendment. They argue that this phrase moves beyond persuasiveness and becomes coercion. Write a 1- or 2-page essay arguing a position concerning this debate. This essay should include an outline with thesis statement, rough draft, several revisions, and a final copy with five new (circled) vocabulary words. The essay must pay particular attention to style (focus, content, organization). Give a copy to instructor/parent to evaluate.

Present a 3-minute coercive speech and persuasive speech on the same topic. A speech is based on an essay, but it is not an essay. There is immediacy in a speech that forces the presenter to be precise and economical in his language. In the speech introduction, clarify the goal of the speech. What are you trying to accomplish? What action do you wish to have result from this speech? A cessation of a behavior? The origination of a behavior? What is your proposition? What does your audience need to believe to be persuaded to your position? Will you be able to provide the proof to accomplish this task?

Final Project

Correct and rewrite all essays and place them in your Final Portfolio.

Persuasive Essay/Speech

The following is the end of an essay/speech on Isaiah 35. To what position is the author persuading the audience?

The really good news of Isaiah 35, and of the gospel, is that as we — the chosen community, today the church — rejoice, grow healthy, and find ourselves living in Zion. So also will the land and those who live in it find hope, health, and wholeness. Health to the Jew, as it was to the Greek, means far more than physical health. It means healing, wholeness. Indeed, the Greek word *salvation* has at its root the word *health*. We are the light of the world, and we can change our world as we share the good news. The Christ whom we represent is the only real hope the world has for wholeness. We should be outspoken and unequivocal with this message. As we sing, with our words and our lives, the land will be saved, made whole. "Say to those with fearful hearts, 'Be strong, do not fear. . . . Then will the eyes of the blind be opened and the ears of the deaf unstopped" (Is. 35:4–5; NIV).

Again, this was awfully good news to a community that faced the awful King Sennacherib. King Hezekiah, Uzziah's successor, was sorely tempted to trust in Egypt, but frankly, Isaiah in chapter 35 is making an offer that Hezekiah cannot refuse. Likewise, today, when we live a holy life, when we trust in God with faith and hope, the land in which we work and live becomes holy. In this God, of whom we bear witness with our words and lives, we, like the faithful Israelites, find wholeness, health, and life. This news is good news!

The speaker is asking the audience to accept the generalization that people find their wholeness and life in Jesus Christ alone.

When you write a persuasive essay, you are creating a paper that will prove a point, which will clarify an is-sue, and, in the process, perhaps change readers' opinions. You won't be able to change anyone's mind, however, until you think clearly about your topic. Using the *Thinking Game* (chapter 1) is a very effective way to clarify your thinking. Talk to your teacher, parents, and friends about the topic. Ask these folks to respond to the position you are arguing. Finally, don't insult your readers by relying only on emotion. Clearly state your case with logic and reason propelling your purpose, not veiled threats, emotion, or fear.

The latter — persuasion by means of threats, emotion, fear — is called coercive persuasion. There are times when this form of persuasion is legitimate. If you were writing an essay concerning the dangers of drug abuse, it would not be inappropriate to remind readers of the consequences of drug addiction, however gruesome the details might be. On the other hand, if you were arguing vigorously that soccer is the "all-American sport" and someone should be arrested for playing another sport, you would be overstating your position and definitely in the inappropriate coercive camp.

What is, then, an appropriate coercive persuasive essay? Use facts, even emotional, disturbing facts, in appropriate ways to coerce readers in a persuasive essay. While you will want to be sensitive to your audience — it is true that cigarette smoking causes millions of deaths a year, but it might not be appropriate to present this fact to a grieving widow whose husband recently died of lung cancer — you are well within your rhetorical bounds to argue persuasively, coercively, for a controversial position — as long as you use indisputable facts to support your case.

Daily Assignment

- Warm-up: Coerce someone to join the army.
- Students will complete Concept Builder 6-A.
- Prayer journal: Students are encouraged to write in their prayer journal every day.
- Students should systematically review their vocabulary words daily.

The Persuasive Essay

The goal of persuasion is to convince someone to adopt a position or an opinion.

Refer to the persuasive essay/speech and complete the chart.

Problem

Solution

End Result

Style (Writing And Speaking): Paragraph — Unity And Coherence

A paragraph must evidence a strategy to convey information. You must not merely "hang out" between the topic sentence and conclusion and hope everything works out. You must project a clear arrangement of ideas — or coherence — in your paragraphs. The interior life of your paragraph is up to you, and you will need to plan it carefully.

You have several options. The purpose of your essay will determine your choices. You may choose to list details according to their importance to your topic. A paragraph in a persuasive essay would normally implement this organizing principle. For instance, if you were arguing for the importance of completing your chores every day, because you think this is the most important reason to do chores, you might suggest first that the completion of these chores is vital to the well-being of the community. And so forth.

In another essay paragraph, you may list details according to their occurrence in your topic. An expository narrative would normally employ this organizing principle. For instance, if you wrote an essay paragraph about how to bake a cake, you would need to mention that baking powder should be placed in the batter before eggs if that is necessary to a successful cake. If you were disorganized in your paragraph arrangement, you would have a terrible cake.

Finally, in a descriptive essay in particular, you may choose to describe details according to their location in your setting. For instance, if you were describing a new car, you likely would not mention the color of the upholstery before you mentioned the outside color of the car.

You must intentionally organize your paragraph. Your subject matter will not automatically fall into organizational patterns. The following are some transitional words that will help you gain coherence:

Temporal order	First, Before, During, Thus, And
Comparison/Contrast	As, either . . . Or, Also, However
Distance	Around, Near
Cause & Effect	If . . . then, Because, Therefore, Since

Daily Assignment

- Warm-up: Coerce someone to attend church.
- Students will complete Concept Builder 6-B.
- Prayer journal.
- Students should outline all assigned essays and speech for the week.

CONCEPT
BUILDER
6-B

Paragraph—Unity and Coherence

Read carefully the following passage and underline words that add coherence to this paragraph:

First, Chinese civilization began around 2500 to 2000 B.C. Contrast this timeline with Western European civilization that began around 1000 B.C. and European-American civilization that began in A.D. 1600. A rich culture thrived in the lower Huang He (or Yellow River) Valley of north China. However, what makes the civilization unique in world history is its continuity through over 4,000 years. No other civilization can make that claim!

Thus, Chinese scholars, from China's earliest pre-history, maintained a cultural identity separate from contiguous neighbors. The Chinese kept voluminous records since very early times. Therefore, they always had a sense of a unique cultural identity.

Chinese history, until recently, was written mostly by royal patrons and scholars. Thus, there is a definite political bias in most Chinese history. Very little social history emerged. Therefore, we know very little about common people in early Chinese history. Also, historians described a Chinese political pattern of dynasties, or political kingdoms, one following another in a cycle of birth and death.

Public Speaking: Delivery and Converting the Persuasive Essay to a Speech

Delivery of a speech is critical to its success. The old cliché is true — sometimes people cannot hear what we say because our appearance and behavior speak too loudly. Dress appropriately for the occasion. Claiming discomfort in a suit or dress is beside the point when you are presenting a formal speech to an audience. Move around enough to show life but not so much that your movement is distracting. Engage your audience through eye contact and appropriate voice inflection. Typically, you should stand straight with one foot slightly forward to naturally focus your attention toward the audience. Posture yourself accordingly.

What if there is a podium? Don't grab it like a steering wheel and don't swing it like a dance partner. Stand behind it, if you must; move beyond it, if you can. It is not there to block you from your audience. It is there to hold your notes. Period. Move away from it. The larger the room and audience, the more animated you should be. However, don't move so close to your first row audience that you invade their body space.

Practice controlling your facial expressions. For example, you should not be smiling while you are talking about death!

In most cases your physical actions and appearance will determine how long your audience will honor you with their attention. You can write and present a highly effective, inspired speech that can end in disappointment if your physical delivery is deficient.

Daily Assignment

- Warm-up: Coerce someone to paint your house.
- Students will complete Concept Builder 6-C.
- Prayer journal.
- Students should write rough drafts of all assigned essays and speech.

Author's Bias

Every author has an opinion, sometimes strong opinions that he wishes to communicate to his audience. He may even want to persuade a reader to accept his position. It is important that readers discern these biases.

Read the following poem by Langston Hughes and answer the questions that follow:

"A Dream Deferred:"

Does it dry up
Like a raisin in the sun?
Or fester like a sore--
And then run?
Does it stink like rotten meat?
Or crust and sugar over--
Like a syrupy sweet?
Maybe it just sags
Like a heavy load.
Or does it explode?

1. Does Hughes sound as if he is frustrated or happy with his world?
   frustrated

2. What sort of images does he offer for "a dream deferred?" Are they pleasant or unpleasant images?
   unpleasant

3. What does he mean "or does it explode?" Why does he put these words in italics? *meaning it all fails instead*

4. Would it matter to the reader that Langston Hughes is an African-American poet? Why or why not?

Lesson 4

Student Sample

One Nation, Under God? The first amendment in the Constitution of the United States reads, *"Congress shall make no law respecting an establishment of religion, or prohibiting the free exercise thereof; or abridging the freedom of speech, or of the press; or the right of the people peaceably to assemble, and to petition the Government for a redress of grievances."* These 45 words spark much controversy about all kinds of issues from flag burning to the phrase "under God" in the Pledge of Allegiance. Since its establishment in the 1950s, the phrase "under God" has had many misconceptions surrounding it. The purpose of this essay is to clarify some of those misconceptions.

First of all, some people point to "separation of church and state" as a reason for opposing "under God" in the Pledge of Allegiance. Where did that phrase come from? It certainly did not come from anywhere in the Constitution. The "separation of church and state" phrase actually originated in 1802 when Thomas Jefferson, one of America's most beloved Founding Fathers, responded to a letter from a concerned church in a correspondence of his own, in which he allayed their fears about having no inalienable right granted them by their state to worship as they chose. Instead, they felt as though their ability to legally worship came only as a favor from their home state of Connecticut. Jefferson, responding with the exact words of the First Amendment and mentioning the "establishment clause," told them it created "a wall of separation between church and state." Read in context, this "separation of church and state" is actually meant to protect the church from the state, not the other way around. Secondly, there is a populace of individuals that would direct attention to the "establishment clause" (*"Congress shall make no law respecting an establishment of religion, or prohibiting the free exercise thereof"*) as a reason

for scrapping the term "under God" in the Pledge of Allegiance. However, their logic is flawed. In what way is the phrase "under God" respecting an establishment of religion, or prohibiting the free exercise thereof? If the definition of religion according to the Merriam-Webster dictionary is *"a personal set or institutionalized system of religious attitudes, beliefs, and practices,"* how is the acknowledgement of God an establishment of a specific system of religious attitudes, beliefs, and practices? Well, one might answer the mere acknowledgement of God is a belief. However, the dictionary clearly states that the definition of religion means not only religious beliefs, but also religious attitudes and practices.

Thus, one can conclude that mentioning God in the Pledge of Allegiance is not a law establishing religion. Furthermore, the "separation of church and state" phrase not only isn't contained in the Constitution, (and therefore it has no legal ramifications) but was originally coined to reassure concerned citizens that the church was protected from the *state*. (J.B.)

Daily Assignment

- Warm-up: Coerce your dog to do tricks.
- Students will complete Concept Builder 6-D.
- Prayer journal
- Review the assigned text. Keep vocabulary cards.
- This is the day that students should write, and then rewrite the final drafts of their assigned essay and speech.

My Own Bias

We have our own biases, and that will color our own reading of a writing. Use the following chart to determine your own bias and the bias of your mom and dad. Rate each situation 1 to 5 — 1 means you value it very little and 5 means you value it very much.

The Situation	My Views	My Mom's Views	My Dad's Views
Going to Church.	1 2 3 4 ⑤	1 2 3 4 ⑤	1 2 3 4 ⑤
Playing sports.	1 2 ③ 4 5	1 ② 3 4 5	1 2 3 ④ 5
Playing video games.	1 ② 3 4 5	① 2 3 4 5	1 2 ③ 4 5
Subscribing to cable television.	① 2 3 4 5	① 2 3 4 5	① 2 3 4 5
Owning the newest computer equipment.	1 ② 3 4 5	1 2 ③ 4 5	1 2 3 ④ 5
Getting a new stove.	1 ② 3 4 5	1 2 3 4 ⑤	1 2 ③ 4 5
Having the house clean.	1 2 3 ④ 5	1 2 3 4 ⑤	1 2 3 ④ 5
Owning a new car.	1 ② 3 4 5	1 2 ③ 4 5	1 2 ③ 4 5
Going on vacation.	1 2 3 4 ⑤	1 2 ③ 4 5	1 2 ③ 4 5
Visiting Grandmother's house at Thanksgiving.	1 2 ③ 4 5	1 2 3 ④ 5	1 2 3 ④ 5
Owning a pet.	1 2 3 4 ⑤	1 2 3 ④ 5	1 2 3 ④ 5
Having a big house.	1 ② 3 4 5	1 ② 3 4 5	1 ② 3 4 5
Valentine's Day.	① 2 3 4 5	1 ② 3 4 5	① 2 3 4 5
Dating.	① 2 3 4 5	① 2 3 4 5	① 2 3 4 5
Shopping at a department store.	1 ② 3 4 5	1 2 ③ 4 5	1 ② 3 4 5
Shopping at a hardware store.	① 2 3 4 5	1 ② 3 4 5	1 ② 3 4 5
Owning a motorcycle.	① 2 3 4 5	① 2 3 4 5	① 2 3 4 5
Saving money in a bank.	1 2 3 4 ⑤	1 2 3 4 ⑤	1 2 3 4 ⑤

Writing Skill: Persuasive Advertisement Essay

Chapter 7

Style (Writing and Speaking): Paragraph - Transitional Devices

Public Speaking Skill: Delivery and Converting the Persuasive Advertisement Essay to a Speech

First Thoughts

The most common persuasive writings concern advertisements. Advertisements commonly rely upon the three appeals of Aristotelian rhetoric to convey their message: logos, pathos, and ethos. Logos pertains to the logical cognitive function of the argument itself; pathos involves the emotion stirred up in the audience, and ethos concerns the credibility of the advertisement. Advertisements may not include all three appeals or draw equally from them, but they are present in the advertisement in one form or another.

Chapter Learning Objectives

In chapter 7 we will explore persuasive advertisements.

Look Ahead for Friday

- Turn in a final copy of essay and speech

- Take Weekly Essay/Test

Write a one-page persuasive advertisement essay for your favorite vacation spot. This essay should include an outline with thesis statement, rough draft, several revisions, final copy with five new (circled) vocabulary words. Pay particular attention to style (focus, content, organization). Give a copy to instructor/parent to evaluate.

Create a persuasive advertisement speech for your favorite vacation spot.

Final Project

Correct and rewrite all essays and place them in your Final Portfolio.

Ethos, Logos, Pathos

Aristotle's *On Rhetoric* describes various modes of persuasion in the following way:

> Persuasion is clearly a sort of demonstration, since we are most fully persuaded when we consider a thing to have been demonstrated. Of the modes of persuasion furnished by the spoken word there are three kinds. [...] Persuasion is achieved by the speaker's personal character when the speech is so spoken as to make us think him credible. [...] Secondly, persuasion may come through the hearers, when the speech stirs their emotions. [...] Thirdly, persuasion is effected through the speech itself when we have proved a truth or an apparent truth by means of the persuasive arguments suitable to the case in question.

The three terms used for these three kinds of persuasion are logos, pathos, and ethos. Logos pertains to the logical cognitive function of the argument itself. Pathos involves the emotion stirred up because of the argument. Finally, ethos concerns the credibility of what is stated.

Daily Assignment

- Warm-up: Persuade someone to join the army.
- Students will complete Concept Builder 7-A.
- Prayer journal: Students are encouraged to write in their prayer journal every day.
- Students should systematically review their vocabulary words daily.

Writing with Emotion II

Using the chart below illustrate an important, emotional experience that you had.

Setting

Character

My Emotional Story
Title

The event that caused
my emotional story.

The outcome of my
emotional story.

Style (Writing and Speaking): Paragraphs — Transitional Devices

Effective transitions perform the critical task of joining parts of a speech or a piece of writing together. Transitions are created by mentioning a previous key word or expression in a new sentence or paragraph. Transitions are also created by using such words as *however, furthermore, in addition to, consequently, next, second,* etc.

Daily Assignment

- Warm-up: Persuade someone to attend church.
- Students will complete Concept Builder 7-B.
- Prayer journal.

- Students should outline all assigned essays and speech for the week.

CONCEPT BUILDER 7-B

Writing Skill: The Persuasive Advertisement Essay

The following was written by World War II correspondent Ernie Pyle. It was used to recruit soldiers. Use the web-diagram on the next page to discuss how Pyle persuades young men to join the army.

Some of the men carried grenades already fixed in the ends of their rifles. All of them had hand grenades. Some had big Browning automatic rifles. One carried a bazooka. Interspersed in the thin line of men every now and then was a medic, with his bags of bandages and a Red Cross arm band on the left arm. The men didn't talk any. They just went. They weren't heroic figures as they moved forward one at a time, a few seconds apart. You think of attackers as being savage and bold. These men were hesitant and cautious. They were really the hunters, but they looked like the hunted. There was a confused excitement and a grim anxiety on their faces.

They weren't warriors. They were American boys who by mere chance of fate had wound up with guns in their hands sneaking up a death-laden street in a strange and shattered city in a faraway country in a driving rain. They were afraid, but it was beyond their power to quit. They had no choice.

They were good boys. I talked with them all afternoon as we sneaked slowly forward along the mysterious and rubbled street, and I know they were good boys.

And even though they aren't warriors born to the kill, they win their battles. That's the point.

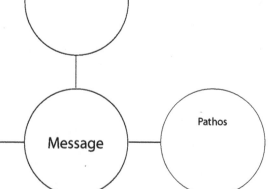

Sample Essay Emphasizing Transitions

Observe the effective way that transitions are used in the following essay:

Religion has always been a central part of American history. We are, and have always been, a religious people. It was, natural then, in the midst of a booming economy of unprecedented prosperity that Americans would fight a religious battle called the Scopes Trial.

Many historians will ask us to see it otherwise. They tell us it was a victory for liberty and justice. It was a landmark case showing the need for separation of Church and state. It emphasized again the need for the separation of Church and state. But they are wrong.

It was a disaster. A sort of spiritual suicide. In the words of the insane but brilliant German nihilist, Frederick Nietzsche, we looked into the abyss.

When you look into an abyss, the abyss also looks into you (Friedrich Nietzsche).[1] *On Looking Into the Abyss: Untimely Thoughts on Culture and Society* by Gertrude Himmelfarb argues that the abyss is the abyss of meaninglessness. The interpreter takes precedence over the thing interpreted, and any interpretation goes. The most obvious aim of such a creed is to weaken our hold on reality, chiefly by denying that there is any reality for us to get hold of; its most probable effect, if we were to take it seriously, would be to induce feelings of despair and dread. This view invites the tyranny of the subjective — anything goes so long as it does not hurt anyone and it is believed sincerely.[2]

In the Scopes Trial, Americans chose to write history to suit themselves and in the process to ignore the Word of God. It was the most natural thing in the world. Americans of the 1920s were dedicated to the pleasure principle. They conceived of history as a form of fiction. Himmelfarb argues that contemporaries play the harlot with words like "freedom" and "liberty." She makes a startling claim: Absolute liberty is itself a form of power — the power to destroy without having to face the consequences.

The Scopes Trial, then, was a pivotal cultural battleground during the mid-1920s; it has remained the battleground to the present age. The roots of this religious conflict were planted in the late 19th century. Before the Civil War, the Protestant denominations were united in a belief that the findings of science confirmed the teachings of religion. But during the 1870s, a lasting division had occurred in American Protestantism over Charles Darwin's theory of evolution. Religious modernists argued that religion had to be accommodated to the teachings of science, while religious traditionalists sought to preserve the basic tenets of their religious faith.

---

1   www.brainyquote.com/quotes/quotes/f/friedrichn161830.html.
2   Gertrude Himmelfarb, *On Looking Into the Abyss: Untimely Thoughts on Culture and Society* (New York: Vintage Press, 1995).

Daily Assignment

- Warm-up: Persuade someone to paint your house.
- Students will complete Concept Builder 7-C.
- Prayer journal.
- Students should write rough drafts of all assigned essays and speech.

Persuasive Techniques

Persuasive writers and speakers trying to persuade the reader of the value of a particular position, attitude, or action. The reader is not interested in fairness or objectivity.

Match these statements with the Persuasive Technique.

Statement	Persuasive Technique
__B.__ Harvard students are all snobs.	**A.** Faulty Reasoning: Writers makes statements that draw readers to a conclusion that is not supported by facts.
__E.__ Either I will go to college or I will fail at everything I try.	**B.** Stereotype: A writer makes unsubstantiated generalizations about groups of people.
__D.__ I drive a car that only the richest people drive.	**C.** Cause and Effect: A writer suggests that some cause leads to an effect that in fact is erroneous.
__A.__ Students will do well on the SAT I if they will only take five or six practice exams.	**D.** Snob Appeal: A writer encourages his reader to adopt a position with the promise that the reader will be joining an "elite group."
__C.__ I know that the election of our president is the cause of my pastor leaving our church.	**E.** Either/Or Fallacy: A writer argues that the reader must accept his position or there will be an effect when in fact the outcome is far more complicated.

we want to avoid these techniques

Public Speaking: Delivery and Converting the Persuasive Advertisement Essay to a Speech

The voice is to the speaker as the ink brush is to the artist or as the pencil is to the writer. The voice is a powerful ally to communicate the message — or it can be a terrible impediment. The speaker must be aware of the speed of the speech — not too fast but not too slow. The speaker must be aware of the volume of the speech — not too low but not too loud. Speak clearly and convincingly. Use pauses to emphasize the points and vary the rhythm in order to help keep the audience's attention. Speaking smoothly, steadily, and candidly earns the audience's respect.

Delivery of the speech is obviously critical to a persuasive advertisement speech. The advertisement speech should be composed and presented like any other persuasive speech; however, the delivery is absolutely crucial. Also, the speaker is acutely aware that the message is cognitive (logos), emotional (pathos), and credible (ethos).

SOME KEYS TO EFFECTIVE SPEECH DELIVERY

Tempo: an appropriate tempo — not too fast, not too slow

Eye contact: look at your audience — make eye contact, or at least appear to make eye contact

Clarity: enunciate plainly with voice tone appropriate to the subject

Body language: face the audience with one foot forward

Facial expressions: exhibit facial responses that match the subject

Daily Assignment

- Warm-up: Persuade your dog to do tricks.
- Students will complete Concept Builder 7-D.
- Prayer journal.
- Review the assigned text. Keep vocabulary cards.
- This is the day that students should write, and then rewrite, the final drafts of their assigned essay and speech.

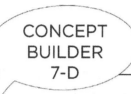

Argumentation

In persuasive writing, argumentation is the technique of choice to persuade the reader to accept a position.

In the following argument identify these three things.

1. The thesis: the purpose of the argument.

2. The counter argument: what the other side believes.

3. The conclusion: a summary or restatement of the thesis.

I heartily accept the motto, — "That government is best which governs least"; and I should like to see it acted up to more rapidly and systematically. Carried out, it finally amounts to this, which also I believe, — "That government is best which governs not at all"; and when men are prepared for it, that will be the kind of government which they will have. Government is at best but an expedient; but most governments are usually, and all governments are sometimes, inexpedient. The objections which have been brought against a standing army, and they are many and weighty, and deserve to prevail, may also at last be brought against a standing government. The standing army is only an arm of the standing government. The government itself, which is only the mode which the people have chosen to execute their will, is equally liable to be abused and perverted before the people can act through it. Witness the present Mexican war, the work of comparatively a few individuals using the standing government as their tool; for, in the outset, the people would not have consented to this measure. —Henry David Thoreau.

The Thesis: the purpose of the argument.

to persuade readers that the goverment is
better when it is not doing anything

The counter argument: what the other side believes.

The conclusion: a summary or restatement of the thesis.

Writing Skill: Summary Report

Chapter 8

Style (Writing and Speaking): Sentences - Overview

Public Speaking Skill: Overcoming Fear and Converting Summary Essay to a Speech

First Thoughts

A summary report is an abbreviated version of a written piece, nonfiction or fiction. Typically, the summary report avoids any value analysis of the piece's argumentation (as a précis would). However, if instructed to do so, you may use a summary report as the first step of serious literary or historical analysis.

Chapter Learning Objectives

In chapter 8 we will look at summary essays. We will focus on the difference between a summary and a précis.

Look Ahead for Friday

- Turn in a final copy of essay and speech

- Take Weekly Essay/Test

Summarize your favorite book, being sure to include all aspects of a good summary. Remember: a summary is an overview — not an analysis — of something. Your essay will include the following literary elements: plot, theme, characters, setting, and tone. This expository essay should be a two-page essay and should include an outline with thesis statement, rough draft, several revisions, final copy with five new (circled) vocabulary words. Give a copy to instructor/parent to evaluate.

In front of an audience, present a one-minute summary of your favorite book. A summary speech has an introduction, body, and a conclusion. It carefully highlights salient components of the book that make it a good book, or, in this case, your favorite book. When you present your speech, give particular attention to your delivery.

You will gain further confidence as you practice the speech out loud — not silently — if possible in the very room where you will present it.

Most importantly, though, pray. Prepare yourself. Memorize a Scripture verse and silently quote it to yourself as you prepare.

Final Project

Correct and rewrite all essays and place them in your Final Portfolio.

Ethos, Logos, Pathos

The main point of the literary piece is succinctly stated in the first paragraph, if not in the first sentence of the précis.

On a first reading of Mark Twain's *Huckleberry Finn*, the reader is tempted to conclude that Twain is writing a humorous happy-go-lucky narrative best read on the side of a tree-covered riverbank. Such a reading is appropriate, but this reading is by a novice, an adolescent, a lover of a frog-jumping contest and of a dangerous rendezvous with Injun Joe in an eerie graveyard. Unfortunately, the more astute, more mature laureates will recognize that Twain is really writing a scathing criticism of an earlier literary movement and worldview called romanticism. The "Arkansaw" feud, for instance, shows Twain's complete disgust with romanticism.

This beginning paragraph of a much larger précis overviews a significant theme of the novel without offering (at this time) much analysis of its value.

Daily Assignment

- Warm-up: Summarize a favorite book.
- Students will complete Concept Builder 8-A.
- Prayer journal: Students are encouraged to write in their prayer journal every day.
- Students should systematically review their vocabulary words daily.

CONCEPT
BUILDER
8-A

Writing Skill: Summary Report

A summary report is an abbreviated version of a written piece, nonfiction or fiction. Typically, the summary report avoids any value analysis of the piece's argumentation.

Using the chart below, summarize a movie, play, or book that you have read.

Title of Movie/Play/Book: The blood of Olympus

Characters: Percy Jackson, Annabeth C., Piper M., Jason G., Leo V., Hazel L., Nico di Angelo, gaea, giants

Setting: Around the world on a ship, present day

Plot Conflicts: The 7 characters have to stop gaea from rising and her monsters from killing the greek gods

Event: Percy and Annabeth out of tartarus, join crew on Argo II

Event: make physicians cure

Event: the fight, and blood of olympus shed / gaea rise

Event: final battle

Resolution (ending): 3 characters put gaea to sleep + win war

Lesson 2

A Summary

A summary, on the other hand, merely summarizes the plot, offers scant comment, and gives no analysis:

> *Huckleberry Finn*, by Mark Twain, is the story of a young Southerner and his attempts to escape with a slave. The entire novel is the narration of this journey. . . .

Daily Assignment

- Warm-up: Summarize a recent sporting event.

- Students will complete Concept Builder 8-B.

- Prayer journal.

- Students should outline all assigned essays and speech for the week.

CONCEPT
BUILDER
8-B

Combining Sentences with Conjunctions

Your writing will be better and will express your thoughts better if you combine sentences with appropriate conjunctions. This is a type of transition (discussed in Lesson 7) and improves paragraph coherence.

Rewrite the following sentences:

1. The mayor is not a mean man. He has limits. (Join with *but*)

2. He was sure there would be an end to the war. The enemy surrendered. (Join with *when*)

3. I really want to go to Dallas, Texas. I want to watch the Steelers beat the Cowboys. (Join with *and*)

Style (Writing And Speaking Skill): Sentences — Overview

In their book *Prose Style: A Handbook for Writers,*[1] Wilfred Stone and J.G. Bell argue that good writers prefer verbs to nouns, the active voice to the passive voice, the concrete to the abstract, the personal to the impersonal, and the shorter to the longer.

When possible, use precise, clear verbs rather than a plethora of nouns however colorful they might be: "The causes of the Civil War are related to the combination of the failure of the political system and the expansion of slavery" is less effective than "Failure of the political system to deal with slavery expansion at least partially caused the Civil War."

Use the active voice: "The skunk stampeded the herd" (active voice) is better than "The herd was stampeded by the skunk" (passive voice).

Use concrete words: "The three-hour tragedy" is better than "The long play."

Use personal nouns: "East coast, classically educated homeschoolers are doing well on the SAT I" is better than "homeschoolers are doing better on tests."

Finally, use shorter expressions when possible to avoid excess words: "I could do nothing to stop my car from hitting the bridge" is better than "There was nothing I could do to stop my car from hitting the bridge."

---

1   Wilfred Stone and J.G. Bell, *Prose Style: A Handbook for Writers* (New York: McGraw-Hill, 1972), p. 72–73.

Daily Assignment

- Warm-up: Summarize a typical family Christmas.
- Students will complete Concept Builder 8-C.
- Prayer journal.

- Students should write rough drafts of all assigned essays and speech.

CONCEPT BUILDER 8-C

Conciseness

Write concisely. Avoid sentences that have unnecessary words. Mark the sentence that is the most concise sentence.

1. _____ I believe that the Germans caused World War II.

    _✓__ The Germans caused World War II.

2. _____ Mary, who was young, published her first novel at age 12.

    _✓__ Mary publisher her first novel at age 12.

3. _____ Although, I never visited Hong Kong, my wife tells me it is beautiful.

    _✓__ I never visited Hong Kong. My wife tells me it is beautiful.

Public Speaking: Overcoming Fear and Converting a Summary Essay to a Speech

Very few of us enjoy speaking in front of a large crowd — we will be nervous, naturally. How can we overcome this fear of exposure that numbs us and makes us dysfunctional? Knowing the material and knowing the speech is of first importance. The speech doesn't have to be memorized; note cards (cue cards) or other props can help you. However, cue cards or props do not substitute for absolutely knowing what you need to say. Know the material well enough that a quick glance will remind you of what comes next in the speech. Be focused and deliberate in your preparation; practice orally delivering the speech several times until presentation day.

Daily Assignment

- Warm-up: Summarize a boring book.

- Students will complete Concept Builder 8-D.

- Prayer journal.

- Review the assigned text. Keep vocabulary cards.

- This is the day that students should write, and then rewrite the final drafts of their assigned essay and speech.

Summary: Poetry

Summarize this poem by Robert Frost.

Mending Wall

Something there is that doesn't love a wall,
That sends the frozen-ground-swell under it,
And spills the upper boulders in the sun,
And makes gaps even two can pass abreast.
The work of hunters is another thing:
I have come after them and made repair
Where they have left not one stone on a stone,
But they would have the rabbit out of hiding,
To please the yelping dogs. The gaps I mean,
No one has seen them made or heard them made,
But at spring mending-time we find them there.
I let my neighbor know beyond the hill;
And on a day we meet to walk the line
And set the wall between us once again.
We keep the wall between us as we go.
To each the boulders that have fallen to each.
And some are loaves and some so nearly balls
We have to use a spell to make them balance:
'Stay where you are until our backs are turned!'
We wear our fingers rough with handling them.
Oh, just another kind of out-door game,
One on a side. It comes to little more:
There where it is we do not need the wall:

He is all pine and I am apple orchard.
My apple trees will never get across
And eat the cones under his pines, I tell him.
He only says, 'Good fences make good neighbors'.
Spring is the mischief in me, and I wonder
If I could put a notion in his head:
'Why do they make good neighbors? Isn't it
Where there are cows?
But here there are no cows.
Before I built a wall I'd ask to know
What I was walling in or walling out,
And to whom I was like to give offence.
Something there is that doesn't love a wall,
That wants it down.' I could say 'Elves' to him,
But it's not elves exactly, and I'd rather
He said it for himself. I see him there
Bringing a stone grasped firmly by the top
In each hand, like an old-stone savage armed.
He moves in darkness as it seems to me~
Not of woods only and the shade of trees.
He will not go behind his father's saying,
And he likes having thought of it so well
He says again, "Good fences make good neighbors."

Writing Skill: Précis

Chapter 9

Style (Writing and Speaking): Sentences - Emphasis

Public Speaking Skill: Presentation Aids and Converting a Précis to a Speech.

First Thoughts

A précis is a summary of a literary work in which the author's story or argument is accurately and fairly reproduced, but in your own words. If there is a story, the précis recounts the basic narrative. If it is a non-fiction piece, the basic arguments are reiterated. In either case, the précis is significantly smaller than the extant piece. A précis employs all levels of critical thinking — analysis, synthesis, and evaluation.

Chapter Learning Objectives

In chapter 9 we will look at précis essays

Look Ahead for Friday

- Turn in a final copy of essay and speech
- Take Weekly Essay/Test

Write a précis of your favorite book, being sure to include all aspects of a good précis. This subject essay should be on two pages and include an outline, rough draft, thesis statement, final copy, and five new (circled) vocabulary words. Give a copy of your paper to your teacher/parent.

Convert a précis of your favorite book into a speech. Remember, in your speech you will need to follow the same guidelines established in the "Writing Skills" section of this lesson. A précis speech is based on a précis manuscript. Identify the salient points of your favorite book and emphasize them. For example, if you were presenting a précis speech on "Charge of the Light Brigade," you would be wise to memorize the refrain and maintain eye contact with your audience as you repeat phrases from it numerous times. It would also allow you to catch your thoughts as you progress through the speech.

Final Project

Correct and rewrite all essays and place them in your Final Portfolio.

Writing Task: Précis

A précis often requires

1. A rearrangement of ideas. It is not longer than the original work, but it is more profound in its analysis of a literary work than is a summary. The précis writer must apprehend and assimilate the complete thought of the passage under discussion. When writers first begin to experiment with précis writing, missing the essential meaning of the text is common.

2. A crystallization of the text in a precise but profound way. A précis addresses intent as well as substance.

   The creation of a précis, whether of a prose or verse passage, involves certain progressive steps that should be followed in a general way by every writer.

   First of all, it is necessary to read the passage attentively and usually more than once, in an effort to grasp the central idea. This preliminary reading is concerned about details.

Often it helps to read the passage aloud, for such a procedure necessitates slowness and may focus attention on some item that would otherwise be missed. At this stage it is actually quite helpful to write a paraphrase or summary of the text. Only on the second reading does the reader ferret out thematic concepts and syllogisms.

3. Analysis — not moralizing or preaching. The sole purpose of précis writers is to interpret the author, not judge the author. Précis writers are not critics; they are interpreters. Frequently, the interpretation of an important part of a passage, or of the passage as a whole, will depend upon the clear under-standing of a single word or a phrase.

   For instance, the refrain "Rode the Six Hundred" by Lord Alfred Tennyson in "Charge of the Light Brigade" is critical to an understanding of the poem:

Half a league, half a league,
Half a league onward,
All in the valley of Death
Rode the six hundred.
"Forward, the Light Brigade!
Charge for the guns!" he said:
Into the valley of Death
Rode the six hundred.
"Forward, the Light Brigade!"
Was there a man dismay'd ?
Not tho' the soldier knew
Some one had blunder'd:
Their's not to make reply,
Their's not to reason why,
Their's but to do and die:
Into the valley of Death
Rode the six hundred.

Cannon to right of them,
Cannon to left of them,

Cannon in front of them
Volley'd and thunder'd;
Storm'd at with shot and shell,
Boldly they rode and well,
Into the jaws of Death,
Into the mouth of Hell
Rode the six hundred.

Flash'd all their sabres bare,
Flash'd as they turn'd in air
Sabring the gunners there,
Charging an army, while
All the world wonder'd:
Plunged in the battery-smoke
Right thro' the line they broke;
Cossack and Russian
Reel'd from the sabre-stroke
Shatter'd and sunder'd.
Then they rode back, but not
Not the six hundred.

Cannon to right of them,
Cannon to left of them,
Cannon behind them
Volley'd and thunder'd;
Storm'd at with shot and shell,
While horse and hero fell,
They that had fought so well
Came thro' the jaws of Death,
Back from the mouth of Hell,
All that was left of them,
Left of six hundred.

When can their glory fade?
O the wild charge they made!
All the world wonder'd.
Honour the charge they made!
Honour the Light Brigade,
Noble six hundred![1]

---

[1]   www.bartleby.com/246/386.html.

The refrain "Rode the six hundred" evolves into "Left of six hundred" and then to "Noble six hundred" and is a critical phrase used in the poem. Its purpose and effect on the substance and theme of the poem is central to understanding the poem. Therefore, a précis would address this element.

A skillful précis writer is on the alert for the meanings and suggestions of individual words and phrases. If they cannot be caught from the context, the dictionary should be consulted. Especially in poetry, précis writers carefully examine all figures of speech to determine precisely what they clarify or illustrate.

Daily Assignment

- Warm-up: Write a précis of your favorite poem.
- Students will complete Concept Builder 9-A.
- Prayer journal: Students are encouraged to write in their prayer journal every day.
- Students should systematically review their vocabulary words daily.

CONCEPT BUILDER 9-A

Writing Task: Précis

By now you are familiar with what is meant by a paraphrase, or a summary, that merely repeats the substance of the original passage in different and usually simpler language, but in approximately the same space. Paraphrasing and summarizing are processes of substituting easy phrases for those that present difficulties. In other words, a paraphrase and a summary are merely restatements of what is in the text

Write a précis of this excerpt from Frederick Douglass's autobiography.

I was born in Tuckahoe, near Hillsborough, and about twelve miles from Easton, in Talbot county, Maryland. I have no accurate knowledge of my age, never having seen any authentic record containing it. By far the larger part of the slaves know as little of their ages as horses know of theirs, and it is the wish of most masters within my knowledge to keep their slaves thus ignorant. I do not remember to have ever met a slave who could tell of his birthday. They seldom come nearer to it than planting-time, harvest-time, cherry-time, spring-time, or fall-time. A want of information concerning my own was a source of unhappiness to me even during childhood. The white children could tell their ages. I could not tell why I ought to be deprived of the same privilege. I was not allowed to make any inquiries of my master concerning it. He deemed all such inquiries on the part of a slave improper and impertinent, and evidence of a restless spirit. The nearest estimate I can give makes me now between twenty-seven and twenty-eight years of age. I come to this, from hearing my master say, sometime during 1835, I was about seventeen years old.

1. A rearrangement of ideas:

2. A crystallization of the text:

Frederick Douglass, *Narrative of the Life of Frederick Douglass, an American Slave*, chapter1; utc.iath.virginia.edu/abolitn/abaufda3t.html.

Lesson 2

Preparation of the Précis

Précis writers must first be effective readers. Effective readers learn to read for comprehension, grasping all the nuances of the text.

Next, précis writers write a cogent but comprehensive discussion of the literary piece. It is more than a summary. It is a new creation.

Last of all, précis writers edit their own work, pruning it of extraneous or useless language, and making sure that it truly reproduces the intent of the author. Usually a précis should be from one-quarter to one-third the length of the original.

In summary, précis writers meet the author halfway: While précis writers may vehemently reject the worldview of the author, they dispassionately must understand the author's point of view. Précis writers analyze; they do not moralize or preach. Their sole purpose is to interpret the author — not judge the author. Précis writers are not critics; they are interpreters.

Précis writers may be surprised at the commitment of time and effort their task requires. However, it is well worth the effort. Writing an effective précis demonstrates the fundamentals of literary criticism and great skill beneficial throughout academic life.

Daily Assignment

- Warm-up: Write a précis of your favorite novel.
- Students will complete Concept Builder 9-B.
- Prayer journal.
- Students should outline all assigned essays and speech for the week.

CONCEPT BUILDER 9-B

Vernacular Language

One should use formal language in most essays. Rewrite the following colloquial (everyday, informal) sentences in a more formal way.

Write in more formal words:

You are one cool dude!

I like the sweet chick!

Write in more colloquial language:

The day was not very good.

It has been a perfect day!

Style (Writing and Speaking Skill): Sentence — Emphasis

Typically, write sentences that are very simple: subject-verb-object. At times, though, let your rhetorical wings fly out and soar with the eagles! Experience with lots of writing in lots of genres with lots of effective evaluation informs the writer when to soar and when to remain simple. Remember: shorter is better, with precision above all. Having said that, the way you craft words will determine the effectiveness of some words. After all, writers can only change the position of words and the punctuation of our sentences to gain emphasis. For example, the sentence "John, please make your bed" is much different from "John Smith, make your bed right now, or you will lose the privilege of having a bed!" Emphasis is a powerful tool in the hand of a skillful writer.

Emphasis is also a very dangerous tool. The young writer typically has a penchant to use too many coordinating and subordinating conjunctions. As one scholar warns, "Sentences of this form have neither the potential elegance and strength of the simple sentence nor the possibilities of emphasis afforded by the complex sentence. They have an inherently boring symmetry." Many of us would rather stay uncommitted in our writing: the compound sentence is a wonderful way to cover all the angles of an issue without committing oneself to any position. "The Romans lost Britain to the barbarians and the barbarians were too strong to conquer" is a lazy way to express this idea "The undermanned Roman army lost Britain to the aggressive barbarians."

Check compound sentences to determine if there really is a legitimate connection. "Mary went to Phoenix, Arizona, but David really likes to paint" is confusing and an example of improperly connected sentences. There is no obvious connection between Mary's trip and David's painting. Creating two separate statements is a better option in this case.

Daily Assignment

- Warm-up: Write a précis of your favorite short story.
- Students will complete Concept Builder 9-C.
- Prayer journal.
- Students should write rough drafts of all assigned essays and speech.

CONCEPT BUILDER 9-C

Active Reading

An effective précis inevitably comes from good reading. You must read the passage well to write about it well! Become an active reader by applying reading strategies:

Predict — figure out what will happen next

Visualize characters, events and setting

Connect personally with what you are reading

Question what happens while you read

Clarify — stop occasionally to review what you understand, expect to have your understanding change and develop as you read on

Evaluate — form opinions about what you read, both while you are reading and after you have finished/ develop your own ideas about characters and events

Answer the following questions from *The Adventures of Huckleberry Finn* by Mark Twain.

Clarify: Why does Twain begin his book this way?

Visualize: Twain is writing to an audience that does not have televisions or computers. Twain has to use language to paint a picture for his audience. Write two.

Connect: Describe someone in your life who is like the Widow Douglas.

Predict: What do you think will happen to Huck Finn?

Question: Why does Twain use colloquial language?

Evaluate: What narrative technique does Twain employ? What advantage does it offer him?

YOU don't know about me without you have read a book by the name of *The Adventures of Tom Sawyer*; but that ain't no matter. That book was made by Mr. Mark Twain, and he told the truth, mainly. There was things which he stretched, but mainly he told the truth. That is nothing. I never seen anybody but lied one time or another, without it was Aunt Polly, or the widow, or maybe Mary. Aunt Polly -- Tom's Aunt Polly, she is -- and Mary, and the Widow Douglas is all told about in that book, which is mostly a true book, with some stretchers, as I said before.

Now the way that the book winds up is this: Tom and me found the money that the robbers hid in the cave, and it made us rich. We got six thousand dollars apiece -- all gold. It was an awful sight of money when it was piled up. Well, Judge Thatcher he took it and put it out at interest, and it fetched us a dollar a day apiece all the year round -- more than a body could tell what to do with. The Widow Douglas she took me for her son, and allowed she would sivilize me; but it was rough living in the house all the time, considering how dismal regular and decent the widow was in all her ways; and so when I couldn't stand it no longer I lit out. I got into my old rags and my sugar-hogshead again, and was free and satisfied. But Tom Sawyer he hunted me up and said he was going to start a band of robbers, and I might join if I would go back to the widow and be respectable. So I went back.

Pretty soon I wanted to smoke, and asked the widow to let me. But she wouldn't. She said it was a mean practice and wasn't clean, and I must try to not do it anymore. That is just the way with some people. They get down on a thing when they don't know nothing about it. Here she was a-bothering about Moses, which was no kin to her, and no use to anybody, being gone, you see, yet finding a power of fault with me for doing a thing that had some good in it. And she took snuff, too; of course that was all right, because she done it herself.

Her sister, Miss Watson, a tolerable slim old maid, with goggles on, had just come to live with her, and took a set at me now with a spelling-book. She worked me middling hard for about an hour, and then the widow made her ease up. I couldn't stood it much longer. Then for an hour it was deadly dull, and I was fidgety. Miss Watson would say, "Don't put your feet up there, Huckleberry;" and "Don't scrunch up like that, Huckleberry -- set up straight;" and pretty soon she would say, "Don't gap and stretch like that, Huckleberry -- why don't you try to behave?" Then she told me all about the bad place, and I said I wished I was there. She got mad then, but I didn't mean no harm. All I wanted was to go somewheres; all I wanted was a change, I warn't particular. She said it was wicked to say what I said; said she wouldn't say it for the whole world; she was going to live so as to go to the good place. Well, I couldn't see no advantage in going where she was going, so I made up my mind I wouldn't try for it. But I never said so, because it would only make trouble, and wouldn't do no good.

Public Speaking Task: Presentation Aids

Presentation aids — especially the PowerPoint presentation — are useful and even expected in some presentations (e.g., business presentations). If you are using PowerPoint, be very careful to maintain eye contact with the audience as you make the presentation. Moving beyond the podium and walking more generally into your audience may be necessary, but awkward unless you have a hand controller to move the presentation forward. Never allow the aid to detract from the content of the speech or the presentation.

Daily Assignment

- Warm-up: Write a précis of your favorite movie.

- Students will complete Concept Builder 9-D.

- Prayer journal

- Review the assigned text. Keep vocabulary cards.

- This is the day that students should write, and then rewrite, the final drafts of their assigned essay and speech.

CONCEPT BUILDER 9-D

Précis: Poetry

Write a précis of the poem "Mending Wall" by Robert Frost (Concept Builder 8-D).

Writing Skill: The Character Profile

Chapter 10

Style (Writing and Speaking): Sentences - Expanding Sentences

Public Speaking Skill: Presentation Aids and Converting a Character Profile to a Speech

First Thoughts

In a character profile, writers highlight the salient components of a person's life. They not only describe the physical appearance of the character, they also offer personality insights.

Chapter Learning Objectives

In chapter 10 we will learn how to write character profiles.

Look Ahead for Friday

- Turn in a final copy of essay and speech
- Take Weekly Essay/Test

Write a character profile of a close friend. Your essay should include an outline, rough draft, thesis statement, final copy, and five new (circled) vocabulary words. Pay particular attention to style (focus, content, organization). Give a copy to instructor/parent to evaluate.

In front of an audience, present a character profile of a close friend.

Final Project

Correct and rewrite all essays and place them in your Final Portfolio.

Sample Character Profile

Character profiles describe the outward appearance as well as the internal person of a character.

While taking a break from my nervous Saturday night sermon review, I discovered my wife holding up to our dull attic light an archaic but still beautiful silver Barbie doll dress. Karen, my wife for almost 15 years, was carefully unpacking her 1960 Barbie dolls.

"Lord," she hopefully prayed, "please don't let Jessica think these clothes are corny."

Some of these 1950ish out-of-style clothes would be part of one of my daughter's Christmas presents. With four children to purchase gifts for, Karen and I found Christmas shopping to be a painful experience. My Scottish wife never hesitated to explore creative alternatives to huge post-Christmas Visa bills. . . .

I owe this woman so much, I thought to myself.

Ebenezer Scrooge

Marley was dead: to begin with. There is no doubt whatever about that. The register of his burial was signed by the clergyman, the clerk, the undertaker, and the chief mourner. Scrooge signed it: and Scrooge's name was good upon 'Change, for anything he chose to put his hand to. Old Marley was as dead as a door-nail.

Mind! I don't mean to say that I know, of my own knowledge, what there is particularly dead about a door-nail. I might have been inclined, myself, to regard a coffin-nail as the deadest piece of ironmongery in the trade. But the wisdom of our ancestors is in the simile; and my unhallowed hands shall not disturb it, or the Country's done for. You will therefore permit me to repeat, emphatically, that Marley was as dead as a door-nail.

Scrooge knew he was dead? Of course he did. How could it be otherwise? Scrooge and he were partners for I don't know how many years. Scrooge was his sole executor, his sole administrator, his sole assign, his sole residuary legatee, his sole friend, and sole mourner. And even Scrooge was not so dreadfully cut up by the sad event, but that he was an excellent man of business on the very day of the funeral, and solemnised it with an undoubted bargain.

The mention of Marley's funeral brings me back to the point I started from. There is no doubt that Marley was dead. This must be distinctly understood, or nothing wonderful can come of the story I am going to relate. If we were not perfectly convinced that Hamlet's Father died before the play began, there would be nothing more remarkable in his taking a stroll at night, in an easterly wind, upon his own ramparts, than there would be in any other middle-aged gentleman rashly turning out after dark in a breezy spot — say Saint Paul's Churchyard for instance — literally to astonish his son's weak mind.

Scrooge never painted out Old Marley's name. There it stood, years afterwards, above the warehouse door: Scrooge and Marley. The firm was known as Scrooge and Marley. Sometimes people new to the business called Scrooge Scrooge, and sometimes Marley, but he answered to both names. It was all the same to him.

Oh! But he was a tight-fisted hand at the grindstone, Scrooge! a squeezing, wrenching, grasping, scraping, clutching, covetous, old sinner! Hard and sharp as flint, from which no steel had ever struck out generous fire; secret, and self-contained, and solitary as an oyster. The cold within him froze his old features, nipped his pointed nose, shriveled his cheek, stiffened his gait; made his eyes red, his thin lips blue; and spoke out shrewdly in his grating voice. A frosty rime was on his head, and on his eyebrows, and his wiry chin. He carried his own low temperature always about with him; he iced his office in the dog-days; and didn't thaw it one degree at Christmas.

External heat and cold had little influence on

Scrooge. No warmth could warm, no wintry weather chill him. No wind that blew was bitterer than he, no falling snow was more intent upon its purpose, no pelting rain less open to entreaty. Foul weather didn't know where to have him. The heaviest rain, and snow, and hail, and sleet, could boast of the advantage over him in only one respect. They often "came down" handsomely, and Scrooge never did.

Nobody ever stopped him in the street to say, with gladsome looks, "My dear Scrooge, how are you? When will you come to see me?" No beggars implored him to bestow a trifle, no children asked him what it was o'clock, no man or woman ever once in all his life inquired the way to such and such a place, of Scrooge. Even the blind men's dogs appeared to know him; and when they saw him coming on, would tug their owners into doorways and up courts; and then would wag their tails as though they said, "No eye at all is better than an evil eye, dark master!"

But what did Scrooge care! It was the very thing he liked. To edge his way along the crowded paths of life, warning all human sympathy to keep its distance, was what the knowing ones call "nuts" to Scrooge. (*A Christmas Carol*, Charles Dickens, p. 1)[1]

_____

1   www.gutenberg.org/ebooks/46.

Daily Assignment

- Warm-up: Write a character profile of yourself.

- Students will complete Concept Builder 10-A.

- Prayer journal: Students are encouraged to write in their prayer journal every day.

- Students should systematically review their vocabulary words daily.

Character Profile I

In a character profile, writers highlight the salient components of a person's life. They not only describe the physical appearance of the character, they also offer personality insights.

Read the following character profile and complete the diagram following.

For over forty years Virgil had worshiped in my small, inner city church in Pittsburgh, PA. Besides being married at our altar and raising his children in our church school, Virgil was an elder, trustee, and superintendent of Sunday schools. He served his God well; he served us well too. But, now, senility had stolen him from us and placed him in an Allison Park Nursing Home.

Serving communion to a saint like Virgil was an inspiring event under any circumstances, but today was turning out to be an extra special day: I was bringing my clerk of Session and good friend, Paul. Paul and Virgil were two of my most faithful members.

While I prepared the elements, I could not help but overhear Paul speaking to Virgil. "Virgil, Virgil, can you hear me? Wink or something!"

Virgil only smiled.

Paul was not to be deterred. "Virgil, it has happened! Can you hear me, Virgil? It has happened! Do you remember, Virgil, all those times we prayed that the children would come. . . well, they've come, Virgil, they have come!"

For the last year our Sunday School had grown from six children to eighty children and, in spite of the fact that it was a mixed blessing to some, to Paul it was the answer to over forty years of prayer. Virgil and Paul had given their life to a worthy dream. They had sacrificed for that dream and, in spite of the fact that Virgil would not enjoy the answer to their prayers, they were still willing to sacrifice, to pray, to work hard, and to let God be responsible for the results. They were, in other words, willing to hope for things that they could not see . . .

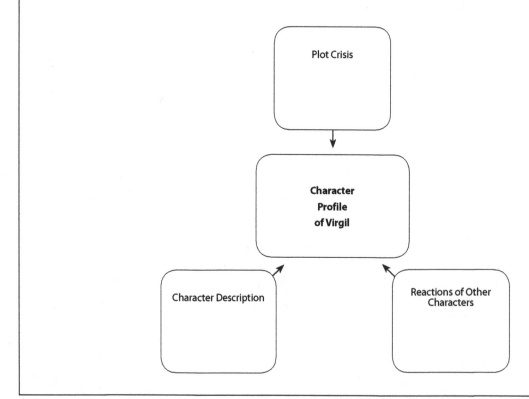

Writing Style: Sentences — Expanding Sentences

An accomplished writer should be able to expand a basic idea with a myriad of vital images and descriptions. Specifically, there are two ways to expand sentences: with cumulative sentences and with details.

Challenge: Contrast the following two paragraphs. Which one is more effective? Why?

1. The pavilion was full of happy children. They were laughing and playing. There was one man who was unhappy, though. He was crying.

2. Across the parking lot, competing with the screams from the adjoining Big Top, children could be heard laughing for at least 50 yards. As I moved closer, however, I saw a peculiar sight: a fat, aging man was crying. In his hand was a picture of a child and a woman. Behind them was the same Big Top, laughing with this frivolous juvenile multitude.

Sometimes shorter is better; however, in the above examples the second, longer passage is much better than the shorter version. Using vivid details and precise language, the second passage is much better than the first passage. The second sentence is an expanded detailed version of the first sentence. The writer develops the paragraph by expanding the details.

Challenge: Consider the following sets of sentences.

Sentences contain words in a series:
The old man was tired, sick, and lost.

Sentences are combined using relative pronouns:
The old man, who was tired, was also sick and lost.

Sentences are combined with an appositive or appositive phrase:
The old man, sick and tired, was also lost.

Daily Assignment

- Warm-up: Write a character profile of your pastor.

- Students will complete Concept Builder 10-B.

- Prayer journal.

- Students should outline all assigned essays and speech for the week.

Character Profile II

Outline a character profile of someone very special to you.

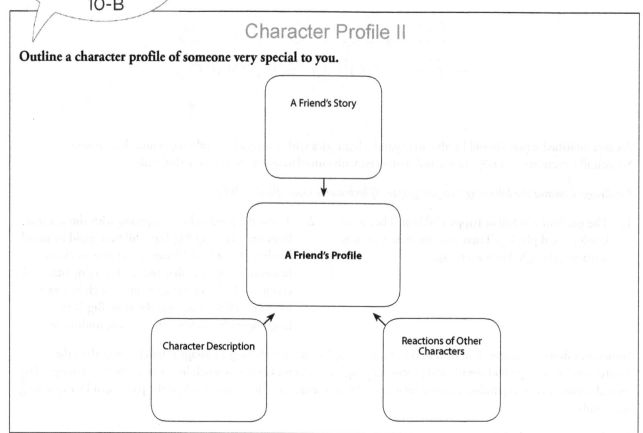

```
                    ┌─────────────────┐
                    │                 │
                    │ A Friend's Story│
                    │                 │
                    └────────┬────────┘
                             │
                             ▼
                    ┌─────────────────┐
                    │                 │
                    │A Friend's Profile│
                    │                 │
                    └─────────────────┘
         ┌─────────────────┐   ┌─────────────────┐
         │                 │   │ Reactions of Other│
         │Character Description│ │    Characters   │
         │                 │   │                 │
         └─────────────────┘   └─────────────────┘
```

Public Speaking: Presentation Aids and Converting a Character Profile to a Speech

In summary, when using any sort of presentation aids, practice using them before the presentation. This is critical in order to check for failure of equipment and to prevent lack of information for operating the equipment. Make sure the presentation aids are large enough and attractive enough. When working with PowerPoint, remember that "less is more." Do not cut and paste large amounts of material for slides. Keep it simple. Finally, for dramatic effect and to prevent distraction, turn off audio-visual equipment when you are not using it.

At their heart, character profile speeches are descriptive essays. The presenter's job is to make characters come alive.

Daily Assignment

- Warm-up: Write a character profile of your pet.

- Students will complete Concept Builder 10-C.

- Prayer journal.

- Students should write rough drafts of all assigned essays and speech.

CONCEPT BUILDER 10-C

Character Profile III

Outline a character profile of yourself. In your profile, highlight your own personality and how others have made you the way you are.

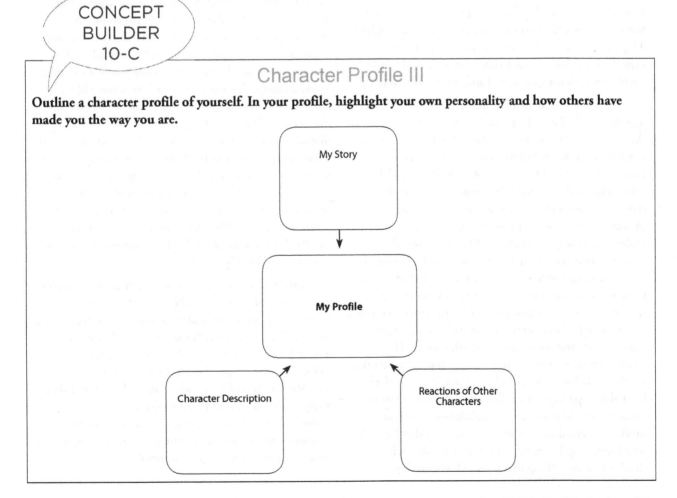

Student Essay

Character Profile: Annika Marisa Lin

This is it, I thought as I boarded the bus with my best friend Annika. It was the very last day of 8th grade, which also meant it was my very last day on Bus 47 with Annika. I thought of all the memories we had together on the bus, when we talked eagerly or sat in companionable silence. The bus played a significant role in our friendship, as it was the only time other than lunch when we could talk and be together. Now it was about to end. After 8th grade, we would be going to the same high school, but it was unlikely we would have the same classes together, which meant no time to visit and talk to each other. We wouldn't even be riding the same bus. In fact, I wouldn't be riding a bus anymore. I lived so close to Century that I would walk there, while Annika would take her usual morning route. After three memorable years, we were going our separate ways. As I was sitting on the seat next to Annika, I sighed. This was one of the last times we may see each other. But even if we see don't see each other much again, I would never forget what a great friend and person she has been.

I can very well remember the very first time we sat together on the bus. I had seen Annika before as we sat at the same table on the first few days of 6th grade, but we never met. At the end of the second or third day, I boarded Bus 47 and filed in along with the formidable 7th graders and towering 8th graders. Even though we didn't know each other at all, it was I who invited her to sit with me. To this day I have no idea what prompted me to do such a thing. Though I had friends, I was an introvert, reserved and sparse with my words. Perhaps I was more outgoing in 6th grade, or maybe I didn't want to be alone. It is also possible that I just wanted to be friends. It was three years ago, and I can't remember much of my thoughts back then. After Annika sat down, we talked a little and got to now each other more. This is also another mystery to me. When I was younger, I wasn't that much of a talker, so it seems like a miracle that we had been able to go beyond the first awkward conversation to being friends. Maybe our personalities were alike, or maybe we deep down we understood each other from the very beginning. But whatever it was, I am sincerely thankful for everything that occurred on that day.

Since the day we met, Annika has always proved to be an amazing friend. She understood everything that I said, she had similar interests as me, she gave me advice, and on top of that, she also loved classical music. This was a rare friend, I realized, not only because she was one of the few my age that understood and loved classical music, but because she was unassuming and was always there for me. Even though she had a punk rockish-type look on the outside, she was caring and honest on the inside. I admired those characteristics and others in her because that's what made her such an awesome friend.

Annika's interest in classical music has especially meant a lot to me. Ever since I was little, I was in love with classical music. However, not many of my friends shared my same views of it; they believed in the common misconception that it was boring. I didn't try to fix their perspective, because pop culture had brainwashed them into narrow-minded conformists. However, with Annika, it was different. She was more of a leader, not a blind follower. She had the guts to dislike something everyone else liked, and like something everyone else disliked. In short, Annika was a nonconformist. This trait gave me the opportunity to discuss openly with someone my views on my favorite topic, music. Her knowledge of composers, famous pianists, and history of music impressed me, and it was a refreshing to have an intelligent conversation with someone once in a while. Our similar interests reassured me that I was not alone, and her courage encouraged me to stand for what I believed in.

Annika is one of the most incredible people I've ever met and one of my best buddies. She is always there for me no matter what, and listens to what I say when no one else will listen to me, much less understand. She is caring, fun, and true to everyone, and as a fellow nonconformist, I will say that she is one of the bravest people I have ever met. She stands up for her beliefs and values even if they disagree with other's beliefs and values. Annika is also someone I can talk freely about my impressions and aspirations toward music. To put it succinctly, Annika is as perfect as a friend could get. (Marissa)

Daily Assignment

- Warm-up: Write a character profile of a sibling.
- Students will complete Concept Builder 10-D.
- Prayer journal.
- Review the assigned text. Keep vocabulary cards.
- This is the day that students should write, and then rewrite, the final drafts of their assigned essay and speech.

CONCEPT
BUILDER
10-D

Elaboration

Good writers include information in their writing that develops their main idea. Here are the types of information that writers provide:

Statistics

Examples

Explanations

Definitions

For example, here is a definition sentence: Love is more than a good feeling or a thoughtful gesture. It is eternal; it is sacrificial; it is real.

Label examples from the following excerpt (one passage has two labels):

1. Immigration is the act or process of moving of people into another nation with the intention of living there permanently. The contrasting term emigration refers to moving from a nation permanently presumably to another nation. Other than Native Americans, the fact is every American family has immigrant roots. Some immigrants were forced to immigrate — African American slaves. Most immigrants, however, came voluntarily.

2. Between 1815 and 1920, about 35 million men, women, and children migrated from Europe, Asia, Canada, and Mexico into the United States. From 1820–1860, for instance, 5 million immigrants came to America. However, from 1860–1900, 15 million immigrants arrived! Many of these migrants ultimately returned to their places of origin. For instance, in 1908 alone, 750,000 people left the United States. Most stayed, however (Ed Fenton et al., *A New History of the United States* (Holt, Rinehart and Winston, 1975).

3. What caused people to immigrate? There were several reasons. Some came to obtain political freedom. For instance, millions of Germans migrated in the middle of the 19th century to escape political unrest.

1. _____ _____

2. _____ _____

3. _____ _____

The General Analysis Essay

Style (Writing and Speaking): Sentences - Writing Complete Sentences

Public Speaking Skill: Converting a General Analysis Essay into a Speech.

First Thoughts

Analysis is a higher-level thinking process. To analyze a problem is to take it apart and understand its parts. Analysis identifies patterns in data and separates parts as a means of recognizing heretofore hidden meanings. Analysis thinking also identifies different meanings of the data.

Chapter Learning Objectives

In chapter 11 we will write analysis essays.

Look Ahead for Friday

- Turn in a final copy of essay and speech
- Take Weekly Essay/Test

Analyze your family by comparing each family member to an animal. Carefully defend your choice. This essay should include an outline, rough draft, thesis statement, final copy, and five new (circled) vocabulary words. The essay must pay particular attention to style (focus, content, organization). Give a copy to instructor/parent to evaluate.

Give a three-minute analysis speech where you compare each family member to an animal. In your speech, em-ploy as many rhetorical questions as you can.

Final Project

Correct and rewrite all essays and place them in your Final Portfolio.

Sample Analysis Essay

The following is an analysis of the evangelical roots of American higher education:

In fact, the American university was built solidly on evangelical principles. An early brochure, published in 1643, stated that the purpose of Harvard University (the oldest American university) was "To advance Learning and perpetuate it to Posterity; dreading to leave an illiterate Ministry to the Churches." Harvard's motto for 300 years was "Christo et Ecclesiae." In fact, most of the U.S. universities founded before the 20th century had a strongly religious, usually Protestant Evangelical Christian character. Yale, Princeton, Chicago, Stanford, Duke, William and Mary, Boston University, Michigan, and the University of Californian had a decidedly evangelical Christian character in the early years of their existence and abandoned it in the 20th century. By the 1920s, the American university had stepped completely back from its evangelical roots. This was true of every American university founded in the first 200 years of our existence.

Universities were founded because early Americans earnestly believed that American society should be governed by evangelical Christian people. They believed that American industry should be run by evangelical Christian entrepreneurs. They believed that American culture should be created by evangelical Christians. The desire to assure that America would be ruled by an evangelical elite was no doubt the primary reason that American universities were founded from 1636–1800.

The marriage of spiritual maturity and elite education is a potent combination and to a large degree assured the success of the American experiment. Its divorce may presage its demise. (James)

The author states his argument quickly (American university was built solidly on evangelical principles) and offers several examples. He advances his argument by arguing that universities were evangelical because "early Americans earnestly believed that American society should be governed by evangelical Christian people." Finally, after analyzing the genesis of American higher education, he finishes by offering an outcome. (The marriage of spiritual maturity and elite education is a potent combination and to a large degree assured the success of the American experiment. Its divorce may presage its demise).

Daily Assignment

- Warm-up: Analyze why your room is so messy.
- Students will complete Concept Builder 11-A.
- Prayer journal: Students are encouraged to write in their prayer journal every day.
- Students should systematically review their vocabulary words daily.

Analysis I

Analysis is a higher-level thinking process. To analyze a problem is to take it apart and understand its parts. Analysis identifies patterns in data and separates parts as a means of recognizing heretofore hidden meanings. Analysis thinking also identifies different meanings of the data.

Analyze the following charts and answer accompanying questions:

Period	Total Immigrants Admitted	Northern and Western Europe		Southern and Eastern Europe	
1861-1870	2,314,824	2,031,624	87.4%	33,628	1.4%
1871-1880	2,812,191	2,070,373	73.6%	201,889	7.2%
1881-1890	5,246,613	3,778,633	72.0%	958,413	18.3%
1891-1900	3,687,564	1,643,492	44.6%	1,915,486	51.9%
1901-1910	8,795,386	1,910,035	21.7%	6,225,486	51.9%
1911-1920	5,735,811	997,438	17.4%	3,379,126	58.9%
1920-1930	4,107,209	1,284,023	31.3%	1,193,830	29.0%

Period	China	Japan	Canada	Mexico
1861-1870	64,301	186	153,878	2,191
1871-1880	123,201	149	383,640	5,162
1881-1890	61,711	2,270	393,304	1,913
1891-1900	14,799	25,942	3,311	971
1901-1910	20,605	129,797	179,226	49,642
1911-1920	21,278	83,837	742,185	219,004
1920-1930	29,907	33,462	942,515	459,287

What one observation can you make from these charts?

There are ALOT of immigrants!! Many immigrants come from Europe. There are not many Japanese immigrants

When did most immigrants arrive?

1901-1910

During which decade did the same immigration originate between two different areas?

Northern/Western Europe and Southern/Eastern Europe in 1920-1930

What can you infer from the fact that Asian immigration was never as much as European immigration?

Not many asians leave Asia, where Europeans seem to trael alot.

Writing Style:
Sentences — Writing Complete Sentences

With few exceptions, use complete sentences when you write. Avoid fragments, comma splices, run-on sentences, and rambling sentences. You will be tempted to write in fragments for the sake of emphasis. Rarely is that acceptable in academic writing.

Generally speaking, at this level, most of you know how to write complete sentences. If there is a need to use a sentence fragment, do so with little fanfare. Do not call attention to the fragment by italics or any other unusual punctuation. The following are examples where sentence fragments may be acceptable:

Rare Use Of A Fragment For Emphasis

1. And, among our own, evangelical professor Mark Noll unkindly observed, "The scandal of the evangelical mind is that there is not much of an evangelical mind." Indeed. Not anymore. Today, more than ever, in the garb of Christian home-schooling, evangelicalism has gained new life.

2. Another time when a sentence fragment might be acceptable is when you ask a question and then answer it for emphasis. "Was I upset?" "Of course!" would be a sentence fragment example that is acceptable when used infrequently.

Comma Splice (Fused Sentence) Commas splices occur when two or more sentences are incorrectly connected with only a comma or with only a conjunction:

"Writing poetry is my favorite, writing prose is okay, too." Notice the use of the comma without a conjunction.

"Writing poetry is my favorite but writing prose is okay, too." Notice the use of the conjunction without a comma.

"Writing poetry is my favorite, but writing prose is okay, too." Notice the use of the conjunction and the comma. Since this example has two complete sentences being used together, they should be joined with a comma and a conjunction. Without the comma and the conjunction, the two sentences are fused together into one — incorrect mechanical construction.

Abbreviating Sentences Sentences may exceed their natural, useful life and may need to be shortened into two sentences, or they may need to be omitted entirely. "Slavery expansion caused the Civil War, but the Second Great Awakening and the ineffectual political process and reform movement exacerbated the situation" is too entangled. Readers forget the main point of the sentence before they finish reading it. Practice breaking this sentence down into two or three more effective sentences. *Slavery expansion caused the Civil War. But, the 2nd great awakening*

Daily Assignment

- Warm-up: Analyze how to eat a piece of pie.
- Students will complete Concept Builder 11-B.
- Prayer journal.
- Students should outline all assigned essays and speech for the week.

Analysis II

Analyze the following charts and answer accompanying questions:

What did the immigrants do? The following is a chart examining the occupations of immigrants to the United States, 1860-1910 (Ernest Rubin, "Immigration and Economic Growth of the U. S.: 1790-1914" *Conference on Income and Wealth*:

Decade	Agriculture	Skilled Labor	Unskilled Labor	Domestic Service	Professional	Misc.
1861-1870	17.6%	24.0%	42.4%	7.2%	0.8%	8.0%
1871-1880	18.2%	23.1%	41.9%	7.7%	1.4%	7.7%
1881-1890	14.0%	20.4%	50.2%	9.4%	1.1%	9.4%
1891-1900	11.4%	20.1%	47.0%	15.1%	0.9%	15.1%
1900-1910	24.3%	20.2%	34.8%	14.1%	1.5%	14.1%

Why was unskilled labor the largest immigration group consistently throughout this time period?

Unskilled labor is the easiest way to work for immigrants because they can get a job fast without having to practice a trade. No slaves mean people need others to work for them

How well have immigrants assimilated in American society?

Immigrants seemed to assimilate well despite the fact that 34-50% of immigrants are in unskilled labor.

New York: National Bureau of Economic Research, 1957); www.nap.edu/openbook

Lesson 3

Public Speaking: Converting a General Analysis Essay into a Speech

You will need to analyze a problem or situation for an analysis speech. In Job 4, Eliphaz the Temanite analyzes Job's problems. He utilizes a time-honored technique commonly employed in analysis speeches: rhetorical questions. A rhetorical question states obvious truth — it is the kind of question that does not need an actual answer. A rhetorical question is used for persuading someone of a truth without the use of argument or to give emphasis to a supposed truth by ironically stating its opposite. Note the repeated use of the rhetorical question in the following passage from Job:

"If someone ventures a word with you, will you be impatient?

But who can keep from speaking?

Think how you have instructed many,

how you have strengthened feeble hands.

Your words have supported those who stumbled;

you have strengthened faltering knees.

But now trouble comes to you, and you are discouraged;

it strikes you, and you are dismayed.

Should not your piety be your confidence

and your blameless ways your hope?

"Consider now: Who, being innocent, has ever perished?

Where were the upright ever destroyed?

As I have observed, those who plow evil

and those who sow trouble reap it.

At the breath of God they are destroyed;

at the blast of his anger they perish.

The lions may roar and growl,

Yet the teeth of the great lions are broken.

The lion perishes for lack of prey,

and the cubs of the lioness are scattered.

"A word was secretly brought to me,

my ears caught a whisper of it.

Amid disquieting dreams in the night,

when deep sleep falls on men,

fear and trembling seized me

and made all my bones shake.

A spirit glided past my face,

and the hair on my body stood on end.

It stopped,

but I could not tell what it was.

A form stood before my eyes,

and I heard a hushed voice:

'Can a mortal be more righteous than God?

Can a man be more pure than his Maker?

If God places no trust in his servants,

if he charges his angels with error,

how much more those who live in houses of clay,

whose foundations are in the dust,

who are crushed more readily than a moth!

Between dawn and dusk they are broken to pieces;

unnoticed, they perish forever. Are not the cords of their tent pulled up,

so that they die without wisdom?' " (Job 4:1–21; NIV).

Additionally, rhetorical questioning is often used for comic effect as in Shakespeare's *King Henry IV, Part 1*, when Falstaff lies about fighting off eleven men single-handedly, then responds to the prince's doubts, "Art thou mad? Is not the truth the truth?"[1]

1   William Shakespeare, *King Henry IV, Part I*, 1597; www.classicreader.com/booktoc.php/sid.5/bookid.807/.

Daily Assignment

- Warm-up: Analyze the causes of your father's baldness.

- Students will complete Concept Builder 11-C.

- Prayer journal.

- Students should write rough drafts of all assigned essays and speech.

CONCEPT
BUILDER
11-C

Analysis III

The structure of an analysis paper, like other academic essays, is traditionally three-part: an introduction in which you introduce your topic and present your thesis; body paragraphs in which you support and explain your analysis with specific evidence and a conclusion that wraps up your paper. You will use this essay again at 12-C. Identify the three parts of this essay in the chart below: Introduction (I), Body (B), Conclusion (C).

I One of the worst monetary investments in the early 17th century was an investment in the Virginia Company. The Virginia Company was a stock-option company set up to raise funds for new colonizing enterprises. It was a bust for its investors.

Its first and only real undertaking was the Jamestown investment. The Jamestown investment proved to be an extraordinarily bad because it lost vast amounts of money for its investors. Principally, this was due to the unwillingness of the early colonizers to do the necessary work of providing for themselves. At the same time, and in defense of the early settlers, the investors never really provided enough capital for adequate supply of the venture. Nevertheless, how extraordinary that the United States, whose business is business President Calvin Coolidge once said, started as a bad business venture!

With very little prospect of profit, the English were much slower than the French, Spanish, Dutch, and even the Portuguese to explore and then to settle the New World. While Drake and others participated in exciting adventures, virtually no Englishman undertook a serious exploration of the New World (except John Cabot). Nonetheless, by 1607, 20 years after the ill-fated colony at Roanoke disappeared, England had a firm geopolitical claim to North America.

Jamestown, Virginia, was the site of the first permanent British settlement in North America. It was founded on May 14, 1607, and was located on a peninsula (later an island) in the James River in Virginia. It was named in honor of King James I.

From the beginning the colony was unsure about its reason for existence. Ostensibly, it was founded for the sole purpose of making profit for its investors. One quick way to make money in the 17th century, of course, was to prospect gold. This possibility was especially appealing to the yeoman (middle class) farmer and second or third son of an aristocratic family (who had scant hope of inheriting any money in England) both of whom made up the majority element of early British settlers. Gold was and still is hard to come by in southeastern, tidewater Virginia.

Finally, after starvation took over half the colony, the new colonists discovered that the cultivation of tobacco was about as good as gold. It was then grown everywhere — including the streets of Jamestown.

No one knows why the early profiteers would choose such an unhealthy place as Jamestown for a settlement. No self-respecting Native American would be caught dead near the place. Situated in an unhealthful marshy area, the colony always had a small population because of a high death rate from disease. What disease did not kill, fire often did. In 1608 Jamestown was accidentally burned, and two years later it was about to be abandoned by its inhabitants when Thomas West, Lord De La Warr, arrived with new energy and new supplies. Other fires occurred in 1676 and 1698. Jamestown fell into decay when the seat of government of Virginia was moved in 1699 to the Middle Plantation (later Williamsburg). By this time quick profit had been abandoned for more long term endeavors — like fishing and agriculture. However, from the beginning the Jamestown experiment was an experiment in profit making.

Saturday Morning Television: An Analysis

The author is remembering his youth and experiences with Saturday morning television and then he offers an analysis of its outcome. (We found, on the little black and white, a place of hope, of continuity, of wholesomeness.)

My brothers Bill and John Hugh and I looked forward to Saturday morning television each week in the 1960s. First came *My Friend Flicka*, snickering and shaking his head on the screen. What a great horse! They don't make them like that anymore. This is not an anthropomorphic George Lucas *War Horse* or a choleric *Black Beauty*. No, this was intrepid but loyal Flicka. What a sensitive horse. He really took care of his boy. We wanted a horse like that. Craig Towles had a horse of sorts — Potato — but he was mean and ugly. Little Ken McLaughlin loved Flicka and Flicka loved Ken. And we loved them both. And they lived happily on Goose Bar Ranch — not a lot like 407 Pine Street but, hey, one can pretend! Remember? And then Roy Rogers. Man, I am still looking for those pants he wore. Sears and Roebuck and Ross Dress For Less has nothing like those things. I think they would look good on my ancient, ever-expanding body. Might help a little. Divert attention from the tummy shelf I so carefully placed above my belt buckle. Next, Hi-yo, Silver, away — the adventures of the masked hero and his Indian — ugh, excuse me — his Native American sidekick. With his faithful Indian (Native American) companion Tonto, the daring and resourceful masked rider of the plains led the fight for law and order in the early West. Return with us now to those thrilling days of yesteryear. The Lone Ranger rides again! After the Lone Ranger it was time for a little serious drama — Johnny Quest. *The Adventures of Johnny Quest* featured teenage adventurers Johnny Quest, Hadji Singh, and Jessie Bannon as they accompanied Dr. Benton Quest and bodyguard Race Bannon to investigate strange things, legends, and mysteries in exotic locales. We could only imagine that the Johnny Quest world was somewhere beyond Texarkana Arkansas — this was as far as we had ever been in our young lives. We hoped to go there someday with a friend as good as Hadji. Johnny had a dog (aka Bandit), too. Even before the 60s began, we were pleasured with Flash Gordon — Luke Skywalker could learn a little bit about courage and fortitude from Flash. No whining on his show. And Flash Gordon never had an identity crisis like whimpy Luke.

Finally, we would end our rich repertoire with Lassie. What a dog! No matter what dog we owned, we all pretended we had a female Collie named Lassie, didn't we? The *Lassie* classic echoed each Saturday morning through my sizzling, flickering black and white 22-inch Philco: "I learned a secret that I will share with you. In the hush, I heard the whippor wills reveal the Secret of the Silent Hills. Not a secret men scheme and plot for, Only true words, we should not forget. 'Love can cure the world of all its ills.' And that's the Secret of the Silent Hills." And for about half a day we would sit in front of our Philco and eat our Frosty Flakes — Little Bill, and John Hugh, and I — and enjoy the safe, child-friendly media world of Saturday morning television. We were not too young to know that the Russians might blow us up next Monday morning or that Ricky Mays might fall asleep in church tomorrow, but today, well, today was Saturday morning. And all was right with the world. It doesn't get much better than that. Happy Saturday morning!

Theologian Walter Brueggemann, in his seminal work called *The Land* argues that, like the wandering Israelites of old, Americans are searching for a "Promised Land." A place of succor, of safety, of love, and of life. Saturday morning, in a caricatured way, in a small way, made the same promises to John Hugh, Little Bill, and to me. We found, on the little black and white, a place of hope, of continuity, of wholesomeness.

Daily Assignment

- Warm-up: Analyze one of your pastor's sermons.

- Students will complete Concept Builder 11-D.

- Prayer journal.

- Review the assigned text. Keep vocabulary cards.

- This is the day that students should write, and then rewrite, the final drafts of their assigned essay and speech.

CONCEPT
BUILDER
11-D

Cause and Effect

Analysis is a good way to show how one event or action directly results in another event or action. Carefully read this passage and complete the accompanying diagram:

The main Native American tribe in the Virginia area in the early 17th century was the Lenape Powhatan Tribe. By the time the English colonists had arrived, the chief of the Powhatans, Chief Powhatan, ruled a formidable 30-tribe confederacy. He allegedly controlled 128 villages with about 9,000 inhabitants. Powhatan initially opposed the English settlement at Jamestown. According to legend, he changed his policy in 1607 when he released the captured Smith. In April 1614, Pocahontas, Powhatan's daughter, married the planter John Rolfe, and afterwards Powhatan negotiated a peace agreement with his son-in-law's people.

Peace reigned until after Powhatan died in 1618. In 1622 a great war broke out between the English settlers and the Powhatan Confederacy. Initially the Powhatan Confederation very nearly destroyed the Jamestown settlement. In the long term, however, the war destroyed the Confederacy as a viable entity Disease and European revenge virtually destroyed the Powhatan Confederacy as a viable element in American history.

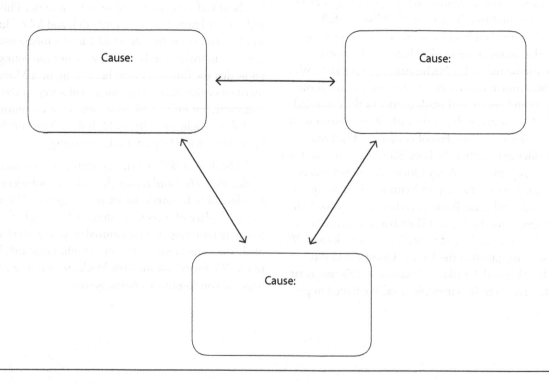

The General Synthesis Essay

Style (Writing and Speaking): Sentences - Writing Clear Sentences

Public Speaking Skill: Converting a General Synthesis Essay into a Speech

First Thoughts

Whenever you report to a friend the things other friends have said about a movie or your pastor's sermon, you engage in synthesis. We synthesize information naturally to understand the connections between things; for example, you have probably stored up a mental data bank of your favorite ice cream flavors. You access that data bank every time you visit an ice cream parlor.

Chapter Learning Objectives

In chapter 12 we will write synthesis essays.

Look Ahead for Friday

- Turn in a final copy of essay and speech
- Take Weekly Essay/Test

Last year, almost a million-plus evangelical Christians graduated from high school. Many of them have gone to college and will become the next generation of leaders. Speculate about what effect this influx of graduates will have on American society and culture. This essay should include an outline with thesis statement, rough draft, revised draft, final copy, and five new (circled) vocabulary words. Pay particular attention to style (focus, content, organization). Give a copy to instructor/parent to evaluate.

While attending a local state university, you have written a very impressive paper entitled, "A Case for the Mosaic Authorship of the Pentateuch." Your unbelieving professor is so impressed that he wants to speak to you privately. You recognize this invitation as an opportunity to share the gospel with this professor. Write a three-minute synthesis speech organizing and presenting evidence for the Mosaic authorship of the Pentateuch.

Final Project

Correct and rewrite all essays and place them in your Final Portfolio.

Sample Family Mission Statement

The following is a synthesis statement of the Stobaugh family mission.

We are called to live radical Christian lives as if we belong to God and not to ourselves (Galatians 2:20). Therefore, we will seek the Lord with all our heart — knowing He will be found. We will have a heart for the lost. He has given us the ministry of reconciliation; indeed, our family is an image of this reconciliation (Romans 8; 2 Corinthians 5). We will be His ambassadors. He has given us a family to rear and people to influence for Him. We want to be world changers. The job(s) to which God has called us is requiring all we have, and it is worthy of our best and total efforts.

We will rear our four children to be world changers. We want them to accept this mission statement, and we want them to discern the times.

Pastoring, writing, lecturing, teaching — all are related to the above-mentioned mission statement.

Henceforth, the Stobaughs will make decisions based on this mission statement — not on circumstances. Every new job or activity must further this mission statement or be rejected.

Daily Assignment

- Warm-up: Create a new game combining baseball and hockey.
- Students will complete Concept Builder 12-A.
- Prayer journal: Students are encouraged to write in their prayer journal every day.
- Students should systematically review their vocabulary words daily.

Synthesis

Synthesis is related to division, classification, or comparison. Instead of finding similarities and differences, synthesizing information is a matter of pulling them together into some kind of perceivable unity. In a way, all your writing is an exercise in synthesis. Synthesis searches for links between information for the purpose of constructing a thesis. It classifies, divides, and compares, and then distills the information into a thesis or purpose statement. Synthesis is a higher-level thinking process. To synthesize a problem is to put things together in another way.

The following is an imaginary problem. Complete the chart to find a solution (synthesis):

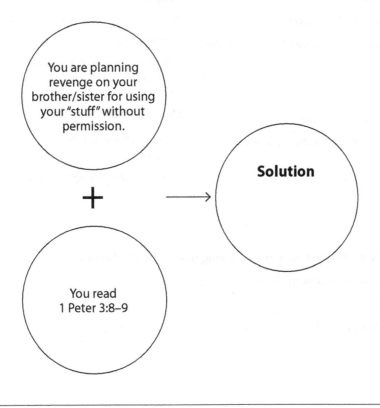

Writing Style: Sentences
— Writing Clear Sentences

Students should avoid incomplete comparisons, ambiguous wording, indefinite references, misplaced modifiers, and dangling modifiers. Here are some examples.

Incomplete Comparison

My home is like an 18-wheeler. (incorrect)

Full of frenetic activity, my home proceeds through time like an 18-wheeler. (correct)

Indefinite Reference

The soldier fought in the war. (incorrect).

The union soldier fought in the Civil War. (correct)

Misplaced Modifier

The man drove by a horse near the barn down the road. (incorrect)

The man drove his car near a horse standing by the barn. (correct)

Dangling Modifier

Standing in the rain four hours, the bus finally came. (incorrect)

After I stood in the rain for four hours, the bus finally came. (correct)

Daily Assignment

- Warm-up: Create a solution to your sister's long times in the bathroom.
- Students will complete Concept Builder 12-B.
- Prayer journal.
- Students should outline all assigned essays and speech for the week.

CONCEPT
BUILDER
12-B

Problem/Solution Chart

Most decisions are a synthesis of data and a resulting solution outcome. Complete the following problem/ solution chart concerning a problem you are facing. An example is provided.

Problem

#1 My brother uses my bicycle without my permission.

#2

Possible Solutions	Results
#1 Wreck my bike.	**Pro**
#2	#1 My brother will not use my bike.
	#2
	Con
	#1 I won't use my bike either!
	#2
#1 Warn my brother. If he stops fine. If he doesn't, tell our parents.	**Pro**
	#1 I give my brother a chance to stop. If he doesn't, he certainly will stop when Mom & Dad intervene!
	#2
	Con
	#1 He may not believe me or he might tell Mom & Dad about something that I have done that will get me into trouble.
	#2

Decision

#1 I will warn my brother and then tell Mom and Dad if he does not stop.

#2

Public Speaking: Converting a Synthesis Essay to a Synthesis Speech

A synthesis speech accurately reports information about a topic using different phrases and sentences. It is organized in such a way that listeners can immediately see where the information overlaps. It defines and interprets the topic and enables the listener to understand the topic in greater depth.

The following is a synthesis essay/speech by the French author Victor Hugo, who discusses the purpose of drama by discussing all the elements that combine to make it drama.

Sample Synthesis Essay/Speech

It seems to us that someone has already said that the drama is a mirror wherein nature is reflected. But if it be an ordinary mirror, a smooth and polished surface, it will give only a dull image of objects, with no relief — faithful, but colourless; everyone knows that colour and light are lost in a simple reflection. The drama, therefore, must be a concentrating mirror, which, instead of weakening, concentrates and condenses the coloured rays, which makes of a mere gleam a light, and of a light a flame. Then only is the drama acknowledged by art.

The stage is an optical point. Everything that exists in the world — in history, in life, in man — should be and can be reflected therein, but under the magic wand of art. Art turns the leaves of the ages, of nature, studies chronicles, strives to reproduce actual facts (especially in respect to manners and peculiarities, which are much less exposed to doubt and contradiction that are concrete facts), restores what the chroniclers have lopped off, harmonises what they have collected, divines and supplies their omissions, fills their gaps with imaginary scenes which have the colour of the time, groups what they have left scattered about, sets in motion anew the threads of Providence which work the human

marionettes, clothes the whole with a form at once poetical and natural, and imparts to it that vitality of truth and brilliancy which gives birth to illusion, that prestige of reality which arouses the enthusiasm of the spectator, and of the poet first of all, for the poet is sincere. Thus the aim of art is almost divine: to bring to life again if it is writing history, to create if it is writing poetry.

It is a grand and beautiful sight to see this broad development of a drama wherein art powerfully seconds nature; of a drama wherein the plot moves on to the conclusion with a firm and unembarrassed step, without diffuseness and without undue compression; of a drama, in short, wherein the poet abundantly fulfills the multifold object of art, which is to open to the spectator a double prospect, to illuminate at the same time the interior and the exterior of mankind: the exterior by their speech and their acts, the interior, by asides and monologues; to bring together, in a word, in the same picture, the drama of life and the drama of conscience.[1]

---

1   Victor Hugo, "Preface to Cromwell," 1827; www.Bartleby.com/39/40.html.

Daily Assignment

- Warm-up: Create a solution to your mother's insistence that you eat broccoli.
- Students will complete Concept Builder 12-C.
- Prayer journal.
- Students should write rough drafts of all assigned essays and speech.

Comparison/Contrast

A primary form of synthesis is the comparison and contrast essay. Reread Concept Builder 11-C and compare and contrast that article with the article below.

Meanwhile, farther north, in New England, Englishmen were starting a holy experiment. The historian Perry Miller wrote, "Without some understanding of Puritanism . . . there is no understanding of America." Indeed. But who were the Puritans? What is the difference between a Boston Puritan and a Plymouth Pilgrim? Were Puritans bigots? Saints? Puritanism, a movement arising within the Church of England in the latter part of the 16th century, sought to carry the reformation of that church beyond the point the early Anglican or Church of England had gone. The Church of England was attempting to establish a middle course between Roman Catholicism and the ideas of the Protestant reformers. This was unacceptable to a growing number of reformers, called Puritans, who wanted the Church of England to reject Anglicanism and embrace Calvinism. The term Puritanism was also used in a broader sense to refer to attitudes and values characteristic of these radical reformers. Thus, the Separatists (i.e., Pilgrims) in the 16th century, the Quakers in the 17th century, and Nonconformists after the Restoration were called Puritans, although they were no longer part of the established church. For our purposes, though, we will refer to the Puritans in two ways: Puritans and Pilgrims.

The Pilgrims, or founders of Plymouth in Massachusetts were, like their countrymen in Virginia, initially dependent upon private investments from profit-minded backers to finance their colony. In other ways, however, these intensely religious people were nothing like the Jamestown settlers.

The stated purpose of the Separatist expedition was to worship God in a place and in a fashion that was more conducive to their world view. This world view was decidedly Theistic/ Calvinistic. These religious Separatists believed that the true church was a voluntary company of the faithful under the spiritual direction of a pastor. In all Puritanism, including Separatism, there was not a clear distinction between what was secular and what was sacred. The Church and state were one and the notion that they were separate was a ludicrous thought indeed to the Puritan. The Pilgrims, unlike the Puritans who settled in Boston, wanted to separate from the Church of England — not merely "purify" the church– but they did not wish to separate the Church from the state.

The Pilgrims, then, were committed Christians but they were also loyal Englishmen. They came to the new world as English patriots with a strong faith in Jesus Christ.

In 1620, the Pilgrims, whose legal destination really lay 300 miles south in Virginia, mistakenly landed on Cape Cod. They called their new settlement Plimouth Plantation. In the first year of settlement, nearly half the settlers died of disease. Thanks to help from the local natives, a few survived. Although none of their principal economic pursuits — farming, hunting, fishing, and trading — promised instant wealth, the Pilgrims were, nonetheless, after only five years, self-sufficient. They were free to focus on more eternal issues — like advancing the Kingdom of God in a wilderness.

Before disembarking from the Mayflower in 1620, William Bradford, demanded that all the adult males sign a compact promising obedience to a legal covenant promoting a very narrow theistic legal plan. The Compact placed biblical law above British common law. The highly religious Mayflower Compact was an important step in the evolution of American democracy.

The Puritans of Boston, Massachusetts Bay, arriving in 1630, like the Pilgrims, sailed to America to worship God freely. As mentioned, unlike the Pilgrims, the Puritans did not desire to separate themselves from the Church of England but, rather, hoped to reform it. Nonetheless, the later notions of freedom and equality, so precious to later New England patriots, were completely foreign to Puritan leaders. The leaders of the Massachusetts Bay enterprise never intended their colony to be a bastion of freedom and toleration in the New World; rather, they intended it to be a "City on a Hill," a model of Christian felicity and fervency.

Massachusetts Bay was not a democracy; it was an autocracy under the law of the land and the perceived laws of the Bible. This was one of the first efforts to create a new society entirely on the Word of God. The first governor John Winthrop believed that it was not the duty of the public officials of the commonwealth to act as the direct representatives of their constituents but rather to act entirely according to the laws of the land and the laws of the World of God. The will of the people was suspect and even spurious when stacked against the Bible.

Nonetheless, in 1634 the General Court, the ruling body of Massachusetts Bay, under the stated authority of Scripture, adopted a new plan of representation that became a prototype for American representative democracy. Each town was allowed to send representatives to a sort of legislature. This was a new phenomenon, even in British political history.

Nonetheless, Puritan society was certainly not egalitarian and several disenchanted Puritans founded other colonies, notably Connecticut and Rhode Island. In fact, Roger Williams ironically founded Rhode Island as a religious sanctuary from orthodox Massachusetts Bay Colony!

One final note: Most of us think of Puritans as colorless, unhappy, stuffy white collared, black coated, frowning saints. Nothing could be farther from the truth. They were fun loving, active people, whose love of life was only surpassed by their love of God. We will discover that the Puritan civilization was a successful marriage between cultural sonority and Christian devotion.

Colonists	Origination	Religious Emphasis	Government
Jamestown			
Plimoth (Pilgrims)			
Boston (Puritans)			
Conclusion Similarities/Differences			

Synthesis Essay Example

Apologetics, the defense of the gospel, is a form of synthesis. It is both the culmination of evidence for Christianity and the refutation of arguments against Christianity. In both cases, the writer must synthesize supporting and opposing arguments and develop a persuasive argument. G.K. Chesterton, in his own indomitable way, does so with élan, acumen, and humor in the following excerpt.

Orthodoxy – Introduction In Defence Of Everything Else

THE only possible excuse for this book is that it is an answer to a challenge. Even a bad shot is dignified when he accepts a duel. When some time ago I published a series of hasty but sincere papers, under the name of "Heretics," several critics for whose intellect I have a warm respect (I may mention specially Mr. G.S. Street) said that it was all very well for me to tell everybody to affirm his cosmic theory, but that I had carefully avoided supporting my precepts with example. "I will begin to worry about my philosophy," said Mr. Street, "when Mr. Chesterton has given us his." It was perhaps an incautious suggestion to make to a person only too ready to write books upon the feeblest provocation. But after all, though Mr. Street has inspired and created this book, he need not read it. If he does read it, he will find that in its pages I have attempted in a vague and personal way, in a set of mental pictures rather than in a series of deductions, to state the philosophy in which I have come to believe. I will not call it my philosophy; for I did not make it. God and humanity made it; and it made me. . . .

To show that a faith or a philosophy is true from every standpoint would be too big an undertaking even for a much bigger book than this; it is necessary to follow one path of argument; and this is the path that I here propose to follow. I wish to set forth my faith as particularly answering this double spiritual need, the need for that mixture of the familiar and the unfamiliar which Christendom has rightly named romance. For the very word "romance" has in it the mystery and ancient meaning of Rome. Any one setting out to dispute anything ought always to begin by saying what he does not dispute. Beyond stating what he proposes to prove he should always state what he does not propose to prove. The thing I do not propose to prove, the thing I propose to take as common ground between myself and any average reader, is this desirability of an active and imaginative life, picturesque and full of a poetical

curiosity, a life such as western man at any rate always seems to have desired. If a man says that extinction is better than existence or blank existence better than variety and adventure, then he is not one of the ordinary people to whom I am talking. If a man prefers nothing I can give him nothing. But nearly all people I have ever met in this western society in which I live would agree to the general proposition that we need this life of practical romance; the combination of something that is strange with something that is secure. We need so to view the world as to combine an idea of wonder and an idea of welcome. We need to be happy in this wonderland without once being merely comfortable. It is THIS achievement of my creed that I shall chiefly pursue in these pages. . . .

I add one purely pedantic note, which comes, as a note naturally should, at the beginning of the book. These essays are concerned only to discuss the actual fact that the central Christian theology (sufficiently summarized in the Apostles' Creed) is the best root of energy and sound ethics. They are not intended to discuss the very fascinating but quite different question of what is the present seat of authority for the proclamation of that creed. When the word "orthodoxy" is used here it means the Apostles' Creed, as understood by everybody calling himself Christian until a very short time ago and the general historic conduct of those who held such a creed. I have been forced by mere space to confine myself to what I have got from this creed; I do not touch the matter much disputed among modern Christians, of where we ourselves got it. This is not an ecclesiastical treatise but a sort of slovenly autobiography. But if any one wants my opinions about the actual nature of the authority, Mr. G.S. Street has only to throw me another challenge, and I will write him another book.[1]

---

1   G.K. Chesterton, *Orthodoxy*, preface; www.pagebypagebooks.com/Gilbert_K_ Chesterton/Orthodoxy/Introduction_in_Defence_of_Everything_Else_ p3.html.

Daily Assignment

- Warm-up: Create an alternative solution to the rule that you cannot watch tv on school nights.

- Students will complete Concept Builder 12-D.

- Prayer journal.

- Review the assigned text. Keep vocabulary cards.

- This is the day that students should write, and then rewrite, the final drafts of their assigned essay and speech.

CONCEPT BUILDER 12-D

Predicting

When you read a story, watch a movie, or listen to a speech, you are figuring out what will happen next. This is a synthesis exercise — you are gathering data, and then predicting an outcome. Read the following story and predict an outcome.

The Camel, the Jackal, and the Crow

In a far off forest, there lived a lion served by a leopard, a jackal and a crow. One day they sighted a camel who lost his way. Thinking the camel they saw was an unusual animal, the lion asked his assistants to find out if he was a wild animal or domestic animal.

The crow said that the camel was a domestic animal fit to be killed and eaten. Refusing to eat the camel the lion said: "I shall not kill someone who came seeking hospitality. According to our elders, you cannot kill even an enemy who came trusting you. Assure him of safety and bring him to me."

The three assistants brought the camel to the presence of the lion. On the lion asking the camel to relate his story, the camel told him how he was part of a trade caravan and how he had lost his way.

The lion told the camel, "Camel, why do you go back to your village and become once again a beast of burden? Remain with us without any hesitation and feast on this tender grass." Thereafter, the camel stayed on to live happily with the lion and his three assistants.

One day, the lion was locked in a battle with an elephant. The elephant badly injured him. The lion became too weak to hunt. Without food he was in no position to do

anything. Then, the lion asked the assistants to go out and look for some animal for his meal. "Bring the animal here. I will kill him somehow and provide food for you all," said the lion.

The leopard, the jackal, and the camel looked everywhere for an animal but could not find anyone. The jackal told his lord, "Oh, lord, we went to every nook and corner of the forest. We could not find a single animal. We are tired, weak and hungry. Since my lord is also in the same condition, I humbly suggest that we make a meal of this camel."

Highly annoyed, the lion said, "I have given him my word. How can I kill him? Haven't our elders said that no gift of land or cow or food is greater than the gift of an assurance?"

"You are right my lord. It is a sin to kill him who has your word. But if the camel voluntarily offers himself as food it is no sin to accept the offer. If he does not volunteer, you can kill anyone of us. You are hungry and close to your end. If we are not of use to you at this time what value has our lives?"

"This seems to be more reasonable," said the lion.

The Camel, the Jackal, and the Crow

Clues from the story	Prediction

"The Camel, the Jackal, and the Crow," Panchatantra Stories; forum1.sahyadri.com/showthread php?tid= 654&pid=1065).

Literary Analysis

Chapter 13

Style (Writing and Speaking): Sentences - Writing Clear Sentences

Public Speaking Skill: Converting a Literary Analysis Essay into a Speech

Chapter Learning Objectives

In chapter 13, we will learn how to write literary analysis. Literary analysis is writing about literature. It is analyzing, taking apart, the components of a literary piece and explaining what they mean. But it is more than that. A first cousin to literary analysis is apologetics, the art of defending the faith. When one learns to analyze literature, one is gaining the same cognitive skills to defend Christianity. Is there any wonder, then, that the greatest apologist of the 20th century — C. S. Lewis — was an English teacher?

Look Ahead for Friday

Write a literary analysis of a favorite short story or novel, from rough draft, to revised draft, to final copy, with five new (circled) vocabulary words. Pay particular attention to style (focus, content, organization). Give a copy to instructor/parent to evaluate.

Final Project

Correct and rewrite all essays and place them in your Final Portfolio.

Background

There are many tools authors employ to convey their message. *Allusion* is a casual and brief reference to a famous historical or literary figure or event: "You must borrow me Gargantua's mouth first. 'Tis a word too great for any mouth of this age's size" (Shakespeare). Shakespeare uses a comparison to help the reader understand his point.

The main character in a literary piece is the *protagonist.* An *antagonist* is the person with whom the main character has the most conflict. He is the enemy of the main character, the protagonist. In *The Scarlet Letter,* by Nathaniel Hawthorne, for instance, Chillingworth is the antagonist. Hester, Chillingworth's wife, the person who wears the scarlet letter, is the *protagonist*. Introduced characters whose sole purpose is to develop the main character are called *foils.* Conflict often occurs within a character. This is called *internal conflict.* An example of this occurs in Stephen Crane's *Red Badge of Courage* when Henry Fleming, the protagonist, is struggling within himself about whether or not he should flee from the battlefield. An *external conflict* is normally an obvious conflict between the protagonist and antagonist(s).

The *plot* is the story. The plot includes the events of the story, in the order the story gives them. A typical plot has five parts: *exposition, rising action, crisis or climax, falling action,* and *resolution.* Crisis or climax is the moment or event in the plot in which the conflict is most directly addressed: the main character "wins" or "loses," or the secret is revealed. After the climax, the *denouement* or *falling* action occurs.

The *setting* is the place(s) and time(s) of the story, including the historical period, social milieu of the characters, geographical location, and descriptions of indoor and outdoor locales. The theme is the one-sentence major purpose of a literary piece, rarely stated but implied. The theme is not a moral, which is a statement of the author's didactic purpose of his literary piece. A *thesis statement* is similar to the theme. A précis is a summary of the plot or a portion of the plot.

The *tone* is the mood of a literary piece. For instance, the tone or mood of Poe's poem "Annabel Lee" is quite somber.

Among others, these terms are the critic's tools to discuss and to analyze literature. As a physician defines his patient in terms of this or that syndrome or physical attribute, the critic describes his literary piece in terms of a credible narrator or an exciting plot or an effective theme.

One final word: Literary criticism papers are more frequently assigned than any other high school or college writing assignment. Therefore, developing this craft and continuing to refine it throughout your writing career is a must in academics.

Daily Assignment

- Warm-up: Write a literary Analysis of your favorite novel.
- Students will complete Concept Builder 13-A.
- Prayer journal: Students are encouraged to write in their prayer journal every day.
- Students should systematically review their vocabulary words daily.

Literary Analysis: Alliteration

Literary analysis or *criticism* is a way to talk about literature. Literary analysis is a way to understand literature better. If we really want to understand something, we need to have a common language with everyone else. If we talk about cooking, for instance, we would need to know certain terminology and use it when describing the process. How lost we might be without knowing what "to cream the butter and sugar" means! Literary analysis employs a common language to take apart and to discuss literary pieces. The following terms are part of a language that critics use to discuss literature.

Authors—especially poets—use sounds to create a mood or to make a particularly important point. *Alliteration* is the repetition of initial consonant sounds. The repetition can be juxtaposed (side-by-side, as in *simply sad*). An example: "I conceive, therefore, as to the business of being profound, that it is with writers, as with wells; a person with good eyes may see to the bottom of the deepest, provided any water be there; and that often, when there is nothing in the world at the bottom, besides dryness and dirt, though it be but a yard and a half underground, it shall pass, however, for wondrous deep, upon no wiser a reason than because it is wondrous dark" (Jonathan Swift). Swift uses alliteration to create a satiric tone.

Read this poem by Eve Merriam and give three examples of alliteration:

Weather

Dot a dot dot dot a dot dot
Spotting the windowpane.

Spack a spack speck flick a flack fleck
Freckling the windowpane.

A spatter a scatter a wet cat a clatter
A splatter a rumble outside.

Umbrella umbrella umbrella umbrella
Bumbershoot barrel of rain.

Slosh a galosh slosh a galosh
Slither and slather a glide

A puddle a jump a puddle a jump
A puddle a jump puddle splosh

A juddle a pump a luddle a dump
A pudmuddle jump in and slide!

1. Dot a dot dot dot a dot dot

2. Spack a spack speck

3. flick a flack fleck... freckling

Sample Student Essay

Note any errors you find in this student's critical analysis.

Crime and Punishment:

Narrative Technique

The book *Crime and Punishment* by the famous Russian author Fyodor Dostoyevsky is a melancholy and yet fascinating story of a young man (Raskolnikov) who commits a crime (he murders an old deceptive hag and her innocent sister) and is punished by his own conscience. It is told through omniscient narration, a nameless voice who reliably reports to the reader everything that the characters do and say and also what they think.

Most of the time the narrator keeps his opinions to himself — simply revealing the thought and actions of Raskolnikov and the other characters. The characters describe or experience the physical environment, the look on people's faces, and the level of tension among them.

However, while the author employs omniscient narration, he seems, at times, to stray into limited narration. Most of the time what the reader learns is what Raskolnikov (the protagonist) sees or feels: that's the clue that he is the central focus of the novel. Since Raskolnikov is the major character, almost everything the narrator tells the reader is about him. The other characters and events are described primarily for what they reveal about Raskolnikov. There are, for instance, only a few scenes in which he does not appear. At such times he remains the focus, even when he is physically absent. The narrator shows the reader the warm affection Raskolinkov's family and friends feel for him in a few scenes where he is absent. While the reader decides what Raskolnikov is really like, these scenes help the reader realize that he has many good qualities after all. The author uses omniscient narration effectively to show how his protagonist develops. Therefore, while it's true that the narrator doesn't say, "Hate this character," or "Love this one," the details observed by the reader in narration lead him to the conclusion Dostoyevsky intends.

Omniscient (or all-knowing) narration is a favorite device of authors writing complicated novels, because it is an effective method for giving the reader some comprehensive views of several characters. While Dostoyevsky writes from omniscient narration, he still has his favorite interpreter: Raskolinkov. (Jessica)

Daily Assignment

- Warm-up: Write a literary Analysis of your favorite poem.
- Students will complete Concept Builder 13-B.
- Prayer journal.
- Students should outline all assigned essays and speech for the week.

Literary Analysis: Characterization

Read the following passage from "Pecos Bill" by Edward S. O'Reilly and complete the chart. Refer to Lesson 1 for additional guidance.

Pecos Bill

Well now Pecos Bill was born in the usual way to a real nice cowpoke and his wife who were journeying west with their eighteen children. Bill's Ma knew right from the start that he was something' else. He started talkin' before he was a month old, did his teething on his Pa's Bowie knife and rode his first horse jest as soon as he learned to sit up on his own. When he started to crawl, Pecos Bill would slither out of the wagon while his Mama was cookin' supper and wrestle with the bear cubs and other wild animals that roamed the prairies.

Well now, Texas jest became too tame for Pecos Bill once he killed off all the bad men, so he struck out for New Mexico, looking for a hard outfit. He asked an old trapper he met on the way where he could find a hard outfit, and the trapper directed Bill to a place where the fellers bit nails in half for fun. It sounded like a promisin' place to Bill, so he set off. But his durned fool hoss got its neck broke on the way, and Bill found himself afoot.

Now everyone in the West knows that Pecos Bill could ride anything. No bronco could throw him, no sir! Fact is, I only heard of Bill getting' throwed once in his whole career as a cowboy. Yep, it was that time he was up Kansas way and decided to ride him a tornado.

Now, Pecos Bill had a way with wimmen. No doubt. But his one true love was Slue-foot Sue. She was his first wife — and she could ride almost as good as Bill himself. Bill first saw Slue-foot Sue ridin' a catfish down the Rio Grande.

Pecos Bill Protagonist	
Pecos Bill	**Internal Conflict**
	Conflict
Antagonist	

O'Reilly, Edward S., *Saga of Pecos Bill*, 1923

Writing Style:
Sentences — Sentence Variety

Use sentence variety. First, vary the beginnings of your sentences. *I was at home yesterday. I saw a television show. I did not like the show* is inferior to *While at home yesterday, I saw a boring television show.* Beginning sentences with modifiers and phrases is a good way to vary sentence structure. Another way is to vary the kinds and lengths of sentences you write.

Daily Assignment

- Warm-up: Write a literary Analysis of your favorite short story.
- Students will complete Concept Builder 13-C.
- Prayer journal.
- Students should write rough drafts of all assigned essays and speech.

CONCEPT BUILDER 13-C

Literary Analysis: Plot

The *plot* is the story. The plot includes the events of the story, in the order the story gives them. A typical plot has five parts: *exposition, rising action, crisis* or *climax, falling action,* and *resolution*. Crisis or climax is the moment or event in the plot in which the conflict is most directly addressed: the main character "wins" or "loses," or the secret is revealed. After the climax, the denouement or falling action occurs.

Complete the following chart using the short story "Pecos Bill."

Plot
Exposition
Rising Action
Crisis
Falling Action
Resolution

Public Speaking:
Literary Analysis

It is quite challenging to convert a literary analysis essay into a literary analysis speech. For one thing, you have the arduous task of analyzing a story, characters, and other literary concepts without giving away the final resolution or even the ultimate theme. For instance, you will lose your audience fairly quickly if you begin an analysis of "The Fall of the House of Usher" by Edgar Allan Poe, with a statement that "the house killed the whole family." The profound insights of a brilliant literary analysis essay may very easily evolve into a superficial discussion of a lukewarm literary piece. The truth is, writing a literary analysis speech (which is a process speech) is really challenging.

So what is one to do? It is critical that you use an outline. Devise an outline before — not after — you write the speech. Be certain that you organize your points well. Use multiple transitions. Do not give away your plot/theme/story line too soon and be sure to analyze carefully each point. Use copious textual evidence. Finally, it is sometimes helpful in the written and spoken literary analysis to compare this literary piece to another piece by the same author and/or a literary piece by another author.

Daily Assignment

- Warm-up: Write a literary Analysis of your favorite movie.
- Students will complete Concept Builder 13-D.
- Prayer journal.
- Review the assigned text. Keep vocabulary cards.
- This is the day that students should write, and then rewrite, the final drafts of their assigned essay and speech.

Literary Analysis: Narration

The *narration* of a story is the way the author chooses to tell the story. In *first-person narration*, a character refers to himself using "I." Example: Huck Finn in *The Adventures of Huckleberry Finn* tells the story from his perspective. This creative way brings humor into the plot. In *second-person narration*, a character addresses the reader and/or the main character as "you" (and may also use first-person narration, but not necessarily). One example is the opening of each of Rudyard Kipling's *Just-So Stories*, in which the narrator refers to the child-listener as "O Best-Beloved." In *third-person narration*, the author, usually not a character in the story, refers to the story's characters as "he" and "she." This form of narration is probably the most common. In *limited narration*, the author is only able to tell what one person is thinking or feeling. Example: In *A Separate Peace*, by John Knowles, the reader only sees the story from Gene's perspective. *Omniscient narration* is when the narrator can tell what any or all characters are thinking and feeling and is what Charles Dickens employs in most of his novels. *Reliable narration* is presented with the stance that everything this story says is true, and the narrator knows everything that is necessary to the story. An *unreliable narrator* may not know all the relevant information, may be intoxicated or mentally ill, and/or may lie to the audience. Example: Edgar Allan Poe's narrators are frequently unreliable. Think of the delusions that the narrator of "The Tell-Tale Heart" has about the old man.

Identify the narration in the following passages:

Passage	Narration
My mother, who walked three miles a day and regularly ate chicken gizzards fried in old lard shrugged her shoulders and forgot about the whole thing. In fact, even after Geritol and BC Powders failed, she refused to visit her doctor. To question a doctor-friend's diagnosis was worse than a serious illness — it was downright unfriendly, something my mother manifestly refused to be.	
Mrs. Smith walked three miles a day and regularly ate chicken gizzards fried in old lard. She shrugged her shoulders and forgot about the whole thing. In fact, even after Geritol and BC Powders failed, she refused to visit her doctor. To question a doctor-friend's diagnosis was worse than a serious illness — it was downright unfriendly, something Mrs. Smith manifestly refused to be.	
Mrs. Smith walked three miles a day and regularly ate chicken gizzards fried in old lard. Even after Geritol and BC Powders failed, Mrs. Smith did not visit her doctor.	
Mrs. Smith walked three miles a day and regularly ate chicken gizzards fried in old lard. She shrugged her shoulders and forgot about the whole thing. In fact, even after Geritol and BC Powders failed, she refused to visit her doctor. To question a doctor-friend's diagnosis was worse than a serious illness — it was downright unfriendly, something Mrs. Smith manifestly refused to be. When she did visit the doctor, he too was afraid of her!	

Evaluation Essay

Chapter 14

Style (Writing and Speaking): Using the Dictionary vs. Thesaurus

Public Speaking Skill: Converting an Evaluation Essay into a Speech

First Thoughts

Evaluation is a higher-level thinking process. To evaluate a problem is to judge the worth of the material. Of course you must use some sort of rating system or criteria to evaluate something. Sometimes the rating criterion is given to you; other times, you must set your own criteria. Then you must use evidence to show that the topic does or does not fit your criteria. You should deal with what the implications are for whether it fits or does not fit (or fits some but not others of) your criteria. Finally, you must make a value judgment concerning the material's veracity.

Chapter Learning Objectives

In chapter 14 we will learn how to write evaluation essays.

Look Ahead for Friday

- Turn in a final copy of essay and speech
- Take Weekly Essay/Test

Evaluate the significance to world history of an important individual. Include an outline with thesis statement, rough draft, revised draft, final copy, and five new (circled) vocabulary words. Pay particular attention to style (focus, content, organization).

In a 3-minute speech, evaluate the significance to world history of a well-recognized individual.

Final Project

Correct and rewrite all essays and place them in your Final Portfolio.

Background

Your thesis is particularly important in an evaluation essay. It is the lodestone to which the rest of the paper is drawn. The thesis of the paper must be clearly stated and appropriately qualified. In other words, in an evaluation essay tell your reader what you value and why.

Next, repeat the standards of judgment you will be using in your paper. Make a judgment. Do not merely mention alternative positions; actually discuss all the alternatives. Offer supporting evidence for your judgment and be certain that your viewpoint is consistent throughout the paper — do not equivocate.

The Gods Return

Hubert Dreyfus and Sean Dorrance Kelly, in their book *All Things Shining,* argue that the Greeks got it right — that polytheism is the answer to 21st-century woes.[1] "Homeric polytheism" is a solution to the lostness of the contemporary world. They state that "the world doesn't matter to us the way it used to."

And they get to be a little bizarre. They compare the ending of *The Iliad* with the ending of the movie *Pulp Fiction.* The author has thankfully not seen the latter but one reviewer points out "that both protagonists succeed in their mission by the slimiest of coincidence."

To Dreyfus and Kelly, if one God is good, many gods is better. In an age of such largesse — the 21st Century — one needs more than one deity. The polytheistic approach is rich in that it "whooshes up." Whooshing up is the sensation we enjoy at a sporting event when the crowd shares a victory celebration with its home team. It is the ubiquitous "wave" that spreads across a stadium. The 7th-inning stretch when the whole community savors a moment.

Whooshing up is communal, it is public, and it is like the experience polytheism can give contemporary man. It invites us to extol great heroes — Lou Gehrig, for instance — whose greatness lay in their ability to let some outside force (i.e., the gods) flow through their souls. Their pathos, in other words, merged with their ethos, to form a logos.

Finally, Dreyfus and Kelly conclude that "the story of how we lost touch with these sacred practices is the hidden history of the West."

"These shining moments" are not to be reclaimed by the likes of Aprophite or Zeus. They will be reclaimed by a people embracing again the God of the Old and the New Testament. Thank you very much! (James)

---

1   Hubert Dreyfus and Sean Dorrance Kelly, *All Things Shining,* books.simonandschuster.com/All-Things-Shining/Hubert-Dreyfus/.

Daily Assignment

- Warm-up: Evaluate your favorite television show.

- Students will complete Concept Builder 14-A.

- Prayer journal: Students are encouraged to write in their prayer journal every day.

- Students should systematically review their vocabulary words daily.

Evaluation

In the following passage evaluate if the narrator is reliable, can be trusted.

The thousand injuries of Fortunato I had borne as I best could, but when he ventured upon insult I vowed revenge. You, who so well know the nature of my soul, will not suppose, however, that gave utterance to a threat. At length I would be avenged; this was a point definitely, settled — but the very definitiveness with which it was resolved precluded the idea of risk. I must not only punish but punish with impunity. A wrong is unredressed when retribution overtakes its redresser. It is equally unredressed when the avenger fails to make himself felt as such to him who has done the wrong.

It must be understood that neither by word nor deed had I given Fortunato cause to doubt my good will. I continued, as was my in to smile in his face, and he did not perceive that my smile now was at the thought of his immolation.

He had a weak point — this Fortunato — although in other regards he was a man to be respected and even feared. He prided himself on his connoisseurship in wine. Few Italians have the true virtuoso spirit. For the most part their enthusiasm is adopted to suit the time and opportunity, to practice imposture upon the British and Austrian millionaires. In painting . . . Fortunato, like his countrymen, was a quack, but in the matter of old wines he was sincere. In this respect I did not differ from him materially — I was skillful in the Italian vintages myself, and bought largely whenever I could.

Evaluation Criteria	Response
Does the narrator appear to be sane?	
Does the narrator have an "axe to grind?"	
Is the narrator reliable? Can the reader believe his narration?	

"The Cast of the Amontillado," Edgar Allan Poe, www.eastoftheweb .com/short-stories/UBooks/CasAmo.shtml)

Writing Style:
Words — Using the Dictionary Vs. the Thesaurus

Words are the building blocks of writing. If you build your essay with precise, inspired words, you will have a precise, inspired essay.

Your friend and companion to good writing is the unabridged dictionary — not the thesaurus. The dictionary defines and uses a word in a sentence. The thesaurus gives you several analogies with no hint at their usage. If you are not careful, you will use a word in the wrong way. For instance, pretend you want to find a word to use that means "bad." Your thesaurus tells you that one word for "bad" is "pejorative." You then write the sentence: "The steak was pejorative." Technically, the sentence is correct because it has a subject and a predicate and makes a complete statement; however, it is also very wrong. "Pejorative" is used to describe abstract things, not concrete things. Thus, a correct usage of "pejorative" is, "That pejorative comment hurt me deeply." An unabridged dictionary would tell you the nuances of meanings surrounding such a word as "pejorative" and would also give you a few sample sentences. Many writers make the mistake of relying on a thesaurus instead of a dictionary when they try to make their writing more sophisticated or scholarly.

Daily Assignment

- Warm-up: Evaluate your favorite sport.
- Students will complete Concept Builder 14-B.
- Prayer journal.
- Students should outline all assigned essays and speech for the week.

CONCEPT BUILDER 14-B

Writing Generalizations

Every writing project requires the writer to make decisions about how he/she will write his/her essay. Use the following charts to guide you as you organize and write your essay this week: Evaluate the significance to world history of an important individual.

Person you will evaluate:

Purpose:
- ☐ to inform
- ☐ to argue
- ☐ to entertain
- ☐ to analyze

Audience:
- Will my readers know this person?
- Will they like him/her?
- What level of language is most appropriate for my audience?

Form
- ☐ Essay
- ☐ Letter
- ☐ Sermon
- ☐ Play

Lesson 3

Public Speaking:
Converting An Evaluation Essay Into A Speech

Basically, an evaluation speech is constructed in a way that is very similar to the evaluation essay. You should be very clear in your introductory comments about what you are evaluating, how you are evaluating it, and what your evaluation conclusions are. As the speech unfolds, clearly state your case and evidence it well.

Daily Assignment

- Warm-up: Evaluate your favorite Bible verse.
- Students will complete Concept Builder 14-C.
- Prayer journal.
- Students should write rough drafts of all assigned essays and speech.

CONCEPT
BUILDER
14-C

Building a Story

Recall a conversation you overheard in the last few days and build a story around the words. Use the diagram below to organize your story.

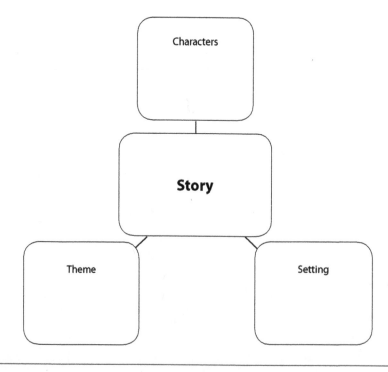

Evaluation Criteria for Choosing the Right Curriculum

Curriculum Evaluation

1. **Inquiry Based** (Does the curriculum invite the student to engage in critical thinking student-centered activities?)

2. **Age Appropriate** (Does the curriculum reflect a vocabulary and sentence structure appropriate to the student?)

3. **Colorful and Interesting** (Does the curriculum appear in columns where appropriate? Are there pictures? Graphs? Is it printed on study materials?)

4. **Answer Key** (Does the curriculum provide a clearly legible answer key?)

5. **Cost** (Is the cost appropriate for high school curriculum? Analyze per unit costs.)

6. **Multicultural** (Does the curriculum seriously deal with multiculturalism?)

7. **Biblically Based** (Is the curriculum Christ-centered?)

8. **Propagandistic** (Does the curriculum reflect serious, objective, carefully researched scholarship?)

9. **Need Based** (Does the curriculum meet your needs? Is the curriculum college-preparatory for those students going to college? Does the curriculum satisfy requirements for an academic core course?)

10. **Organization** (Is the curriculum organized in a user-friendly manner?)

Daily Assignment

- Warm-up: Evaluate your favorite meal.
- Students will complete Concept Builder 14-D.
- Prayer journal.
- Review the assigned text. Keep vocabulary cards.
- This is the day that students should write, and then rewrite, the final drafts of their assigned essay and speech.

Making Judgments

Read the following excerpt from a newspaper article and make a judgment.

Jonathan Prevette was famous last week, but he didn't enjoy it much. The first-grader from Lexington, North Carolina, found his front yard full of news cameras and reporters. He was on CNN, the *Today Show* and NBC News. How did he get so much attention?

"I kissed a girl on the cheek," Jonathan, 6, told news reporters.

When a teacher saw him kiss that girl, the trouble began. Jonathan was sent away from his class for a whole day. He even missed a school ice-cream party for kids with perfect attendance.

Many people who heard about Jonathan's punishment thought it was too harsh, including his parents. "Jonathan is very friendly and affectionate," said his mother Jackie Prevette. "He doesn't understand why he was punished."

The school's leaders say the teacher did the right thing. "A 6-year-old kissing another 6-year-old is inappropriate behavior," said school-district spokeswoman Jane Martin. Jonathan attends Southwest Elementary, which has a rule against "unwelcome touching of one student by another."

Most grownups say that kids should follow the rules. "Kids must be respectful of other kids' bodies," says Dr. Joseph Hagan, an expert on kids' behavior. "If the kiss was done on a dare, then maybe someone should be punished. But an adult should find out if the kiss was O.K. with both kids and ask them why it happened."

Jonathan says the girl told him he could kiss her.

That doesn't mean he's going to do it again anytime soon. He knows what will happen the next time he smooches at school: "I'll get suspended," he says.

Do you think Jonathan's punishment was fair? Why or why not?

Yes	Why or why not?
No	Why or why not?

(www.factmonster.com/tfk/magazines/story/0,6277,94574,00.html)

The Cause/Effect Essay

Chapter 15

Style (Writing and Speaking): Words — Connotation vs. Denotation

Public Speaking Skill: Converting a Cause/Effect Essay into a Speech

First Thoughts

What causes exorbitant fuel prices? What caused the American Civil War? A cause/effect paper invites you to consider a problem, define the problem, and offer a solution to the problem. Cause/effect papers are the most common and perhaps the most fun to write. There are two strategic points that are critical to a cause/effect paper. First, you must be clear about whether you are going to discus *causes* or *effects* or *both*. Secondly, you must be clear about the order of the causes or effects you're going to discuss. Not all causes/effects are of equal importance or impact. Will you begin with the most important or the least important cause/effect? Decide and then stick with your decision for the rest of your paper. Also, you may discuss the most important causes/effects and concede that there are less important causes/effects that you will have to overlook. Finally, one of the most challenging parts to writing cause/effect essays is ending them. Be careful to avoid a "preachy" attitude but feel free to lobby hard for one or two causes/effects or to even suggest a new one no one has noticed. Be careful, though, to avoid making this a cause/solution essay. Solution is beyond the scope of this particular essay.

Chapter Learning Objectives

In chapter 15 we will learn how to write cause/effect essays.

Look Ahead for Friday

- Turn in a final copy of essay and speech
- Take Weekly Essay/Test

Evaluate the last time you made some bad choices. What were the causes of these bad choices? What was the outcome? This essay should include an outline with thesis statement, rough draft, revised draft, final copy, and five new (circled) vocabulary words. Give a copy to instructor/parent to evaluate.

Convert a cause/effect essay into a speech.

Final Project

Correct and rewrite all essays and place them in your Final Portfolio.

Sample Cause/Effect Essay

The Dialectic Process: A Struggle for Truth

Communism is a worldview in retreat. Communism in Russia has failed. However, at the heart of communism is a reasoning process called dialectical materialism, which is very much alive. Karl Marx and Frederick Engels, fathers of communism, base their views of communism on the works of G.W.F. Hegel.

At the heart of dialectic materialism is the notion of conflict. It is within struggle that truth emerges. The philosopher Hegel characterizes dialectic as the tendency of a notion to pass over into its own negation as the result of conflict between its inherent contradictory aspects. Karl Marx and Friedrich Engels adopt Hegel's definition and apply it to social and economic processes. To Marx, history is a process. It is dialectic, but it is not a "spirit" that drives it. In other words, Hegelian dialectics are opposed to metaphysics (the notion that a trans-cendent power or entity determines the course of history). It is materialism, industry, and power that really drives the whole thing.

Therefore, Marx argues that if one wants to control ideals, if he wants a revolution, if he wants progress, he will have to stimulate a struggle.

Where is dialectic materialism alive in America today? Consider the way America makes policy decisions. When America decides to legalize abortion, it compromises between two positions. Truth supposedly arises out of the struggle. The pro-life position is wrong, but so are the pro-choice folks. The truth lies somewhere between these two positions. The struggle between these two polarities will bring forth the truth. Another example is the present debate over homosexuality. Some people argue that homosexuality is wrong. Others argue that it is right. Dialectic materialism leads many to conclude that neither position is right. In the struggle, a new truth emerges, a compromise. This would be the argument used by people who really love each other and are faithful to each other to allow participation in homosexual behavior.

The flaws in these arguments are obvious. Regardless of how long Americans seek to compromise, abortion will always be murder, and homosexuality will always be sinful. The struggle does not lead America to truth — it leads America into error. Truth is not found in the dialectic; it is found in the Word of God. (Jessica)

Daily Assignment

- Warm-up: What causes inflation? What is its effect?
- Students will complete Concept Builder 15-A.
- Prayer journal: Students are encouraged to write in their prayer journal every day.
- Students should systematically review their vocabulary words daily.

Cause and Effect Essay

Read Chapter 15 "First Thoughts," and then consider the following 1912 essay on the causes of racial skin differences and complete the accompanying graph.

You have noticed, yourself, that when you expose the skin of your face or arms to the hot sun, you become freckled, or tanned. This tanning, or browning, of the outer layer of the skin protects the more delicate coats of skin below from being scorched or injured by the strong light. When you are playing and running with your schoolmates, you see that their faces grow very red, and even their hands. Why is this? Because the heart has been pumping hard and has sent the red blood out toward the skin. The red color shines through the outer part of the skin. The pigment in the Native American skin, or the African-American's, prevents the red blood underneath from shining through, as it does through a Caucasian.

Skin Color Changes

Causes

A.

B.

C.

Effect: Different Skin Tone

Woods Hutchinson, M.D., *The Child's Day* (Boston, MA: Houghton Mifflin Company, 1912); www.gutenberg.org/files/18559/18559-8.txt.

Writing Style:
Words—Connotation Vs. Denotation

Words have different meanings in different contexts. In fact, the meaning of a word has two components: *denotative* and *connotative*. The word's denotation is what it actually means — according to the dictionary. The word's connotation is what it implies. For instance, the word "propaganda" means "sharing a biased position in order to convert." Originally, the word was used to describe missionaries who shared propaganda. We, of course, have no problem with this definition of propaganda. Unfortunately, though, during World War II, German Nazis, among others, used propaganda to influence people in adverse ways. Thus, the word gained a very negative connotation.

Exercise care with word choice. The connotation of some words may offend some people. For instance, if I said you were "absent-minded," you would probably not be offended. The connotation of "absent-minded" connotes harmless forgetfulness. On the other hand, if I called you "scatter-brained," you might be offended. Absent-minded and scatter-brained denote approximately the same thing; however, scatter-brained connotes something far more pejorative than absent-minded.

Daily Assignment

- Warm-up: What is the cause of crime? What is its effect?

- Students will complete Concept Builder 15-B.

- Prayer journal.

- Students should outline all assigned essays and speech for the week.

CONCEPT
BUILDER
15-B

Connotation/Denotation

What is the main purpose of this poster?

In what way does the above poster connote negative things about the enemies of the United States in World War II?

How would you feel if you were an Italian American, German American, or Japanese American when you view this poster?

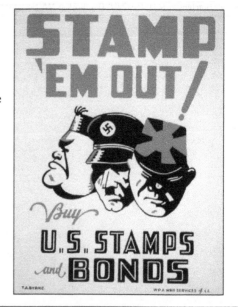

Lesson 3

Public Speaking: Converting the Cause/Effect Essay to a Speech

The cause/effect speech includes some elements of writing that might be considered more professional, even pedantic, than other process speeches might include. It is very important, for instance, that the tone of a cause/effect speech be reflective and serious and that your presentation be factual and believable. Sources are often required in a cause/effect paper, and your choice of these sources is important since they will determine whether or not your audience will accept your conclusions. Finally, in both the cause/effect essay and speech, the first-person point of view does not work. The *professional opinion* is more important than your *considered opinion*. It is important to keep your speaking voice modulated. It can be playful, even a little whimsical, but it must be authoritative. You must not sound uncertain and, above all, you must not be vitriolic.

Daily Assignment

- Warm-up: What were the causes of the Gulf War? What was its outcome?

- Students will complete Concept Builder 15-C.

- Prayer journal

- Students should write rough drafts of all assigned essays and speech.

CONCEPT BUILDER 15-C

Analyzing Emotional Appeal

Writers frequently appeal directly to their readers' feelings. They do this by using words whose connotative meaning suits the purpose of the excerpt. The connotative meaning goes far beyond the denotative meaning.

If you really want to hear about it, the first thing you'll probably want to know is where I was born, and what my lousy childhood was like, and how my parents were occupied and all before they had me, and all that David Copperfield kind of crap, but I don't feel like going into it, if you want to know the truth.

— Holden Caulfield, the protagonist in *Catcher In The Rye.*

Word/Concept	Denotation	Connotation	Purpose
lousy	Something bad		
occupied	To own a place		
David Copperfield	A Charles Dickens's character who rises from poverty to riches		
crap	Animal or human waste		
I don't feel like it	The speaker does not have the strength to do the task.		

Student Essay

Cause — Effect

About a week ago, I made a choice. As with all choices, it had an outcome. In this case, I had decided that day to have something other than breakfast food for breakfast. My alternative was easy to prepare, delicious, and tasty. I had made up my mind to have cake for breakfast and never forgot my decision for the rest of the day.

It all started with my mom's birthday. As is usually the case with birthdays, we had cake. However, this was not just any cake; it was homemade chocolate cake. Baked by my sister, the family cook, it was so good that it lasted only about one and a half days, on average. In our family, one had to scramble to obtain their share, especially with my dad around.

That was exactly what I was thinking the morning after my mom's birthday, when there were only a few pieces of the mouthwatering cake left. Of course, I thought, I also didn't really have anything else to eat for breakfast, and this was quick and easy. Then again, it probably wasn't a good idea to have a dessert for break-fast, but . . . it looked so good. I just had to have the dark brown, moist cake, which was delectably fluffy to the touch of a fork — just the kind of cake that needs ice cream!

After loading my bowl with cake and ice cream, I took my feast to the table and ate every bite. At first, it was just as delicious as it looked, the cake virtually melting in my mouth and the cold vanilla ice cream complementing the already wonderful taste. If only I could have this every morning! Unfortunately, my bliss soon came to an end right around the last few bites of my "breakfast," as the sweets lost their delectability, giving way to downright bitterness in my mouth. Still, I persevered, finished my meal, and forgot about my cake and ice cream escapade within about an hour.

Unfortunately, my stomach did not forget my foolish meal. Around two o'clock that afternoon, it started to hurt. A half hour later, it started to rumble, and all I could think about was that errant breakfast and my painful stomach. Later, I had to lie down, and my evening was in large part ruined, just because of one little piece of cake and one small scoop of ice cream. (JB)

Daily Assignment

- Warm-up: What causes snow? What is its effect?
- Students will complete Concept Builder 15-D.
- Prayer journal.
- Review the assigned text. Keep vocabulary cards.
- This is the day that students should write, and then rewrite, the final drafts of their assigned essay and speech.

Celebration Of The Self

In modern cause and effect essays that are emerging today, it is difficult to identify any particular cause — the effect is evident — but no one is willing to accept the cause. This is a celebration of "subjectivity" or a celebration of the "self."

Examine the painting below and discuss your subjective understanding of what it means. You cannot be wrong, because the ultimate authority here is your own understanding. What happens if we, rather than an outside source (e.g., the Bible), become the ultimate authority in our lives?

"The Scream" by Edvard Munch, 1893 (PD-US).

warm	unfriendly	hate	smiles	chocolate ice cream
cold	terror	love	frowns	green beans
friendly	fear	emptiness	fulfillment	stormy

The Comparison/Contrast Essay

Chapter 16

Style (Writing and Speaking): Words — Standard and Substandard English

Public Speaking Skill: Converting a Comparison/Contrast Essay into a Speech

First Thoughts

We can really understand only those things that are familiar to us or similar to things we already understand. Therefore, a comparison/contrast paper stretches our understanding to another level. It reaches out to the familiar to help its reader understand the unfamiliar. You may compare/contrast the unfamiliar with the familiar and vice versa. You can, and probably do, use comparison/contrast to solve problems, to describe issues, to define things, and to analyze issues; comparison and contrast is useful even to make an argument.

Chapter Learning Objectives

In chapter 16 we will learn how to write comparison/contrast essays.

Look Ahead for Friday

- Turn in a final copy of essay and speech
- Take Weekly Essay/Test

Compare and contrast two personal friends. Your essay should include an outline with thesis statement, rough draft, revised draft, final copy, and five new (circled) vocabulary words. Pay particular attention to style (focus, content, organization). Give a copy to instructor/parent to evaluate.

In a 2- or 3-minute speech, compare and contrast two personal friends.

Final Project

Correct and rewrite all essays and place them in your Final Portfolio.

Sample Comparison/Contrast Essay

A good way to begin a comparison/contrast paper is to discuss the ways in which objects are similar. That is not enough, however. Within the introduction you also will need to describe the ways in which the two ideas are different.

Also, comparing and contrasting ideas can be accomplished by treating one idea thoroughly before discussing the second one. Many writers prefer this style of comparison and contrast.

The intricate plots of authors Mary Shelley and Robert Louis Stevenson, their vivid imaginations, their knowledge of science, and their whimsical but credible characters all conspire to make their writings excellent. There are differences, though, in their writings, all of which are theistic in substance and remarkably different in tone. The following paper will examine these differences. The works being compared are the book *Frankenstein* by Mary Shelley, the poem "Dirge" by Mary Shelley, the book *Dr. Jekyll and Mr. Hyde* by Robert Louis Stevenson, and the poem "Requiem" by Robert Louis Stevenson.

Both Shelley and Stevenson created protagonists who wanted to produce life outside normal human events and divine purpose. Victor Frankenstein created the monster Frankenstein, and Henry Jekyll created the monster Hyde. Both were monstrosities in physical appearance and in philosophical intent. They did not have souls. Throughout the entire undertaking, Frankenstein felt that no human has the right, even if he has the means, to create another human being. Jekyll only felt remorse at the end of his life. Victor Frankenstein and Henry Jekyll created monsters, but their author/creators had a greater purpose.

Shelley and Stevenson illustrated the excesses of the Victorian Age. Like many British subjects overburdened by Victorian morality, Frankenstein and Jekyll were discontent with the limits imposed on them as mortal humans. They wished to push beyond those limits and found themselves in an overabundance of trouble. Their vocation of "god-playing" was hazardous to their health and to everyone around them. Eventually, they regretted their excesses and tried to destroy their monsters, but it was too late. In fact, their monsters destroyed them.

In *Dr. Jekyll* and his poem "Requiem," Stevenson advances a theistic worldview. Dr. Jekyll in effect ends his life because Hyde has broken Christian moral laws, and Dr. Jekyll cannot see a way to stop Hyde unless Jekyll dies: "Henry Jekyll [was] aghast at the acts of Edward Hyde" (p. 87). In "Requiem" Stevenson writes, "Glad did I live and die. I laid me down with a will." Stevenson's view of death is not gloomy. One could even suppose Stevenson believes in heaven. On the other hand, in her works Shelley revels in gloominess and despair. *Frankenstein* offers the reader no hope. The romantic English writer Shelley invites readers into the deep, dreary caves of hopelessness. She obviously has no Christian theistic bent.

Shelley and Stevenson are surely grand writers. At times, though, their characters and plots seem grotesque and even evil. However, the authors promote their characters in such a way that readers feel the grotesque evil is necessary. No one escapes justice in these works. In a culture flirting with Social Darwinism, it seems fitting that an author presents human nature in a monstrous, grotesque way. (Jessica)

Daily Assignment

- Warm-up: Compare your brother to Matt Damon.

- Students will complete Concept Builder 16-A.

- Prayer journal: Students are encouraged to write in their prayer journal every day.

- Students should systematically review their vocabulary words daily.

Comparison/Contrast Essays

When you compare things, you show their similarities; when you contrast things, you show their differences. A *comparison* and *contrast* paper does both.

A good way to begin a comparison/contrast paper is to discuss the ways in which objects are similar. That is not enough, however. Within the introduction you also will need to describe the ways in which the two ideas are different.

Complete the following chart:

Books Being Compared/Contrasted: *Rascal* and *Little Women*		
Characteristics	**Similarities**	**Differences**
Plot		
Theme		
Characters		
Setting		

Writing Style:
Words — Standard and Substandard English

One of the most important aspects of connotation is historical usage. There is a standard (good) and a substandard (poor) usage of most words. This standard is often determined by the purpose of and audience for the writing. For instance, the sentence "I am feeling groovy today" might be substandard English if you were presenting a sociological lecture at Harvard University. On the other hand, "I am feeling groovy today" would be entirely appropriate in Harvard Yard among other students. You have to be exceptionally discerning in your use of standard and substandard English.

Carefully avoid slang in writing. For example, using the world "ain't" in a formal, expository essay is inappropriate. So, too, is the use of vulgarity.

While avoiding slang and vulgarity, you will also need to avoid clichés and the use of contractions, except in dialogue. On the other hand, proper use of abbreviations (Ms., Dr., Mr., Mrs., and U.S. Postal Service) is expected.

Daily Assignment

- Warm-up: Compare your dad to Harrison Ford.
- Students will complete Concept Builder 16-B.
- Prayer journal.
- Students should outline all assigned essays and speech for the week.

Standard and Substandard English

Read the slang term on the left and provide the word or phrase that best describes this in Standard English.

Slang	Standard English
tight	
chilling	
my bad	
off the hook, off the chain	
peace out	
bring it on	
sku me	
whas goin' down?	
what up?	
whatever!	
flow	

Lesson 3

Public Speaking: Converting a Comparison/ Contrast Essay to a Speech

The comparison/contrast speech is organized much like the comparison/contrast essay. A rhetorical question is one way to begin a comparison/contrast speech. "What is the difference between the causes of World War I and World War II?" you may ask. Another great way to begin is to use a quote: "World War II was much more violent than World War I," says Professor John Smiths. However you begin your speech, be very sure that you include a thesis statement in your introduction.

Daily Assignment

- Warm-up: Compare your favorite car to the car your family owns.
- Students will complete Concept Builder 16-C.
- Prayer journal.
- Students should write rough drafts of all assigned essays and speech.

CONCEPT BUILDER 16-C

Analogies I

Analogies enable writers to enrich their vocabularies. An analogy is a sort of comparison: it consists of two pairs of words that are related. You will use the same analogies in 16-D.

Give a sentence that shows the relationship between these words:

A. gasoline: motion

Gasoline is the fuel a car uses while in motion

B. artist: studio

Artists work in art studios.

C. succor: harm

When someone is in harm all they is succor

D. architect: house

Architects build houses.

Sample Student Essay

"Byrdes of on kynde and color flok and flye allwayes together." This proverb, written by William Turner in 1545, was the precursor to the familiar saying, "Birds of a feather flock together." In other words, people with similar tastes and personalities congregate. However, this is not the case two of my friends, David Thurston and David McArthur — they have nothing in common except that they are both boys (as are all of my friends).

David Thurston, whom I have known for eight years, is the son of my church's pastor. A home-schooled senior, he hopes to get an athletic scholarship in football for college. To this end, he lifts weights three times a week (he has a squat of over 400 pounds), and plays on the Arvada West football team — which nearly advanced to the state championship multiple times. Though he works hard in schoolwork, he only does one extra activity — football. Occasionally he will play airsoft with a group of boys at our church — a game where teenage boys (and adults) don paintball masks and camouflage, trek out to a wooded area, and shoot each other with low-powered BB guns. He is never arrogant; instead he is humble, and soft-spoken.

Mr. McArthur, another friend, is almost the polar opposite of David. Instead of playing sports, he is a doctoral student in Piano Performance at the University of Colorado at Boulder. He spends most of his time practicing piano, and it shows — though he has more than 20 minutes of music at his fingertips, he has a hard time getting up more than around 3 flights of stairs. Last fall we were hiking up to a lake in Rocky Mountain National Park, and he was getting fairly winded. My dad let him know, "The trail climbs up for just a little bit more, then falls to the lake and stops."

"Oh, good," he panted. "Just like my heart rate." Even when he is exhausted, he still devotes much of his energy to being witty. Due to his physical stamina — or lack thereof — he never plays airsoft or hunts. Instead, he practices, arranges choral music for the church choir, and listens to classical recordings. In his disposition, he is the complete opposite of David. He is assertive, loud, and unpredictable — especially in conversations about music.

Other than their similarity in gender, my two friends are nothing like each other. Both are boys, but their secular lives revolve around completely different things — one around football, the other around music. Not only that, but their physical appearance is completely different; David Thurston is tall and muscular, Mr. McArthur is slightly overweight with long black hair and a full beard. Some birds of a feather may flock together. However, this is not the case with my "flock." (Alouette)

Daily Assignment

- Warm-up: Compare a movie you saw with the book you read on the same movie.
- Students will complete Concept Builder 16-D.
- Prayer journal.
- Review the assigned text. Keep vocabulary cards.
- This is the day that students should write, and then rewrite, the final drafts of their assigned essay and speech.

CONCEPT
BUILDER
16-D

Analogies II

Match the analogy types in 16-C with the following analogies.

Analogy Type	Choose one of the following
Gasoline: motion	Wheel: race (Wind: flight) Stars: gas
Artist: studio	Bus: garage Mail: mailbox (Surgeon: operating room)
Succour: harm	Fear: anxiety Love: marriage (Happiness: sadness)
Architect: house	(Artist: painting) Smooth: hard Skier: skis

The Problem/Solution Essay

Chapter 17

Style (Writing and Speaking): Words — Idioms

Public Speaking Skill: Converting The Problem/Solution Essay into a Speech

First Thoughts

A problem/solution essay is an argumentative essay. Everything, really, about a problem/solution paper is argumentative. It argues for defining a problem in a certain way, and then it argues for a specific solution or solutions to a specified problem. This paper is most common in the social sciences and business, but it is fair to say that it is one of the most important essay types in all disciplines.

Chapter Learning Objectives

In chapter 17 we will learn how to write problem/solution essays.

Look Ahead for Friday

- Turn in a final copy of essay and speech
- Take Weekly Essay/Test

As this century begins, Christians are becoming a declining minority in American culture and society. In a one-page essay, answer this question, "Is this a problem? Why? What are some solutions?" Your essay should include an outline with thesis statement, rough draft, revised draft, final copy, and five new (circled) vocabulary words. Pay particular attention to style (focus, content, organization). Give a copy to instructor/parent to evaluate.

Present a 2- or 3-minute speech on this topic: As this century begins, Christians are becoming a declining minority in American culture and society. In a one-page essay, answer these questions, "Is this a problem? Why? What are some solutions?"

Final Project

Correct and rewrite all essays and place them in your Final Portfolio.

Background

A problem/solution essay inevitably begins with some sort of a problem — statement. In fact, the way the problem is introduced is extremely important with this paper.

There are several ways to introduce a problem. In the context-problem type of introduction, using references from professionals, you will offer evidence that the problem is indeed a problem recognized as such by numerous, well-informed sources. In the introduction you prove that there is indeed a major problem here. A good way to provide such proof is to demonstrate how your problem has caused a lot of other problems. For instance, you could establish that drug use is a real problem by proving that it leads to juvenile crime. In other words, a common problem-posing introduction begins with a large issue that almost all audience members will recognize as important. That gives your solution — which occurs later in the paper — a much larger target audience.

Another way to begin a problem and solution paper is to argue that there is really no problem after all. In this essay you would begin with a statement of the problem and a brief review of the solutions offered, ending with a statement about why we need to look at the problem from a different perspective and, in the process, we see that it is not a problem after all. You may even be offering an *opportunity* instead of a *solution*. For instance, the Russian intervention in Afghanistan in the late 1970s, perceived by many as a major problem, could be redefined as an opportunity because it ultimately led to the collapse of the Iron Curtain in Central Europe.

A more complicated version of a problem/solution argument evaluates the solutions currently offered as a way of arguing for a new solution rather than suggesting there is no problem. In these types of essays, you would begin with a statement of the problem and a brief review of the solutions offered, ending with a statement about why none of the solutions currently is adequate. Of course, in this instance you will want to offer alternative solutions. In other words, a critique of other solutions will provide you with the proof for an argument for a new solution. This approach can be very effective and convincing.

Daily Assignment

- Warm-up: What do we do about children watching too much tv violence?
- Students will complete Concept Builder 17-A.
- Prayer journal: Students are encouraged to write in their prayer journal every day.
- Students should systematically review their vocabulary words daily.

Problem/Solution I

A problem/solution essay is an argumentative essay. Everything, really, about a problem/solution paper is argumentative. It argues for defining a problem in a certain way, and then it argues for a specific solution or solutions to a specified problem. This paper is most common in the social sciences and business, but it is fair to say that it is one of the most important essay types in all disciplines.

Read the following essay Beginner's American History (1893) and discuss the problems and solutions offered.

Captain John Smith
(1579-1631)

One of the leaders in the new expedition sent out to make a settlement in Virginia was Captain John Smith. He began life as a clerk in England. Not liking his work, he ran away and turned soldier. After many strange adventures, he was captured by the Turks and sold as a slave. His master, who was a Turk, riveted a heavy iron collar around his neck and set him to thrashing grain with a big wooden bat like a ball-club. One day the Turk rode up ad struck his slave with his riding-whip. This was more than Smith could bear; he rushed at his master, and with one blow of his bat knocked his brains out. He then mounted the dead man's horse and escaped. After a time he got back to England; but as England seemed a little dull to Captain Smith, he resolved to join some emigrants who were going to Virginia.

On the way to America, Smith was accused of plotting to murder the chief men among the settlers so that he might make himself "King of Virginia." The accusation was false, but he was put in irons and kept a prisoner for the rest of the voyage.

In the spring of 1607 the emigrants reached Chesapeake Bay, and sailed up a river which they named the James in honor of King James of England; when they landed they named the settlement Jamestown for the same reason. Here they built a log fort, and placed three or four small cannon on its walls. Most of the men who settled Jamestown came hoping to find mines of gold in Virginia, or else a way through to the Pacific Ocean and to the Indies, which they thought could not be very far away. But Captain Smith wanted to help his countrymen to make homes here for themselves and their children.

As soon as Captain Smith landed, he demanded to be tried by a jury of twelve men. The trial took place. It was the first English court and the first English jury that ever sat in America. The captain proved his innocence and was set free. His chief accuser was condemned to pay him a large sum of money for damages. Smith generously gave this money to help the settlement.

Problem	Solution
John Smith is accused of treason.	

Sample Problem/Solution Essay

It seems at times that Americans are lost. I am a pastor, and in spite of our hedonistic bravado, I generally find some of my congregation members — who generally are not living a life centered on Jesus Christ — are in fact desperately unhappy. No wonder. This world does not provide what we need. I once thought it did. I can remember being seduced by the august institution, Harvard University. In 1976, I really believed my university chaplain who told the incoming Harvard class, "You are the next history makers of America." I wanted to believe it. I needed to believe it. My acquaintance and colleague from Harvard Divinity School, Dr. Forrest Church, now pastor in a Unitarian Church in New York City, was fond of saying, "In our faith God is not a given; God is a question . . . God is defined by us. Our views are shaped and changed by our experiences. We create a faith in which we can live and struggle to live up to it . . . compared to love, a distant God had no allure." Indeed. This thinking has gotten us into quite a mess.

What kind of mess? While I attended seminary, I remember hurrying to the opening ceremony of the academic year held every September at Harvard Memorial Chapel in the Yard. Spying an impressive group of Harvard professors, decked out in all their academic robes, capes, and histrionic sententiousness, I decided to follow them to Memorial Chapel, a landmark in Harvard Yard. Although I knew one way to go there, they were not going my way, so, I trusted these sagacious gentlemen to show me a better way. Well, we got lost! And I was late! In spite of their august credentials, they did not know the way after all.

One of the most disturbing essays I have ever read is an essay by Thomas Merton entitled "A Devout Meditation in Memory of Adolf Eichmann." "One of the most disturbing facts," Merton begins, "that came out in the Eichmann trial was that a psychiatrist examined him and pronounced him perfectly sane." The fact is, given our world, we can no longer assume that because a person is "sane" or "adjusted" that he/she is okay. Merton re-minds us that such people can be well adjusted even in hell itself! "The whole concept of sanity in a society where spiritual values have lost their meaning is itself meaningless."

The central symbol for every 21st-century Christian must be the Cross. At least from the second century onward, Christians used the Cross as their central symbol. I yearn, as Dietrich Bonhoeffer did at the end of his life, for the crucified Lord to return again — as the rediscovered center — to the center of the Church and American society. America does not need a new religion; it needs Jesus Christ — crucified and resurrected.

With John Stott, in *The Cross of Christ*, my prayer is that this new generation, haunted by so many bad memories, so bewitched by technology and social science theories, would again come to the Cross of our Lord Jesus Christ. And, at the same time, I want us to reclaim the joy of this adventure — so persuasively presented by John Piper in *Desiring God*. Steering right into the storm, armed with God's divine presence and teachings, can affect the end results of this spiritual storm we Americans are experiencing. (James Stobaugh).

The author establishes the problem clearly and then offers a solution. Notice how much time he spends making sure that the reader agrees with him that there is a problem.

Daily Assignment

- Warm-up: What do we do about teenage pregnancy?

- Students will complete Concept Builder 17-B.

- Prayer journal.

- Students should outline all assigned essays and speech for the week.

Problem/Solution II

As the weather was warm, the emigrants did not begin building log cabins at once, but slept on the ground, sheltered by boughs of trees. For a church they had an old tent, in which they met on Sunday. They were all members of the Church of England, or the Episcopal Church, and that tent was the first place of worship that we know of that was opened by Englishmen in America. When the hot weather came, many fell sick. Soon the whole settlement was like a hospital. Sometimes three or four would die in one night. Captain Smith, though not well himself, did everything he could for those who needed his help.

When the sickness was over, some of the settlers were so discontented that they determined to seize the only vessel there was at Jamestown and go back to England. Captain Smith turned the cannon of the fort against them. The deserters saw that if they tried to leave the harbor he would knock their vessel to pieces, so they came back. One of the leaders of these men was tried and shot; the other was sent to England in disgrace.

Problem	Solution
The settlers grew discontent and tried to mutiny.	

After that first long, hot summer was over, some of the settlers wished to explore the country and see if they could not find a short way through to the Pacific Ocean. Captain Smith led the expedition. The Indians attacked them, killed three of the men, and took the captain prisoner. To amuse the Indians, Smith showed them his pocket compass. When the savages saw that the needle always pointed toward the north they were greatly astonished, and instead of killing their prisoner they decided to take him to their chief. This chief was named Powhatan. He was a tall, grim-looking old man, and he hated the settlers at Jamestown, because he believed that they had come to steal the land from the Indians.

Smith was dragged into the chief's wigwam; his head was laid on a large, flat stone, and a tall savage with a big club stood ready to dash out his brains. Just as Powhatan was about to cry "Strike!" his daughter Pocahontas, a girl of 12 or 13, ran up, and, putting her arms round the prisoner's head, she laid her own head on his — now let the Indian with his uplifted club strike if he dare. Instead of being angry with his daughter, Powhatan promised her that he would spare Smith's life. When an Indian made such a promise as that he kept it, so the captain knew that his head was safe. Powhatan released his prisoner and soon sent him back to Jamestown, and Pocahontas, followed by a number of Indians, carried presents of corn and venison to the settlers.

Problem	Solution
John Smith is captured by Native Americans.	

Lesson 3

Writing Style:
Words — Idioms

Idioms are special constructions of words determined by history and usage. The choice of words, or idioms, is always a knotty problem. Informal, even substandard, expressions are so common that you will be tempted to use them. In some cases this will be acceptable; in other cases it will not. First, of course, the purpose of the writing and the makeup of the audience will determine to a large degree which idioms are acceptable and which are not. A word of caution: While some idioms are acceptable in formal writing, most are not, and, as a general usage rule, if you write like you speak, you most assuredly will have too many idioms. Unless you have a pretty stiff speaking style, your writing should be much different. Thus, you might say, "My opinion is the opposite *to* yours" and get away with it. In a formal essay, however, no matter how weird it may sound to you, you must write the correct form of this sentence: "My opinion is the opposite *of* yours." One more example: the idiomatic expression "You did good" might work at the beach but would never work in a formal paper. "You accomplished the task well" or even "You did well" is the correct way to express this thought in written form.

Daily Assignment

- Warm-up: What do we do about the fact that 80% of urban children have no father?

- Students will complete Concept Builder 17-C.

- Prayer journal.

- Students should write rough drafts of all assigned essays and speech.

Problem/Solution III

Some of the emigrants found some glittering earth that they thought was gold. Soon nearly everyone was hard at work digging it. Smith laughed at them, but they insisted on loading a ship with the worthless stuff and sending it to London. That was the last that was heard of it.

The people had wasted their time digging this shining dirt when they should have been hoeing their gardens. Soon they began to be in great want of food. The captain started off with a party of men to buy corn from the Indians. The Indians contrived a cunning plot to kill the whole party. Smith luckily found it out, and seizing the chief by the hair, he pressed the muzzle of a pistol against his heart and gave him his choice: "Corn, or your life!" He got the corn, and plenty of it.

Captain Smith then set part of the men to planting corn, so that they might raise what they needed. The rest of the settlers he took with him into the woods to chop down trees and saw them into boards to send to England. Many tried to escape from this labor; but Smith said,

"Men who are able to dig for gold are able to chop." Then he made this rule: "He who will not work shall not eat." Rather than lose his dinner, the laziest man now took his axe and set off for the woods.

But though the choppers worked, they grumbled. They liked to see the chips fly and to hear the great trees "thunder as they fell," but the axe-handles raised blisters on their fingers. These blisters made the men swear, so that often one would hear an oath for every stroke of the axe. Smith said the swearing must be stopped. He had each man's oaths set down in a book. When the day's work was done, every offender was called up; his oaths were counted; then he was told to hold up his right hand, and a can of cold water was poured down his sleeve for each oath. This new style of water cure did wonders; in a short time not an oath was heard: it was just chop, chop, chop, and the madder the men got, the more the chips would fly.

Problem	Solution
The men find gold and stop working.	

Sample Student Essay

The Decline of Christianity: An Urgent Response Required

". . . one nation, *under God*, indivisible, with liberty and justice for all." The United States was founded on Christian principles, and the Christian religion was the center of American society for almost two hundred years! However, the number of Christians and the influence of Christianity in this nation has been dwindling rapidly for a couple of decades. After careful research and surveys it has become evident that over half of the next generation will leave the Christian church and the Christian faith by the time they graduate from college. Something has changed for the worse! This is indeed a major problem, but a solution is within reach.

When Christianity dwindles, so does Judeo-Christian morality. Christians have made an impact on society. During the fight for abolition of slavery, both sides attempted to use the Bible to support their claims. Although those fighting to maintain slavery misapplied the Bible by saying that since Ephesians 6:5 stated, "Slaves, be obedient to those who are your masters," slavery was justified, the point is that they were still attempting to justify their claims through Scripture. Christian arguments were also used in the fight for women's suffrage and equal rights with men. One example is in Sojourner Truth's famous speech *Ain't I a Woman*, "That little man in black there, he says women can't have as much rights as man, 'cause Christ wasn't a woman. . . . Where did your Christ come from? From God and a woman." Christian preachers also played a large part in the prohibition movement. Although it was repealed shortly after its ratification by Amendment XXI, Amendment XVIII of the Constitution states, "After one year from the ratification of this article the manufacture, sale, or transportation of intoxicating liquors . . . is hereby prohibited." It was through the passionate speeches of the preachers of the time that this amendment was even considered. Christian influence is seen yet again in the Civil Rights Movement. Martin Luther King Jr. was a zealous Christian pastor and leader of the Civil Rights Movement. He used support from the Bible in his arguments for racial equality. Rejecting Christianity would be indirectly rejecting the arguments for slaves' freedom, women's rights, and racial equality!

Christianity historically has been at the heart of America's culture since the nation's beginning. The founding fathers were stark supporters of Christianity. John Hancock once wrote that "Resistance to tyranny becomes the Christian and social duty of each individual. . . . Continue steadfast and, with a proper sense of your dependence on God, nobly defend those rights which heaven gave, and no man ought to take from us."[1] John Adams said, "The general principles on which the fathers achieved independence were the general principles of Christianity. I will avow that I then believed, and now believe, that those general principles of Christianity are as eternal and immutable as the existence and attributes of God."[2] George Washington clearly states that "While we are zealously performing the duties of good citizens and soldiers, we certainly ought not to be inattentive to the higher duties of religion. To the distinguished character of Patriot, it should be our highest glory to add the more distinguished character of Christian."[3] The main reason for the founding fathers' support of "separation of church and state" was to prevent a situation as in England where the monarch established what denominations were allowed. One must notice that the question in mind was not of religion such as Muslim or Christian, but of denomination such as Catholic or Protestant. Proof of this is evident in the rejection of early Mormons attempting to spread their faith. Rejecting Christianity would be rejecting that which men such as George Washington and John Adams considered even more important than patriotism.

So what is the solution? First, the Church needs to return to a literal interpretation of Scripture. When pastors turn simple phrases like, "And there was evening

---

1   John Hancock, *History of the United States of America* Vol. II, p. 229.

2   Adams wrote this on June 28, 1813, in a letter to Thomas Jefferson.

3   George Washington, *The Writings of Washington*, p. 342–343.

and there was morning, one day,"[4] into symbols representing million-year-long periods of time, Christians lose the foundation for their faith. Pastors often neglect to teach Genesis. Those who do sometimes allow false heretical teachings such as the gap theory to eventually be taught as truth. Genesis is the foundation of the Christian faith. When it is omitted or taught falsely, the rest of the faith is weak and easily demolished by a secular humanistic world. Second, Christians need to restore the biblical principle of parents teaching their own children rather than turning them over to teachers. Deuteronomy 6:6–7 reminds us that it is the parents' job to teach their children. "These words which I command you today shall be in your heart. You shall teach them diligently to your children, and shall talk of them when you sit in your house and when you walk by the way, when you lie down, and when you rise up." Ephesians 6:4 again emphasizes this point when it states, "Fathers . . . bring [your children] up in the training and admonition of the Lord."

James H. Rutz once wrote, "God's plan for religious education is Dad. It's a 4,000-year-old plan that's worked like a watch since the days of Abraham. But if your weekly gathering doesn't equip Dad to open his mouth at home and be a teacher of the Word — well, Sunday school is your next best bet. (Programming Dad would be easier.)"[5] This quote also emphasizes the third part of the solution to the problem of the decline of Christianity. We need to revive the art of apologetics. In most cases, neither pastor nor Sunday school teacher are providing the required biblical defenses that children need to face a pagan world. If the pastor doesn't equip the father to teach the children how to defend the faith, then who will? We need to return to a literal interpretation of Scripture, restore the biblical principle of parents teaching their own children, and revive the art of apologetics. (John)

---

4   Genesis 1:5; NASB.

5   James H. Rutz, *The Open Church: How to Bring Back the Exciting Life of the First Century Church* (Auburn, ME: SeedSowers, 1992).

Daily Assignment

- Warm-up: What do we do about the disappearance of Judeo-Christian morality in our culture?

- Students will complete Concept Builder 17-D.

- Prayer journal.

- Review the assigned text. Keep vocabulary cards.

- This is the day that students should write, and then rewrite, the final drafts of their assigned essay and speech.

CONCEPT BUILDER 17-D

Idioms

Use the following idioms in more standard English sentences.

Idiom	Standard English
Oliver Twist was beside himself when joy when he was adopted.	
Buck was up in arms when his master was attacked by Native Americans.	
Aunt Polly took Tom Sawyer to task for his lies.	

The Definition Essay

Style (Writing and Speaking): Words — Adjectives and Adverbs in Comparative and Superlative Cases

Public Speaking Skill: Converting a Definition Essay into a Speech

First Thoughts

A definition essay explains a common word or expression that is not easily defined. Definition is a method of analysis, as logical as possible, in which the subject is located in a general class and then distinguished from all other members of that class.

Chapter Learning Objectives

In chapter 18 we will learn how to write definition essays.

Look Ahead for Friday

- Turn in a final copy of essay and speech
- Take Weekly Essay/Test

In a one-page essay, define sound. Does a tree falling in the forest make sound if no human hears it? This essay should include an outline, rough draft, thesis statement, final copy, and five new (circled) vocabulary words. The essay must pay particular attention to style (focus, content, organization). Give a copy to instructor/parent to evaluate.

Present a 2- or 3-minute speech defining sound.

Final Project

Correct and rewrite all essays and place them in your Final Portfolio.

Background

Please don't start your definition essay with either a dictionary or an encyclopedia definition of your word or comment. This approach is so often used that it is almost trite. After all, your essay is by definition (no pun intended!) your definition — not someone else's.

One good strategy of defining something is to say what it is not. The following is a portion of a sermon where the speaker has to make sure his reader understands the definition of *death*. He does this by reminding the reader what death "is not."

Jesus really died on the Cross.

This was not some metaphorical event, some dramatic hoax. No, He really died. He died as in "stopped breathing." He really died.

Today, it seems to me, we have as much of a problem in believing that Jesus died as we do in believing that He arose from the grave. Our ubiquitous media promises us eternal bliss and immortality — just put this cream on and the wrinkles will go away. Let's take these vitamins, and we will live forever, and so on.

It was not always so. Death was something our parents and grandparents had to face with more finality and frequency. The average life span was lower than it is now. Medical science was not as successful as now in saving human life. Infant mortality was higher. Since there were fewer hospitals and no nursing homes, sick and dying relatives died at home. Years ago it was the custom for a "wake" to be held in the family's living room. Then the deceased was buried in a local church cemetery. Every Sunday when our grandparents went to church, they were reminded of the reality of death as they passed the marble grave markers of their loved ones.

Jesus Christ was dead. And, I mean, really dead — however, He did not die quietly in bed with all His friends surrounding Him. No, He died a humiliating, messy, public death. And the world had no doubt of one salient fact on that first Easter morning: Jesus bar Joseph was very, very dead. The good news, however, is that he did not stay that way!

Before you write a definition essay, you should answer these three questions: What is the term to be defined? What is the purpose for the intended definition? Who is the intended audience? Is this a general audience for whom terms must be broken down in simple sentences, or is it a special audience whose knowledge of the terminology will not require further definition?

Daily Assignment

- Warm-up: Define love.
- Students will complete Concept Builder 18-A.
- Prayer journal: Students are encouraged to write in their prayer journal every day.
- Students should systematically review their vocabulary words daily.

Definition Essay

A *definition* essay explains a common word or expression that is not easily defined. Definition is a method of analysis, as logical as possible, in which the subject is located in a general class and then distinguished from all other members of that class.

Please don't start your definition essay with either a dictionary or an encyclopedia definition of your word or comment. This approach is so often used that it is almost trite. After all, your essay is by definition (no pun intended!) your definition—not someone else's.

What is wrong with the following definition essay/paragraph? Rewrite it in a better way.

According to the Encarta Dictionary, the Pilgrims were English Puritans who founded Plymouth Colony in Massachusetts in 1620. They sought to worship God in a place and in a fashion that was more conducive to their worldview. That worldview was decidedly theistic/ Calvinistic. These religious separatists believed that the true church was a voluntary company of the faithful under the spiritual direction of a pastor. In all Puritanism, including separatism, there was not a clear distinction between what was secular and what was sacred. The Church and state were one, and the notion that they were separate was a ludicrous thought indeed to the Puritan. The Pilgrims, unlike the Puritans who settled in Boston, wanted to separate from the Church of England — not merely "purify" the church — but they did not wish to separate the Church from the state.

Writing Style: Words — Adjectives and Adverbs In Comparative and Superlative Cases

Students should avoid incomplete comparisons, ambiguous wording, indefinite references, misplaced modifiers, and dangling modifiers. Here are some examples:

This topic is better than that one. (correct)

This topic is the best of all. (correct)

Writing a research paper requires more carefully planned details than writing a paragraph. (correct).

Daily Assignment

- Warm-up: Define hope.
- Students will complete Concept Builder 18-B.
- Prayer journal.
- Students should outline all assigned essays and speech for the week.

CONCEPT
BUILDER
18-B

Identifying Definition Essays

Did you ever have an identity crisis? You know: "Who am I? Why am I here?" I blame my father for my inability to have an identity crisis. He constantly was there to identify me! I "found myself" as it were while Dad and I looked for an elusive dove-hunting Shangri-la — a desolate milo maze field or late autumn corn field — good for nothing at that point except to feed an anemic game animal or two. But we looked anyway. But we looked for a lot of things we never found — for instance we never saw a bluebird and we looked for 20 years. Ironically, every year I see bluebirds on my farm and my dad is not here to see them. I had no time for identity crises — I was busy getting my line untangled from ungracious cypress knees. I learned that there were more important things than my own desires — like what God wanted me to do and what I would be willing to sacrifice to catch that prize-winning goal.

What is the author defining?

Public Speaking: Converting a Definition Essay into a Speech

When you present a definition speech, your introduction should include the term to be defined, the definition of the term, and reason(s) for giving a more detailed definition. Also in the introduction, you should provide the listener with a notice about the kinds of additional information you will use to develop the definition. In the body of your speech use a systematic organization technique that advances your purposes. Usually there is no formal closing that is specific to the definition speech. Perhaps you will want to end with a rhetorical question, or you can conclude with a comparison/contrast with another similar/dissimilar term.

Daily Assignment

- Warm-up: Define finite.
- Students will complete Concept Builder 18-C.
- Prayer journal.
- Students should write rough drafts of all assigned essays and speech.

CONCEPT
BUILDER
18-C

Defining Abstract Terms

Define the following terms without using a dictionary.

Word	Definition
Loneliness	
Happiness	
Tomorrow	

Draw pictures to illustrate the following terms.

Word	Drawing
Loneliness	
Happiness	
Tomorrow	

Sample Student Essay

There are some things we know exist, but we usually don't think of them. Sound is one of them. Does a tree falling in a forest make sound, if nobody hears it? The obvious answer that comes to mind is yes. But is that just because we think of sound as noise? Would sound be only what the ear hears? Or is sound noise? Sound must be simply noise, because whether or not the human ear hears it, something does. (Jonathan)

Daily Assignment

- Warm-up: Define infinite.
- Students will complete Concept Builder 18-D.
- Prayer journal.
- Review the assigned text. Keep vocabulary cards.
- This is the day that students should write, and then rewrite, the final drafts of their assigned essay and speech.

CONCEPT
BUILDER
18-D

My Values

Good writing is concerned with values. Mark the following either 1, 2, or 3 according to their value to you (1 is least valuable, 3 is most).

Getting good grades	
Being different	
Winning	
Reading	
Watching movies	
Going on vacation	
Going to Church	
Christmas	

The Explanatory Essay

Chapter 19

Style (Writing and Speaking): Words — Precise Language

Public Speaking Skill: Converting a Explanatory Essay into a Speech

First Thoughts

An explanatory essay provides an explanation of a certain viewpoint. It is essential that the explanation simplify what is otherwise difficult to understand. When writing an explanatory essay, the audience is critical. You will have to tailor your explanation to suit your audience. An explanation is an informed opinion. Its value will be determined by the credibility of your sources.

Chapter Learning Objectives

In chapter 19 we will learn how to write explanatory essays.

Look Ahead for Friday

- Turn in a final copy of essay and speech
- Take Weekly Essay/Test

In a one-page essay, explain what caused World War I. Include an outline, rough draft, thesis statement, final copy, and five new (circled) vocabulary words. Your essay must pay particular attention to style (focus, content, organization). Give a copy to instructor/parent to evaluate.

Present a 3- to 5-minute speech explaining the causes of World War I."

Final Project

Correct and rewrite all essays and place them in your Final Portfolio.

Background

An explanatory essay explains something or advances a particular point. The following is an explanatory essay that develops a position and then argues a point. It is written in the form of an imaginary letter to an editor.

Dear Editor:

I read your article on "China's One-Child Policy," and I found it very disconcerting. Your editorial manifests bad morality and bad science.

For one thing, forced sterilization and infanticide (both practiced in China to maintain the one-child policy) are clearly against Scripture. From the very beginning, mankind was given the mandate to be fruitful and to multiply and to fulfill the earth and to subdue it (Genesis 1:28). The commandment was repeated to Noah and his sons after the Flood, which shows how important it was (Genesis 9:1). The promise of fruitfulness in procreation is an important feature of the Abrahamic covenant (Genesis 12:2). Therefore, if you are supporting China's policy of one child per family, you are supporting a policy that invites people to disobey the Word of God.

With married couples, birth control is acceptable (however, not with unwed teens) and can even be encouraged by the state. In China, as documented by many different sources, married couples are required to have one child and only one child. If they become pregnant again, many times the child is aborted, and the woman is sterilized. Abortion is murder; abortion is wrong. Therefore, again, the one-child policy is wrong.

As common in the Marxist/Leninist worldview, man is often making his own decisions and relying on his own "wisdom" to choose for the "good" (or what is thought to be good). In *Understanding the Times*, Dr. David Noebel states, "Because social and economic status are by Karl Marx's definition always changing according to the law of the dialectic, mankind's ideas about morality must also be in a state of change."[1] Obviously, making a decision based upon what seems right, what advances the Communist agenda, does not have the moral imperative to murder unborn children and to sterilize unwilling mothers.

Furthermore, Dr. John Jefferson Davis in his book *Evangelical Ethics*[2] correctly argues that the population explosion is a hoax. In fact, there is no evidence to support that the world will be overpopulated any time soon. There is much evidence that the opposite is true. Most population theories of the 1960s have proven to be absolutely false. There is no reason to doubt that future agricultural advances will be able to meet the nutritional needs of a growing population. So, China is misguided in its pursuit of population decline.

Therefore, because the one-child policy violates the Word of God, I oppose it. At the same time, the policy betrays bad science — there is no evidence that the world will be overpopulated any time soon. (Jessica)

---

1   David A. Noebel, *Understanding the Times* (Eugene, OR: Harvest House Publishers, 1994).

2   John Jefferson Davis, *Evangelical Ethics* (Phillipsburg, NJ: Presbyterian & Reformed Pub. Co., 2004).

Daily Assignment

- Warm-up: Explain how to bake a chocolate cake.

- Students will complete Concept Builder 19-A.

- Prayer journal: Students are encouraged to write in their prayer journal every day.

- Students should systematically review their vocabulary words daily.

Explanatory Essay

An *explanatory* essay explains something or advances a particular point.

What is the point being argued in this essay and how does the author develop it?

The terms "minutemen" and "militia" are often thought of as one and the same. However, in early America — especially in the 18th century — there was a distinct difference.

Minutemen represented a small hand-picked force selected from the ranks of local militia companies and regiments. Approximately one-third of the men in each militia unit were chosen "to be ready to march or fight at a minute's notice."

The true minutemen — always the first to appear at or await a battle — stood at Lexington Green on the morning of April 19, 1775, and led the attack on Concord Bridge. Their numbers were reinforced by the regular militia that turned out in that day's historic battles.

Actually, the concept of minutemen existed in America as early as the 17th century, while the term itself came into use in 1759 during the French and Indian War.

The title "minutemen" was formally adopted the year before the American Revolution started. At that time, in October of 1774, the Provincial Congress of Massachusetts voted to enroll 12,000 men under the title of Minute Men — volunteers who would be ready at a minute's warning to take to the field with arms.

After Congress authorized a Continental Army under the command of George Washington, minutemen units eventually ceased to exist. But their contribution as a trained and battle-hardened corps of veterans was an important and significant force as patriots took up arms to oppose the British army in the Revolutionary War.

Point Being Argued	How the Author Develops It

www.earlyamerica.com/earlyamerica/bookmarks/minutemen/

Lesson 2

Writing Style:
Words — Precise Language

Generally speaking, less is more in writing. In other words, if you can say it in three words, say it in three words — not in four or more. Use no more words than is absolutely necessary to express your thoughts. Use familiar words, not esoteric, fancy words. Most of all, though, use words that exactly mean what you want to say. That means you may have to use "perfunctory" instead of "ordinary."

There are other things you can do, too. To write precisely, you can:

Use action, colorful verbs.

The energetic boy kicked the slightly deflated soccer ball is better than *The boy kicked the ball.*

Use as few words as possible and give only relevant details.

The energetic boy kicked the slightly deflated soccer ball is better than *The boy with a tired look be-cause he did not eat breakfast kicked the deflated soccer ball owned by his neighbor whose wife was in the hospital.*

Reduce the number of prepositional phrases.

The energetic, blue-clothed boy in the center of the field kicked the slightly deflated soccer ball is better than *In the center of the field, the energetic boy with a blue shirt kicked the soccer ball with a deflated appearance.*

Reduce expletive constructions.

The energetic, blue-clothed boy in the center of the field kicked the slightly deflated soccer ball is better than *Do you know what? That boy — yes, that blue-clothed boy! — kicked the slightly deflated ball.*

Avoid using vague nouns that lead to wordiness.

The energetic, blue-clothed boy in the center of the field kicked the slightly deflated soccer ball is better than *The good player on the field, the large soccer field, which is not as big as a football field, hit the ball, or at least he touched it softly with his right foot.*

Avoid big words that don't fit the context or tone of the writing.

The energetic, blue-clothed boy in the center of the field kicked the slightly deflated soccer ball is better than *The dynamical, azure-attired male in the choicest and most vital part of the sports field drove with a heavy foot the soccer sphere.*

Avoid noun strings.

The energetic, blue-clothed boy in the center of the field kicked the slightly deflated soccer ball is better than *The energetic, blue-clothed boy, son, brother, and classmate, in the center of the field kicked the slightly deflated soccer ball.*

Daily Assignment

- Warm-up: Explain how to go to your best friend's house.
- Students will complete Concept Builder 19-B.
- Prayer journal.
- Students should outline all assigned essays and speech for the week.

Dislikes/Likes

Every writer is strengthened, or weakened, by his beliefs. A part of our beliefs is our likes and dislikes. Rank the following items starting with those you like most and ending with those you like least. Next, rank the following items starting with those your parents like most and ending with those your parents like least.

	Me	My Parents
Making a decision		
Loneliness		
Winning		
Reading		
Watching movies		
Going on vacation		
Going to Church		
Chores		

Public Speaking: Converting An Explanatory Essay To A Speech

The explanatory speech (like the explanatory essay) has four components:

Introductory comments: background information on the process/controversy that your readers need to know. If the explanatory speech is less controversial, the introduction would tell readers why this subject would matter to them.

Statement of argument/belief/process: lobbies hard for your process/belief/thesis. Readers need to know why they need to continue listening to this process speech. Even if your explanatory paper is about how to bake a cake, you need to make this part interesting.

Explanation/Process: explain the issue/process. Spare no detail. Assume nothing. Assume your reader needs every concept explained, every argument disclosed, and every fallacy exposed.

Conclusion: In a clever, exciting way, conclude this inspired speech.

Daily Assignment

- Warm-up: Explain how to ice skate.
- Students will complete Concept Builder 19-C.
- Prayer journal.
- Students should write rough drafts of all assigned essays and speech.

CONCEPT
BUILDER
19-C

Explaining Who a Person Is

Discussing the motivation of a character in literature is one of the most demanding essays. Circle words on the following figure that describe yourself. Box the words that describe your mom/guardian. Check the words that describe your father/guardian. Underline the words that describe a character in your favorite novel. Finally, use the words in the boxes to label each person. For example, you might be a phlegmatic sanguine.

Melancholic

moody
anxious
rigid
sober
pessimistic
reserved
unsociable
quiet

Choleric

touchy
restless
aggressive
excitable
changeable
impulsive
optimistic
active

Myself
Mom
Dad
Novel Character

Phlegmatic

passive
careful
thoughtful
peaceful
controlled
reliable
even-tempered
calm

Sanguine

sociable
outgoing
talkative
responsive
easy-going
lively
carefree
leadership

Sample Student Essay

Causes of World War I

There are many causes to World War I. Each country had its own reason in joining the war. The war first started with only two countries, but then those two countries caused a chain reaction around the world, which led to the Great War.

The spark of World War I was from the assassination of Archduke Franz Ferdinand. He was the heir to the Austro-Hungarian throne. The Austro-Hungarians accused a Serbian. They issued an ultimatum to Serbia, which demanded assassins be brought to justice and effectively nullified the Serbian sovereignty. The Austria-Hungary expectation was that Serbia would reject the severe terms of the ultimatum, giving them the pretext for launching a limited war against Serbia. However, Serbia had ties with Russia, and asked them to be on their side. Austria-Hungary did not expect that, so they then asked their ally, Germany, to help them just in case Russia would attack them. Germany agreed and encouraged Austria-Hungary's warlike stance.

After the assassination and the asking of allies to help Austria-Hungary and Serbia, a chain reaction started. Austria-Hungary was not satisfied with Serbia's response to the ultimatum, so they declared war on Serbia on July 28, 1914. Because Russia had an alliance with Serbia, they announced mobilization of their troops to help defend Serbia. Germany, who sided with Austria-Hungary, viewed Russia's mobilization as a plan of attack. They then declared war on Russia on August 1. The French had a treaty with Russia, so they declared war on Germany.

After the French declared war on Germany, Germany decided to attack Paris. The shortest route involved invading Belgium. The Germans did not care and invaded Belgium. Great Britain had a 75-year-old agreement with Belgium that it would protect Belgium. When the Germans invaded Belgium, Belgium's king appealed to Great Britain. The British stayed with their agreement and declared war on Germany. Other British colonies and dominions such as Australia, Canada, India, New Zealand, and the Union of South Africa, helped Great Britain. Japan had a military agreement with Britain, so they also declared war on Germany on August 23. Italy was allied with Germany and Austria-Hungary, but wanted to avoid the conflict. One year later on May 1915, Italy entered the war and sided with Germany and Austria-Hungary. Italy, Germany, and Austria-Hungary formed the Triple Alliance while the United Kingdom, France, and Russia formed the Triple Entente.

On the other side of the world, the United States was upholding an isolationist policy. They wanted stay out of the war. The *Lusitania* was an American ship filled with six million rounds of ammunition to be sold to the French and British. President Woodrow Wilson warned American citizens not to go aboard the Lusitania be-cause it was entering the war zone. Not many people listened to him, and the *Lusitania* set sail. On May 7, 1915, the *Lusitania* sank off the coast of Ireland. There were three U-boats waiting there. It was obvious that the Germans had planned the attack. Soon after, America declared war on Germany.

There were many causes to World War I, but the first spark was the assassination of Archduke Franz Ferdinand. Each country had their own reason to declare war on each other, but it mainly was a chain reaction from one country declaring war on another. (Hannah)

Daily Assignment

- Warm-up: Explain whether pizza should be eaten from the pointed end or outside edge.

- Students will complete Concept Builder 19-D.

- Prayer journal.

- Review the assigned text. Keep vocabulary cards.

- This is the day that students should write, and then rewrite, the final drafts of their assigned essay and speech.

Other People Explaining Who I Am

Now have your parents/guardians do the same thing. Have your parents circle words on the following figure that describe you. Have them box the words that describe themselves. Finally, use the words in capital letters to label each person.

Melancholic	**Choleric**
moody	touchy
anxious	restless
rigid	aggressive
sober	excitable
pessimistic	changeable
reserved	impulsive
unsociable	optimistic
quiet	active

Myself

Mom

Dad

Phlegmatic	**Sanguine**
passive	sociable
careful	outgoing
thoughtful	talkative
peaceful	responsive
controlled	easy-going
reliable	lively
even-tempered	carefree
calm	leadership

Fact, Inference, and Opinion

Chapter 20

Style (Writing and Speaking): Usage — Pronoun and Subject/Verb Agreement

Public Speaking Skill: Converting the Historical Profile into a Speech

First Thoughts

Facts can be verified or disproved. An *inference* is a statement about the unknown made on the basis of the known. *Opinion* is a statement of a writer's personal judgment. Students should recognize the difference between each type of writing and be able to create essays in each sphere.

Chapter Learning Objectives

In chapter 20 we will write and identify fact, inference, and opinion essays.

Look Ahead for Friday

- Turn in a final copy of essay and speech
- Take Weekly Essay/Test

In a one-page essay, write about the Lord's Supper. In your essay, examine other opinions but state what you see as the facts. This essay should include an outline, rough draft, thesis statement, final copy, and five new (circled) vocabulary words. The essay must pay particular attention to style (focus, content, organization). Give a copy to instructor/parent to evaluate.

Present a 3- to 5-minute speech on some aspect of the Christian life.

Final Project

Correct and rewrite all essays and place them in your Final Portfolio.

Background

The following essay is full of inference, opinion, and a few facts. Identify each highlighted sentence as fact, inference, or opinion.

Southern Arkansas was a generous but exhausted land. Cotton grew to bountiful heights. Southwest winds permanently bent rice plants pregnant with pounds and pounds of offspring. Pecan trees cradled whole acres of antediluvian loam with their gigantic arms. **Every spring, bayous and rivers deposited a rich delta gift along the banks of grateful farmland.** It was a gift from Minnesota and Ohio, freely given by the ubiquitous Mississippi River. This was really an unselfish land, a land that seemed to give more than it took.

The house in which I lived was a natural addition to this magnificent land. Built during the Depression years of cheap labor, "The House" — so named by Helen — reflected my grandparents' unbounded optimism. **Even to a young child, it appeared bigger than life. In fact, that mansion defied hyperbole.** They had built it with a profitable business and Depression-priced labor. They shamelessly flaunted their prosperity in a culture that was painfully impoverished. No one seemed to mind. The South has always been kind to its elitists. They were a chosen people, or so they claimed with every offering of ebullience. No one questioned their credentials — especially when my grandmother imported bricks from New Orleans streets, painted wicker chairs from replete Havana shops, and hung crystal chandeliers from abandoned Liverpool mansions. **I remember that the bricks surrounding our fireplace evoked a faint smell of horse manure as we enjoyed our winter fires.**

The House was a testimony both to my grandmother's generosity and to her eccentricity: five thousand square feet, six bedrooms, five full baths, and a full basement — the only full basement in my below-river-level community. The House appeared in *Southern Living*. The servants' quarters were above the kennel, and they were better than many of our neighbors' houses. The kitchen was built of cool New Orleans bricks and attached to The House by a closed walkway.

Our neighbors were mostly black. My grandmother had begged Old Man Parker to loan her money to build The House, but no bank would loan her money to build it. Or at least no banker would loan it to my grandfather. He had only solvency and prosperity to offer.

The problem was, as I intimated, my grandparents wanted to build their mansion too close to what my community called "— Town." At least my grandmother Helen wanted to build it there; my grandfather most assuredly did not. He wanted to build his house in the new Wolf Project, where all sensible, prosperous, blue-blooded white Southerners lived. **But he lacked imagination and he knew it, so he dutifully submitted the decision to Helen.** Not that he could do anything else. No one ever denied Helen anything that she really wanted. (James)

Daily Assignment

- Warm-up: Give a fact about yourself.
- Students will complete Concept Builder 20-A.
- Prayer journal: Students are encouraged to write in their prayer journal every day.
- Students should systematically review their vocabulary words daily.

Facts/Inference/Opinion

You should recognize the difference between each type of writing and be able to create essays in each sphere. Find an example of a fact, inference, and opinion in the following World War II German propaganda writing.

A catastrophe has broken over Europe like a sudden hurricane. Even those not directly involved in the struggle are shocked by its elemental rage. We Germans were not as surprised, since we had long understood the enemy's policies and had assumed the day might come when he would carry out his plans and intentions.

Why are we fighting?

Because we were forced into it by England and its Polish friends. If the enemy had not begun the fight now, they would have within two or three years. England and France began the war in 1939 because they feared that in two or three years Germany would be militarily stronger and harder to defeat. The deepest roots of this war are in England's old claim to rule the world, and Europe in particular. Although its homeland is relatively small, England has understood how to cleverly exploit others to expand its possessions. It controls the seas, the important points along major sea routes, and the richest parts of our planet. The contrast between England itself and its overseas territories is so grotesque that England has always has a certain inferiority complex with respect to the European continent. Whenever a continental power reached a certain strength, England believed itself and its empire to be threatened. Every continental flowering made England nervous, every attempt at growth by nations wanting their place in the sun led England to take on the policeman's role.

Fact	
Inference	
Opinion	

Grammar Review:
Usage—Pronoun and Subject/Verb Agreement

Match pronouns in gender and number with their antecedents. Likewise, verbs should match their subject in number. "Everyone should finish their dessert" seems accurate but actually, "everyone" is a singular indefinite pronoun antecedent that requires a singular possessive pronoun. "Everyone should finish her dessert."

Daily Assignment

- Warm-up: What can we infer about you.
- Students will complete Concept Builder 20-B.
- Prayer journal.
- Students should outline all assigned essays and speech for the week.

CONCEPT
BUILDER
20-B

Inference I

What can you infer from this 1893 illustration of Native Americans?

Inference 1
Inference 2

Lesson 3

Public Speaking: Converting the Fact, Inference, Opinion Essay into a Speech

When you are presenting a speech, you must be able to distinguish between fact, inference, and opinion. Great speeches emerge from sound reasoning and logic. When you present your speech, ask pertinent questions, evaluate arguments, and if necessary, admit a lack of understanding. Be willing to examine beliefs, assumptions, and opinions that differ, even contrast, your own. Weigh all views against facts. Fairly and honestly tell your reader these other views. In your speech, suspend judgment until all facts have been gathered and considered, but once you have moved beyond opinion and you know your facts, state them clearly and forcefully.

Daily Assignment

- Warm-up: What sort of opinions do people have about you.
- Students will complete Concept Builder 20-C.
- Prayer journal.
- Students should write rough drafts of all assigned essays and speech.

CONCEPT BUILDER 20-C

Inference II

What can you infer from this World War II German poster?

Inference 1

Inference 2

Sample Student Essay

Fact, Inference, and Opinion Essay on the Lord's Supper

In Acts 2:46, Luke writes that the first Christians "devoted themselves to the apostles' teaching and to the fellowship, to the breaking of bread and to prayer" (NIV). Breaking bread, or having communion, as Christians today call it, was one of the four activities that the Apostles obviously considered of utmost importance. However, there are differing opinions as to how this sacrament should be perceived. Which of the three opinions on communion is correct? To answer this question, it is important to examine Scripture, and then compare each opinion to the facts.

First, it is vital to investigate the scriptural origins. Communion is very obviously a symbol of Christ's death on the Cross. It is written in Matthew 26:26–28, "As they were eating, Jesus took bread, blessed and broke it, and gave it to the disciples and said, 'Take, eat; this is my body.' Then He took the cup, and gave thanks, and gave it to them, saying, 'Drink from it, all of you. For this is my blood of the new covenant, which is shed for many for the remission of sins.' " Communion is a symbol of forgiveness made possible through Christ's sacrifice. However, even though the first communion was administered at Jesus' Last Supper, the derivation of this sacrament can be traced all the way back to the Old Testament. The Last Supper took place during an annual Jewish celebration, the Passover. God had commanded the Jews to repeat the Passover meal annually so they would remember when God had mightily rescued the Israelites from slavery in Egypt. This feast included, among many other dishes, unleavened bread and four cups of wine. The particular bread referred to in Matthew 26 is the Afikoman. The Afikoman was the piece of matzo (unleavened bread) that was broken and then hidden. This piece of bread was a symbol of Jesus Christ. When he states, "This is my body," he is claiming to be the Savior that the Jews have been searching for. Additionally, the wine in Matthew 26 is the fourth cup of wine. This last cup was to represent the future Messiah. When Jesus says, "This is my blood," He claims that He is the Messiah and the fulfillment of the prophecy. The context of the Lord's Supper originates in the Old Testament and is fulfilled in the New Testament.

Communion is very significant to Christians because of what the sacrament symbolizes. However, there are more meanings of the Lord's Supper than simply forgiveness. First, the meal represents all Christians' participation in the benefits of Christ's death. Paul writes in Romans 5:19 that "For just as through one man's disobedience the many were made sinners, so also through the one man's obedience the many will be made righteous" (HCSB). It is through Jesus that our conscience is cleansed from sin, and that we can be reunited with God, our Father. This leads to the next symbol, spiritual nourishment. Just like breakfast, lunch, and dinner are meant to nourish the body; communion is meant to nourish the soul. The sin and despair that weighs down a person's heart is removed when Jesus forgives. Since communion symbolizes Jesus' forgiveness, the Lord's Supper is a tangible metaphor that helps people understand the refreshing factor of forgiveness. Communion also unites Christians together as one. First Corinthians 10:17 states that, "Because there is one bread, we who are many are one body, for all of us share that one bread" (HCSB). As believers look toward Jesus for forgiveness, they are made one. All humans have a common origin, Adam and Eve. All Christians, however, are united even further because of a common path, Jesus on the Cross, to a common goal, God in heaven. Communion is also a way for Christ to affirm His love toward us. Receiving communion is a reminder of God's ultimate act of love when He sent His only Son to die for all mankind's sins. It is also a reminder that God has unimaginable blessings stored up for us that we will receive in the end. The final symbolic meaning of communion is the receiver's affirmation of faith. When a person eats the bread and drinks the wine of communion, he or she is personally confessing, "I know that I am sinful and I want God to forgive me." This confession is restated in a subtle way every time a Christian receives communion.[1] Communion is extremely significant to the Christian faith. (John)

---

1   Wayne Grudem *Systematic Theology* Ch. 50

Daily Assignment

- Warm-up: What do you infer from a smile.
- Students will complete Concept Builder 20-D.
- Prayer journal.
- Review the assigned text. Keep vocabulary cards.
- This is the day that students should write, and then rewrite, the final drafts of their assigned essay and speech.

CONCEPT
BUILDER
20-D

Fact vs. Opinion

Find opinions and facts in the following passage:

In this dreadful war with the savages there were times when even the women had to fight for their lives. In one case, a woman had been left in a house with two young children. She heard a noise at the window, and looking up, saw an Indian trying to raise the sash. Quick as thought, she clapped the two little children under two large brass kettles which stood near. Then, seizing a shovel-full of red-hot coals from the open fire, she stood ready, and just as the Indian thrust his head into the room, she dashed the coals right into his face and eyes. With a yell of agony the Indian let go his hold, dropped to the ground as though he had been shot, and ran howling to the woods.

Facts	Opinions

(D.H. Montgomery, *The Beginner's American History*, 1893; www.gutenberg.org/files/18127/18127-h/18127-h.htm)

Historical Profile

Chapter 21

Style (Writing and Speaking): Usage — Pronouns

Public Speaking Skill: Converting the Historical Profile into a Speech

First Thoughts

In a history profile, you should write highlights giving the salient components of a historical person's life. Normally, historical profiles will be written in your humanities classes. Whenever you write one, be certain to invest enough time in the project to bring the person(s) alive to your readers!

Chapter Learning Objectives

In chapter 21 we will write a historical profile.

Look Ahead for Friday

- Turn in a final copy of essay and speech
- Take Weekly Essay/Test

Write a historical profile of William Wilberforce. This essay should include an outline, rough draft, thesis statement, final copy, and five new (circled) vocabulary words. Pay particular attention to style (focus, content, organization). Give a copy to instructor/parent to evaluate.

Present a 1- to 3-minute historical profile of William Wilberforce.

Final Project

Correct and rewrite all essays and place them in your Final Portfolio.

Sample Essay

Historical profiles have an organizational structure. The most common approach is a chronological one.

Carl Henry was born to a Roman Catholic mother and a Lutheran father, but religion was a matter of private indifference to his parents. During his early teens, Henry was baptized and confirmed in the Episcopal Church but later became a church dropout. He began a career by selling newspaper subscriptions. By 1933 he was Long Island's youngest editor of the *Port Jefferson Times Echo*. During this time he had a profound ecumenical experience. Henry said, "A Seventh-Day Adventist plied me with catastrophic forebodings from the book of Daniel. An elderly Methodist lady stressed my need to be born again. A Presbyterian minister deplored my newspaper coverage for the New York press in contrast to his coverage of Long Island for God. A university graduate in the Oxford Group pushed me to a personal decision for Christ." While he was at Wheaton College, he joined a Baptist Church. By 1949, Henry had finished his formal education (B.A. and M.A, Wheaton; B.D. and Th.D., Northern Baptist Theological Seminary; Ph.D., Boston University). He joined Harold Ockenga and Charles E. Fuller in founding Fuller Theological Seminary. (James)

Other historical profiles are organized topically:

Virgil was a broken, tired, old man. Strapped to a wheelchair, with his hands cupped in his lap, his left foot slowly moving his chair back and forth, Virgil silently smiled into empty space.

For over 40 years Virgil had worshiped in my small, inner-city church in Pittsburgh, Pennsylvania. Besides being married at our altar and raising his children in our church school, Virgil was an elder, trustee, and superintendent of Sunday schools. He served his God well; he served us well, too. But, now, senility had stolen him from us and placed him in an Allison Park Nursing Home.

Serving communion to a saint like Virgil was an inspiring event under any circumstances, but today was turning out to be an extra special day: I was bringing my clerk of Session and good friend, Paul, with me. Paul and Virgil were two of my most faithful members. . . . (James)

Daily Assignment

- Warm-up: Write a historical profile of your next door neighbor.
- Students will complete Concept Builder 21-A.
- Prayer journal: Students are encouraged to write in their prayer journal every day.
- Students should systematically review their vocabulary words daily.

Historical Profile: Original Documents

In a historical profile, you should write highlights giving the salient components of a historical person's life. Often these facts are drawn from original documents. The following are original documents sent from my grandmother, Helen Parris Stobaugh, to my cousin, Win Farrell. Read carefully this document and record important facts.

Dear Win,

I intend to write this before the postman came but got busy so didn't start until lunch time.

I have our family Bible and intended to give it to you when you were down here as I know you would appreciate it.

Sammy, being the oldest son, should have it as I was supposed to have it, but Mama gave it to Mary since she got everything else that wasn't tied down. Stella Joe gave it to me after she and George divorced and I am glad she did as I don't think Richard would care for it. I think it should belong to Ronny, but he will never return to McGee to live.

It is too fragile to ship to you so when you come out you can take it back with.

Mama's people settled Ft. Pitt which is now Pittsburg, I think. I saw a picture of a Major Cobb in an old home in New Hampshire and he was a large man like Mama's brothers Mark and Vernon.

There was a Methodist Church in Charlston West Virginia that Uncle Vernon built as the Vernon Memorial and Mama made fun of it as she said memorials are supposed to be built by your family after you die, but Uncle Vernon was afraid no one would do it.

She said Uncle Mark and he stole all the land her mother owned, as her daddy was killed in a coal mine when she was little.

She also said that some of our relatives came over on the Mayflower or soon after. So many of Will Rogers relatives greeted hers. I think you would find out about some of them by visiting the libraries in West Virginia. She also had relatives named Parker.

But so did Mrs. Stobaugh.

My mama was the youngest of ten children and she had three half brothers and sisters.

She started school before she was five years old as her mother couldn't take care of her and she lived with Uncle Mark, a school teacher. So when she finished school before she was 15, she taught school. I believe she taught in Charleston.

Any way she and Daddy Sam ran off and got married and they rode to Charleston on a frieght train in an empty boxcar.

He was railroading and made $50 a month. They rented a three story house in Charleston for eight dollars a month. She showed it to me one time when she was mad at Daddy Sam. It was on the river bank.

When you come down, I will see what else I can think of to tell you. When I have time I will get the Bible out and see whom I can find in it.

Love,
Mama

Fact 1

_____

Fact 2

_____

Fact 3

_____

Fact 4

Student Essay

Historical profiles are the perfect way to make a statement about world society or culture.

William Wilberforce was a man of many talents. He was a philanthropist, politician, and parliament member. His most outstanding achievements, however, were that of abolishing slave trade in Britain and the revival of the Christian religion. Wilberforce once said, "God Almighty has set before me two great objects — the suppression of the slave trade and the reformation of manners." The abolishment of the slave trade and the reformation of manners were indeed Wilberforce's two goals.

Wilberforce was adamant in his plea for reform of slavery. His cause for slavery started after he began his career in parliament. Having been introduced into polite society, he formed an acquaintance with Rev. James Ramsay, who educated him about the horrors of slavery. From thence on he met Hannah More, Thomas Clarkson, and other abolitionary activists who wished to end the horrors of slavery. But the real impetus to start the end of slavery did not come until a late conversation with William Pitt. Under an oak tree that has become known as the Wilberforce Oak, William Pitt asked, "Wilberforce, why don't you give notice of a motion on the subject of the slave trade? You have already taken great pains to collect evidence, and are therefore fully entitled to the credit which doing so will ensure you. Do not lose time, or the ground will be occupied by another."

Wilberforce's answer was yes. A grueling campaign of around 20 years inspired Parliament to pass his act. The Slave Trade Act received the Royal Assent on March 25, 1807.

The other major factor in Wilberforce's life, and indeed the impetus for his campaign against slavery was his religion. Wilberforce believed that a reintroduction of Christian morals and manners would save his beloved country from utter ruin. He sought to make piety a fashion among the rich and poor both, and to this end he wrote *Practical View of the Prevailing Religious System of Professed Christians in the Higher and Middle Classes of This Country Contrasted with Real Christianity*." Wilberforce felt that his love for his Lord and Savior could be broadcasted to the rest of the world, and cure it's problems.

"Is it not the great end of religion, and, in particular, the glory of Christianity, to extinguish the malignant passions; to curb the violence, to control the appetites, and to smooth the asperities of man; to make us compassionate and kind, and forgiving one to another; to make us good husbands, good fathers, good friends; and to render us active and useful in the discharge of the relative social and civil duties?"

William Wilberforce was truly a man of many talents. His love for his religion, his passion to abolish the horrors of slavery, and his drive to meet his goals all construed to make the man of character and will that we know as William Wilberforce. (Alouette)

Daily Assignment

- Warm-up: Write a historical profile of your pastor.
- Students will complete Concept Builder 21-B.
- Prayer journal.
- Students should outline all assigned essays and speech for the week.

Historical Narrative

A historical narrative is an account of a real-life experience. It is written by a person who actually experienced these events. Using the story written by Helen Stobaugh, complete the following chart.

Author	
Type of Document	
Purpose	
Primary or Secondary Audience	
Intended Audience	

Lesson 3

Grammar Review:
Usage — Pronoun Usage

Nominative case forms of pronouns are used in subject and nominative positions. Objective case forms of pronouns are used as objects.

Him and me went to the store is incorrect.

He and I went to the store is correct.

Mary and Susan spoke to he and I is incorrect.

Mary and Susan spoke to him and me is correct.

Daily Assignment

- Warm-up: Write a historical profile of your teacher.
- Students will complete Concept Builder 21-C.
- Prayer journal.
- Students should write rough drafts of all assigned essays and speech.

Historical Profile: Character Analysis

Circle words on the following figure that describe Helen Stobaugh. Under what character heading (choleric, melancholic, sanguine, phlegmatic) does she lie?

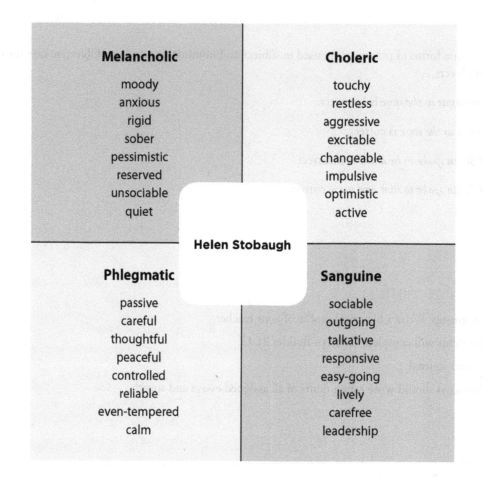

Melancholic

moody
anxious
rigid
sober
pessimistic
reserved
unsociable
quiet

Choleric

touchy
restless
aggressive
excitable
changeable
impulsive
optimistic
active

Helen Stobaugh

Phlegmatic

passive
careful
thoughtful
peaceful
controlled
reliable
even-tempered
calm

Sanguine

sociable
outgoing
talkative
responsive
easy-going
lively
carefree
leadership

Public Speaking: Converting the Historical Profile Essay into a Speech

The historical profile speech is basically the historical profile essay in speech form. You must be careful to give the details in some sort of order — sequential or temporal.

William Wilberforce

On August 24, 1759, William Wilberforce was born to Robert and Elizabeth Wilberforce in Kingston upon Hull. When he was only a young boy of seven, his father passed away. He was then sent to be raised by his aunt and uncle, who were devout evangelical Christians. He was greatly influenced by them, specifically his aunt. However, his mother brought him back to Hull to discourage such beliefs.

After finishing school, he was accepted at St. John's College in Cambridge. However, he was hardly the diligent student. He partied his way through college and took up gambling and drinking. The deaths of his grandfather and uncle had left him extremely wealthy and encouraged this loose living. After his college education, William showed a keen interest in politics and eventually ran for parliamentary election in his town, and after spending £8,000, he won. Despite his rowdy college life, William gave his life to the Lord in 1784. He deeply regretted his wasted time during his young adulthood and became very interested in social reforms.

Thus begins his extensive campaign toward the abolition of the slave trade. His interest in this campaign began when he was asked by Lady Middleton to lobby against the slave trade. As he dug deeper, William became more and more involved. He viewed the cause as his personal responsibility. In 1789, the movement proposed its first bill to parliament to abolish the slave trade. Even with a three and a half hour moving speech by William, the motion did not pass. Many Englishmen were worried that the economy would collapse if the slave traded ended. Main sources of income during that time were plantations in the West Indies, which were run by countless slaves. Despite the resistance and his frail health, William kept fighting. This, at times, made him an unpopular figure. But William and others like him kept the cause alive. Year after year, the bills were continually blocked by parliament. In 1805, the anti-slave movement began gaining ground, as a bill banning the slave trade passed the House of Commons, but was blocked by the House of Lords. Finally, in 1807, the bill was passed by an incredible 283 to 16 vote! The parliament even gave Wilberforce a standing ovation. However, the fight wasn't over. William continually fought for emancipation throughout his carrier. His works also encouraged the fight against slavery for years to come.

In the end, William Wilberforce made a profound impact on the anti-slavery campaign in England. He laid the groundwork for additional anti-slavery laws to come. William's life and career also bring valuable lessons to light, such as his perseverance through all of the resistance and health troubles. He also taught that we should be diligent and good stewards with education, unlike himself — he regretted his poor decisions. (Nick)

Daily Assignment

- Warm-up: Write a historical profile of the president.
- Students will complete Concept Builder 21-D.
- Prayer journal.
- Review the assigned text. Keep vocabulary cards.
- This is the day that students should write, and then rewrite, the final drafts of their assigned essay and speech.

Historical Profile: Secondary Source

The following is a secondary source historical profile of Helen Stobaugh. What new facts emerge from this account?

My grandparents wanted to build their mansion too close to what my community called "Colored Town." At least my grandmother Helen wanted to built it there; my grandfather most assuredly did not. He wanted to build his house in the new Wolf Project where all sensible, prosperous, blue-blooded white southerners lived. But he lacked imagination and he knew it, so he dutifully submitted the decision to Helen. Not that he could do anything else. No one ever denied Helen anything that she really wanted. Helen was no Civil Rights activist nor did she pretend that she had any high moral standards. Helen was no hypocrite. She was a cold realist and she cared for no one more than herself. Her egotism was unalloyed with any idealism. She loved us, her family, dearly but she loved herself more. She knew a propitious place to build a house and was not going to let the absence of money or the pretension of Southern society stop her.

Old man John John Parker at the bank at first denied her request. But Helen walked into his business, the Fitzgerald County stock exchange, sat on his lap, kissed him on the mouth (not the cheek!), and asked in her most polished and sophisticated Southern accent, "Please, Mr. John John, will you loan me the money to build my house?" Whether from warm enticement of pecan pies, or from cold fear that she would do something else to embarrass him, Old Man Parker loaned her the money at no interest. The deal was sealed when Helen promised to bake him a Christmas pecan pie for the rest of his life. And she did. Parker ate pecan pie every Christmas until he died (in fact it may have killed him — when he died he weighed a whopping 330 pounds). Only once did Helen fail to live up to her bargain — one season the pecan crop was abysmally bad and she had to substitute Vermont walnuts. Old Man Parker hardly noticed because Helen compensated the loss with her 100 proof rum cakes! Helen did not like to cook — nor did she have to cook — she always had servants. But when she did anything, cooking, building a house, playing hide and seek with her grandchildren, she played and cooked to win.

Helen is an enigma that greatly bothered our arcane Southern society. Again, Helen was an iconoclast. She cared nothing about what others thought — except to irritate potential critics. For instance, Helen , a fourth-generation Methodist, loved to visit the Presbyterian Church because the pastor's wife wore stylist dresses. Helen wore scandalously short dresses and, while she refused to inhale, she nonetheless carried a lit cigarette in her right hand to pique scurrilous busybodies.

New Fact 1

New Fact 2

New Fact 3

Writing the Research Paper

Chapter 22

Style (Writing and Speaking): Different writing styles will be continued to be emphasized

Public Speaking Skill: You should continue to journal

Writing Assignments: Over the next 12 lessons, you will write a research paper.

Final Portfolio Due

The focus of this chapter is the final portfolio. (No concept builders are included in this chapter. You will give your instructor/parent your corrected essays, speech evaluations, and other material in an attractive, organized, and labeled folder. You will include evidence that you have produced at least three weekly journal entries (a total of 63).

The Research Paper

Rarely, if ever, are college students evaluated through objective tests (e.g., multiple choice, true-false). Most professors prefer to have their students write two or three short papers (or three to five papers) and one large, final research paper. Therefore, the ability to read vast amounts of material (500–1,500 pages per week) and to write large numbers of manuscripts is part of the American college scene. Prepare now!

Background

For the next few weeks, you will be writing a research paper. The research paper is really only a long explanatory paper. Like all papers, it has pre-writing, writing, and rewriting phases. The pre-writing part of preparing a research paper includes the following: selecting an interesting topic, gathering information, and limiting the topic.

In a few weeks, when you finish your research paper, you will have a thesis statement, preliminary outline, many notes, a thorough outline, an inspiring outline, a thoroughly developed main body, a satisfying conclusion, and a complete works cited page. You will write and rewrite this research paper until you are a specialist in your topic.

Use the Thinking Game (see Appendix in teacher guide or in Chapter 23) to help you narrow your topic, and, later, to sharpen your thesis statement. *The first step in all pre-writing is articulating a thesis statement.* Next, even though it is still early, you should begin to collect resources about your topic and even begin to take notes.

Daily Assignment

- Warm-up: Research different ways to hang toilet rolls.
- Prayer journal.

Lesson 2

Style (Writing and Speaking): Usage — Fewer Vs. Less, Good Vs. Well, and Double Negatives

Fewer refers to the number of separate units; less refers to bulk quantity. If you can count the item, it is fewer; if you cannot, it is less.

Good is used as an adjective; *well* is used as an adverb.

Avoid double negatives:

I can't hardly read the signs (incorrect).

I can hardly read the signs (correct).

Daily Assignment

- Warm-up: Describe the best park benches.
- Prayer journal.

Public Speaking: Effective Listening

Every great orator is a great listener. First, you must desire to become a better listener. Stop talking. Look at the speaker. Listening is an active process. Try to listen objectively. Get rid of distractions. As you listen, make a note of the main points. Don't be quick to judge. Don't mentally offer a response until you have heard everything. Avoid jumping to conclusions. Finally, most importantly, decide what is not said. Only respond to what is said, not what is unsaid.

The inability to listen may have disastrous results. At the end of the Civil War, knowing that the end of the war was near, Jefferson Davis, the president of the Southern Confederacy, was greatly encouraged by President Abraham Lincoln's second inaugural speech. After this speech, Davis saw Lincoln as the South's best friend and the only hope that the South had to obtain a just peace. On the other hand, the misguided, Southern patriot John Wilkes Booth heard the following speech and decided that Abraham Lincoln was the South's worst enemy. As a result, Booth assassinated President Lincoln a month after this speech was presented. Listen to the following speech and decide who was a better listener — Jefferson Davis or John Wilkes Booth.

Fellow countrymen: At this second appearing to take the oath of the presidential office, there is less occasion for an extended address than there was at the first. Then a statement, somewhat in detail, of a course to be pursued, seemed fitting and proper. Now, at the expiration of four years, during which public declarations have been constantly called forth on every point and phase of the great contest which still absorbs the attention and engrosses the energies of the nation, little that is new could be presented. The progress of our arms, upon which all else chiefly depends, is as well known to the public as to myself; and it is, I trust, reasonably satisfactory and encouraging to all. With high hope for the future, no prediction in regard to it is ventured.

On the occasion corresponding to this four years ago, all thoughts were anxiously directed to an impending civil war. All dreaded it — all sought to avert it. While the inaugural address was being delivered from this place, devoted altogether to saving the Union without war, insurgent agents were in the city seeking to destroy it without war — seeking to dissolve the Union, and divide effects, by negotiation. Both parties deprecated war; but one of them would make war rather than let the nation survive; and the other would accept war rather than let it perish. And the war came.

One-eighth of the whole population were colored slaves, not distributed generally over the Union, but localized in the Southern part of it. These slaves constituted a peculiar and powerful interest. All knew that this interest was, somehow, the cause of the war. To strengthen, perpetuate, and extend this interest was the object for which the insurgents would rend the Union, even by war; while the government claimed no right to do more than to restrict the territorial enlargement of it.

Neither party expected for the war the magnitude or the duration which it has already attained. Neither anticipated that the cause of the conflict might cease with, or even before, the conflict itself should cease. Each looked for an easier triumph, and a result less fundamental and astounding. Both read the same Bible, and pray to the same God; and each invokes his aid against the other. It may seem strange that any men should dare to ask a just God's assistance in wringing their bread from the sweat of other men's faces; but let us judge not, that we be not judged. The prayers of both could not be answered — that of neither has been answered fully.

The Almighty has his own purposes. "Woe unto the world because of offenses! for it must needs be that offenses come; but woe to that man by whom the offense cometh." If we shall suppose that American slavery is one of those offenses which, in the providence of God, must needs come, but which, having continued through his appointed time, he now wills to remove, and that he gives to both North and South this terrible war, as the woe due to those by whom the offense came, shall we discern therein any departure from those divine attributes which the believers in a living God always ascribe to him? Fondly do we hope — fervently do we pray — that this mighty scourge of war may speedily pass away. Yet, if God wills that it continue until all the wealth piled by the bondsman's two hundred and fifty years of unrequited toil shall be sunk, and until every drop of blood drawn by the lash shall be paid by another drawn with the sword, as was said three thousand years ago, so still it must be said, "The judgments of the Lord are true and righteous altogether."

With malice toward none; with charity for all; with firmness in the right, as God gives us to see the right, let us strive on to finish the work we are in; to bind up the nation's wounds; to care for him who shall have borne the battle, and for his widow, and his orphan — to do all which may achieve and cherish a just and lasting peace among ourselves, and with all nations. (Abraham Lincoln)[1]

---

1   www.bartleby.com/124/pres32.html.

Daily Assignment

- Warm-up: Research the best way to climb a pine tree.
- Prayer journal.

Public Speaking:
Controversial Subjects

It is important for the speaker to clarify his goals and to make sure that his audience knows his goals. The amount of controversy surrounding the proposition and the attitudes of the audience will determine how much time and rhetoric the speaker devotes to convincing the audience of the veracity of his position. How persuasive is the following Christmas Eve sermon?

I want to suggest something so obvious, but so radical, that it seems silly for me to say it: God is always with us; God is everywhere; God can do all things. If I can convince you that this is true, I want to show you through the Christmas story that this omniscient, omnipresent God loves us, too.

We wonder, I fear, whether it is true — whether or not God is real, whether or not He is here among us. We can believe in the stock market, in the Pittsburgh Pirates, in post-Christmas sales, but can we believe that God is right here, right now, in our midst, right next to us even in our hearts? Can we believe this? I hope we can. Statisticians tell us that almost 75 percent of us believe in miracles, and more that that believe that there is a God. But how many of us live our lives as though God knew everything that we are doing, thinking, saying? I imagine if we really understood, our actions and words would probably change!

No doubt, Joseph and Mary's generation wondered if there was a God at all. That is, I fear, a perennial question. As Gideon watched his people being persecuted by enemy armies, he wondered where God had gone. David, as he grieved over the death of his son Absalom, wondered if God really cared. Thomas Jefferson, the author of the Declaration of Independence, sincerely held that God was no longer present or concerned about the world He had created. Jefferson thought God had placed the world in the universe, wound up as a clock, and then backed off to let things happen according to natural law. The great Colonial Awakening preacher Jonathan Edwards shared genuine concern that God was still active in his world — at least, he lamented that no one seemed to act like it!

The great English Christian apologist C.S. Lewis, when his cherished wife Joy Davidman died, wished that God were not so present! Listen to Lewis — and remember that this is a man who loved Jesus Christ with all his heart.

Where is God? This is one of the most disquieting symptoms. When you are happy, so happy that you have no sense of needing Him, so happy that you are tempted to feel His claims on you as an interruption, if you remember yourself and turn to Him with gratitude and praise, you will be welcomed with open arms. But go to Him when your need is desperate, when all other help is in vain, and what do you find? . . . Silence. . . . There are no lights in the window.

Are there no lights in your windows? Have you given up on God? Surely the generation in our gospel lesson had reason to give up, to lose hope. Why not? When was the last time God had done anything for them? From their perspective, the hated Romans had subjected God's people to unthinkable indignities, with no end in sight. Where was God? Where was the light?

This generation, as our own, echoes the words of C.S. Lewis, "Not that I am thinking that there is no God. . . . The real danger is of coming to believe such dreadful things about Him." How is God doing in your book? Do you still believe in Him? How near is God? As near as one born as we were born, albeit in a stable, among most primitive conditions. As near as one who announces a new Way, a new Life, a new Hope. As near as one who died a horrible death on a cross — because He loved me — and then arose from the grave. . . . He is here.

Daily Assignment

- Warm-up: Research the best way to remove stains from towels.

- Prayer journal.

Research Paper: Prewriting

Style (Writing and Speaking): Usage

Public Speaking Skill: Effective Listening

First Thoughts

For the next 11 lessons you will write a research paper. At times it will seem that we are going too slow; at other times, too fast. But a research paper by definition is a long, arduous process. It is not a fast, creative essay. It is a thorough, in some cases innovative, look at an important subject or corpus of information. Enjoy!

Chapter Learning Objectives

In chapter 23 we will begin the process of designing a working plan for a research paper by narrowing our topic.

Look Ahead for Friday

- Turn in a final copy of essay and speech
- Take Weekly Essay/Test

You will be assigned a research topic this week. After being assigned a paper topic, narrow that topic by using the Thinking Game.

Listen carefully to a speech or sermon and relate the main points to your teacher/parent.

Research Paper Benchmark

If you complete the assignments for each lesson, by Lesson 34 you will have a complete research paper. Do not skip any step! During this lesson you will obtain/choose and narrow your research paper topic.

Background

Use the Thinking Game to help you narrow your topic, and, later, to sharpen your thesis statement. *The first step in all pre-writing is articulating a thesis statement.* Next, even though it is still early, you should begin to collect resources about your topic and even begin to take notes.

Let's begin!

The Thinking Game (put in a box)

State problem/issue:

in five sentences

in two sentences

in one sentence

Name three or more subtopics of the problem.

Name three or more subtopics of the subtopics

What information must be known in order to solve the problem or to answer the question?

State the answer to the question/problem:

in five sentences.

in two sentences.

in one sentence.

Stated in terms of outcomes, what evidences will I see to confirm that I have made the right decision?

Once the problem/question is answered/solved, what one or two new problems/answers will arise?

Daily Assignment

- Warm-up: Discuss adolescent pimples.
- Students will complete Concept Builder 23-A.
- Prayer journal.

Pre-Writing: Brainstorming

This week you will brainstorm concerning your topic.

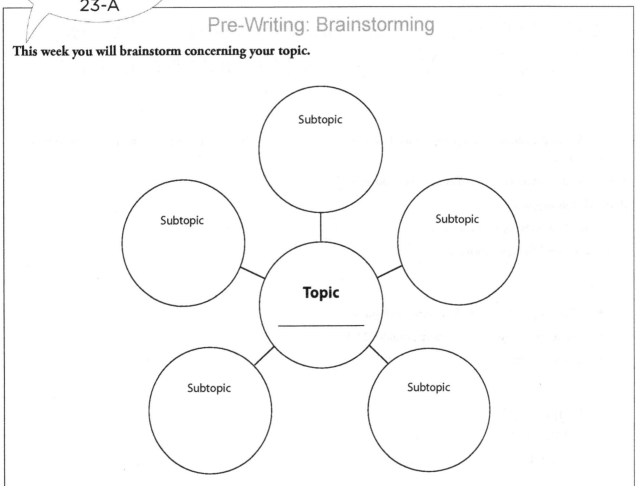

Style (Writing and Speaking): Usage — Fewer Vs. Less, Good Vs. Well, and Double Negatives

Fewer refers to the number of separate units; less refers to bulk quantity. If you can count the item, it is fewer; if you cannot, it is less.

Good is used as an adjective; *well* is used as an adverb.

Avoid double negatives:

I can't hardly read the signs (incorrect).

I can hardly read the signs (correct).

Daily Assignment

- Warm-up: Discuss drinking milk with pizza.
- Students will complete Concept Builder 23-B.
- Prayer journal.

CONCEPT
BUILDER
23-B

A Chronological Chart

One effective brainstorming strategy is to organize information chronologically. Based on your topic, complete the following chart.

Event 1	
Event 2	
Event 3	

Public Speaking: Slips of Speech

By John Bechtel

"We should be as careful of our words as of our actions," Roman Orator Cicero explained. And so we should. At the heart of great speech writing is great writing in general. One cannot have an effective spoken speech if it is not based on an effective written piece.

Good taste is a universal gift. It has been found in some degree in all nations, races, and ages. It is shown by the savage in his love of personal decoration; by the civilized man in his love of art. But while it is thus universal, it is as different among men as their faces, complexions, characters, or languages. Even among people of the same nation, it is as different as the degrees of society. The same individual at different periods of life, shows this variableness of taste. These diversities of taste imply a susceptibility to improvement. Good taste in writing forms no exception to the rule. While it seems to require some basis in nature, no degree of inborn aptitude will compensate for the lack of careful training.

To give his natural taste firmness and fineness a [speech] writer needs to read the best literature, not merely so as to know it, but so as to feel the beauty, the fitness, the charm, the strength, the delicacy of a well-chosen word. The study of the proper arrangement and the most effective expression of our thoughts prompts us to think more accurately. So close is the connection between the thought and its expression that looseness of style in speaking and writing may nearly always be traced to indistinctness and feebleness in the grasp of the subject. No degree of polish in expression will compensate for inadequacy of knowledge. But with the fullest information upon any subject, there is still room for the highest exercise of judgment and good sense in the proper choice and arrangement of the thoughts, and of the words with which to express them. The concurrent testimony of those best qualified to render a decision, has determined what authors reflect the finest literary taste, and these writers should be carefully studied by all who aspire to elegance, accuracy, and strength in literary expression.

Never hesitate to call a spade a spade. One of the most frequent violations of good taste consists in the effort to dress a common subject in high-sounding language. The ass in the fable showed his stupidity when he put on the lion's skin and expected the other animals to declare him to be the king of beasts. The distinction of a subject lies in its own inherent character, and no pompous parade of words will serve to exalt a commonplace theme.

In the expression of homely ideas and the discussion of affairs of every-day life, avoid such poetic forms as o'er for over, ne'er for never, 'mid for amid, e'en for even, 'gan for began, 'twixt for betwixt, 'neath for beneath, list for listen, oft for often, morn for morning, eve for evening, e'er for ever, ere for before, 'tis for it is, 'twas for it was. In all prose composition, avoid such poetic forms as swain, wight, mead, brake, dingle, dell, zephyr.

The unrestrained use of foreign words, whether from the ancient or from the modern languages, savors of pedantry and affectation. The ripest scholars, in speaking and writing English, make least use of foreign words or phrases. Persons who indulge in their use incur the risk of being charged with a desire to exhibit their linguistic attainments. On the other hand, occasions arise when the use of words from a foreign tongue by one who is thoroughly familiar with them, will add both grace and exactness to his style.

Rarely use a foreign term when your meaning can be as well expressed in English. Instead of blase, use surfeited, or wearied; for cortege use procession for couleur de rose, rose-color; for dejeuner, breakfast; for employe, employee; for en route, on the way; for entre nous, between ourselves; for fait accompli, an accomplished fact; for in toto, wholly, entirely; for penchant, inclination; for raison d'etre, reason for existence; for recherche, choice, refined; for role, part; for soiree dansante, an evening dancing party; for sub rosa, secretly, etc.

The following incident from the *Detroit Free Press* is on point:

The gentleman from the West pulled his chair up to the hotel table, tucked his napkin under his chin, picked up the bill-of-fare and began to study it intently. Everything was in restaurant French, and he didn't like it.

"Here, waiter," he said, sternly, "there's nothing on this I want."

"Ain't there nothin' else you would like for dinner, sir?" inquired the waiter, politely.

"Have you got any sine qua non?"

The waiter gasped.

"No, sir," he replied."

"Got any bon mots?"

"N— no, sir."

"Got any semper idem?"

"No, sir, we hain't."

"Got any jeu d'esprits?"

"No, sir; not a one."

"Got any tempus fugit?"

"I reckon not, sir."

"Got any soiree dansante?"

"No, sir."

The waiter was edging off.

"Got any sine die?"

"We hain't, sir."

"Got any e pluribus unum?"

The waiter's face showed some sign of intelligence.

"Seems like I heard ob dat, sir," and he rushed out to the kitchen, only to return empty-handed.

"We ain't got none, sir," he said, in a tone of disappointment.

"Got any mal de mer?"

"N— no, sir."

The waiter was going to pieces fast.

The gentleman from the West, was as serene as a May morning.

"Got any vice versa?" he inquired again.

The waiter could only shake his head.

"No? Well, maybe you've got some bacon and cabbage, and a corn dodger?"

"'Deed we have, sir," exclaimed the waiter, in a tone of the utmost relief, and he fairly flew out to the kitchen.[1]

---

1   Bechtel, John H., *Slips of Speech*, The Penn Publishing Company, Philadelphia, 1901, www.gutenberg.org/dirs/etext04/slpsp10h.htm

Daily Assignment

- Warm-up: Discuss pesky little brothers/sisters.
- Students will complete Concept Builder 23-C.
- Prayer journal.

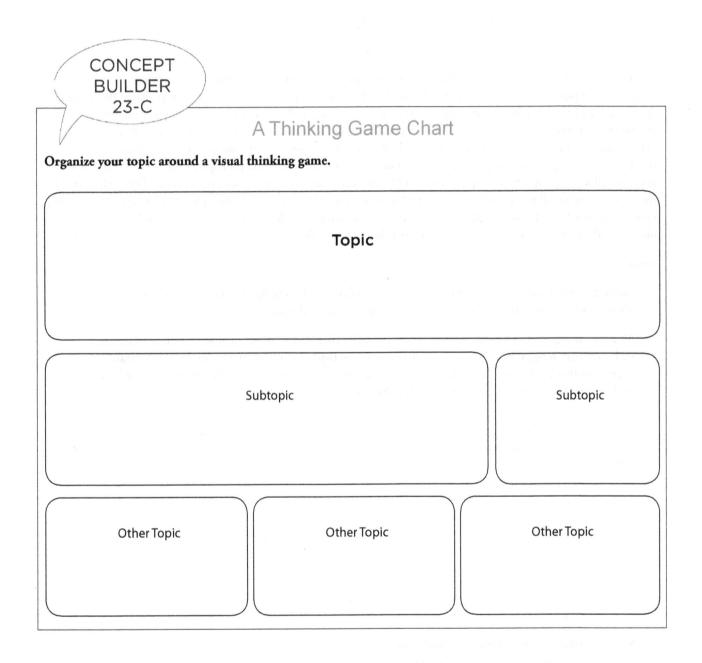

CONCEPT BUILDER 23-C

A Thinking Game Chart

Organize your topic around a visual thinking game.

Topic

Subtopic

Subtopic

Other Topic

Other Topic

Other Topic

Public Speaking:
The Gettysburg Address

The Gettysburg Address presented by Abraham Lincoln is perhaps the most perfect speech ever written. As scholar Merwin Roe explains, "It is a short speech. It is wonderfully terse in expression. It is quiet, so quiet that at the moment it did not make upon the audience, an audience wrought up by a long and highly-decorated harangue from one of the prominent orators of the day, an impression at all commensurate to that which it began to make as soon as it was read over America and Europe. There is in it not a touch of what we call rhetoric, or of any striving after effect. Alike in thought and in language it is simple, plain, direct. But it states certain truths and principles in phrases so aptly chosen and so forcible, that one feels as if those truths could have been conveyed in no other words, and as if this deliverance of them were made for all time. Words so simple and so strong could have come only from one who had meditated so long upon the primal facts of American history and popular government that the truths those facts taught him had become like the truths of mathematics in their clearness, their breadth, and their precision."

Excerpt:

Fourscore and seven years ago our fathers brought forth upon this continent a new nation, conceived in liberty, and dedicated to the proposition that all men are created equal.

Now we are engaged in a great civil war, testing whether that nation, or any nation so conceived and so dedicated, can long endure. We are met on a great battle-field of that war. We have come to dedicate a portion of that field as a final resting-place for those who here gave their lives that that nation might live. It is altogether fitting and proper that we should do this.

Daily Assignment

- Warm-up: Discuss curfew: Should it be negotiated?
- Students will complete Concept Builder 23-D.
- Prayer journal.

Venn Diagram

The overlapping circles of a Venn diagram can help you see clearly the similarities and differences between two similar topics.

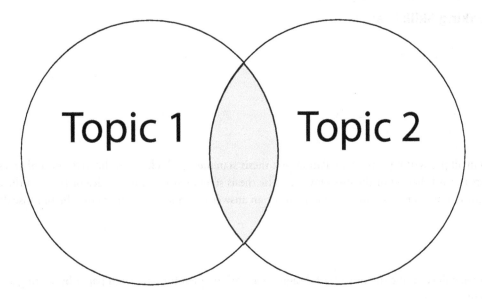

Research Paper: Thesis Statement

Chapter 24

Style (Writing and Speaking): Usage

Public Speaking Skill: Oratory

First Thoughts

The first step in all pre-writing is the articulation of a thesis statement, which states the main idea of an essay. It usually appears toward the end of the introduction. The thesis statement is the main idea or point of the essay. A thesis statement is a one- or two-sentence statement or an answer to a question concerning the purpose of the writing assignment.

Chapter Learning Objectives

In chapter 24 we will continue the process of designing a working plan for a research paper by writing a thesis statement.

Look Ahead for Friday

- Turn in a final copy of essay and speech
- Take Weekly Essay/Test

Write and then present a three-minute oratory on a subject of your choice.

The Roman statesman Cicero, in "To Cerealis,"[1] discusses how you should create your oratory:

1. The entrance, or the introduction
2. The narration, or the background details
3. The proposition, or the thesis
4. The division, or a brief list of your points
5. The confirmation, or the evidence for these points
6. The confutation, or anticipation of the rebuttal
7. The conclusion

You will be assigned a research topic this week. After being assigned a paper topic, narrow that topic by using the Thinking Game (see Appendix).

---

1   www.bartleby.com/9/4/1024.html.

Research Paper Benchmark

In the last chapter you determined and narrowed your topic. During this lesson you will write your research paper thesis statement.

Background

All writing assignments, no matter how complicated or how long, can be reduced to a single statement. For example, if the paper topic assigned is "The Causes of the American Civil War," the thesis statement must answer the question "What Caused the American Civil War?" Again, the answer to this question is the thesis statement for the paper. A thesis statement must be interesting, as specific as possible, and manageable in scope. A good way to ferret out a thesis statement is to write something like this:

In this essay, I plan to explain or argue that

_____ because of

(1) _____,

(2) _____,

(3) _____, and

(4) _____.

In summary, an effective thesis statement is a one-sentence statement of truth about a topic. "Slavery caused the Civil War" is a correctly formed thesis statement, but it is too broad and incomplete. "The failure of the American political system to manage the problem of slavery expansion in antebellum America caused the Civil War" is more defined. This statement presents a topic and an opinion about a topic in a sufficiently broad way to summarize the purpose of the research paper and in a sufficiently narrow way to have precise application to this particular research paper.

Daily Assignment

- Warm-up: Write a paragraph on this topics as if it is the first paragraph of a research paper. Topic: Adolescent pimples.

- Students will complete Concept Builder 24-A.

- Prayer journal: Students are encouraged to write in their prayer journal every day.

- Students should systematically review their vocabulary words daily.

Narrowing Your Topic: The Thesis Statement

The first step in all pre-writing is the articulation of a thesis statement, which states the main idea of an essay. It usually appears toward the end of the introduction. The thesis statement is the main idea or point of the essay. A thesis statement is a one or two-sentence statement or an answer to a question concerning the purpose of the writing assignment. All writing assignments, no matter how complicated or how long, can be reduced to a single statement.

Using the diagram below, narrow the topic of your research essay. Your goal is to create a thesis statement.

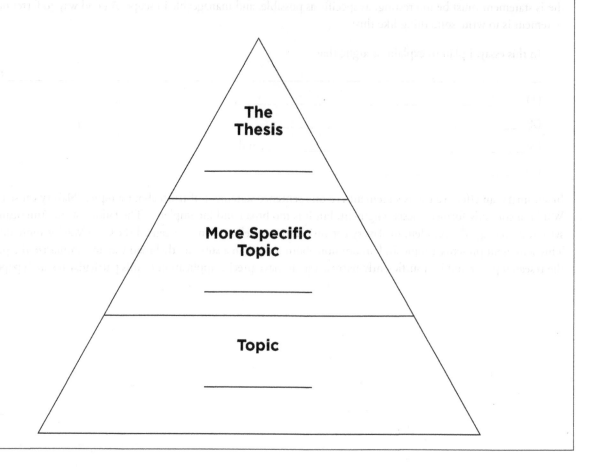

Lesson 2

Using the Computer

While some of you will use 3 x 5 cards and hard copy folders, the vast majority of you will write your essay on a computer. The diagram below would be the organization strategy you should use whether you use cards or a computer:

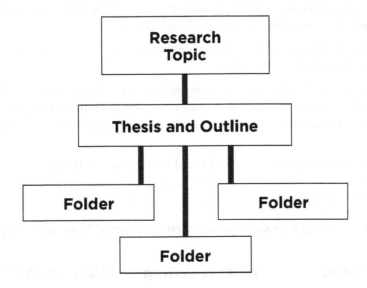

Daily Assignment

- Warm-up: Write a paragraph on this topics as if it is the first paragraph of a research paper. Topic: Drinking milk with pizza.
- Students will complete Concept Builder 24-B.
- Prayer journal.
- Students should outline all assigned essays and speech for the week.

What is a Good Thesis Statement

The faculty of the University of North Carolina argues that these questions must be answered in the affirmative if a statement is a good thesis statement. (www.unc.edu/depts/wcweb/handouts/thesis.html)

- *Do I answer the question?* Re-reading the question prompt after constructing a working thesis can help you fix an argument that misses the focus of the question.

- *Have I taken a position that others might challenge or oppose?* If your thesis simply states facts that no one would, or even could, disagree with, it's possible that you are simply providing a summary, rather than making an argument.

- Is my thesis statement specific enough? Thesis statements that are too vague often do not have a strong argument. If your thesis contains words like "good" or "successful," see if you could be more specific: why is something "good"; *what specifically* makes something "successful"?

- *Does my thesis pass the "So what?" test?* If a reader's first response is, "So what?" then you need to clarify, to forge a relationship, or to connect to a larger issue.

- *Does my essay support my thesis specifically and without wandering?* If your thesis and the body of your essay do not seem to go together, one of them has to change. It's okay to change your working thesis to reflect things you have figured out in the course of writing your paper. Remember, always reassess and revise your writing as necessary.

- *Does my thesis pass the "how and why?" test?* If a reader's first response is "how?" or "why?" your thesis may be too open-ended and lack guidance for the reader. See what you can add to give the reader a better take on your position right from the beginning.

Given these criteria, what is wrong with the following thesis statements? Next, correct the thesis statements.

Thesis Statement	What is Wrong	Corrected Thesis Statement
Both soccer and football are popular sports but for different reasons.		
William Faulkner's novel *The Sound and the Fury* is a great novel.		

Writing Style:
Usage — Who Vs. Whom

The case of the pronoun beginning a subordinate clause is determined by its use in the clause that it begins. The case and number of the pronoun is not affected by any word outside the clause. In the case of *who* and *whom*, who functions in the subjective case (subject, predicate noun) and *whom* functions in the objective case (direct object, indirect object, object of a preposition).

The new Sunday school teacher, whom came from Chicago, was very effective. (incorrect)

The new Sunday school teacher, who came from Chicago, was very effective. (correct)

Daily Assignment

- Warm-up: Write a paragraph on this topics as if it is the first paragraph of a research paper. Topic: Pesky little brothers/sisters.

- Students will complete Concept Builder 24-C.

- Prayer journal.

- Students should write rough drafts of all assigned essays and speech.

Find the Thesis Statement

Underline the thesis statement in this short essay.

The U. S. Constitution, then, was birthed in the midst of discord and rebellion.

In 1775, the 13 colonies — it would be inaccurate to call them a "nation" — were ill-prepared to wage war against the most powerful nation on the face of the earth. The American colonies had no army. The first military force consisted of colonial militia (untrained volunteers) headed by local leaders with virtually no military training and unaccustomed to taking orders from a commander. There was no central system of housing, paying, or feeding the troops, and supplies of gunpowder and clothing were inadequate. When a national army was formed, enlistments were short and often soldiers were mustered out about the time they were most effective! The American army — called the Continental army — never contained more than one-tenth of military-age Americans. Even worse, states — particularly Southern states — were full of Tories or Loyalists. Perhaps a third of Americans remained faithful to the king. As one historian stated, "All in all, it was a stupendous task that faced the patriots. They had to improvise an army and a new government at the same time, to meet unusual situations arising daily, to find trusted leaders, and to get 13 proud states to work for the common cause. And all this had to be done with little preparation, at a time when the menace of defeat and reprisals for rebellion and treason cast dark shadows over the land.

On the other hand, the American colonies had substantial advantages. For one thing, they were defending their homeland; the British were enforcing their national will. The American nation was huge and a long way from England. Essentially, all America had to do was to hold out until Great Britain grew too tired to fight. Finally, if disorganized, the Americans were natural soldiers and showed ingenuity and poise in the face of adversity. Given time, the Americans would win. General George Washington knew it. A mediocre general at best, George Washington managed to lose virtually every battle he fought, but he won the war! Washington knew that eventually the British would grow tired and abandon their efforts to subjugate the colonists. They eventually did, and surrendered at Yorktown, Virginia, in 1781.

The War was won, but there was no American nation. There were now 13 autonomous free countries in place of the 13 colonies. Most of the jealousies of colonial times still continued. America was more like the German states in Europe than a unified nation. They were tentatively held together by a document known as the Articles of Confederation. It was not a constitution; it was a sort of "gentleman's agreement."

Drafted in 1777 by the same Continental Congress that passed the Declaration of Independence, the articles established a covenant among the 13 states. The fact is, though, there was not much love lost among states, and the Confederation could do little to ameliorate petty state rivalries. In the Continental Congress, which consisted of a single legislative chamber, each state had one equal vote. When a federal decision was necessary each state delegation would struggle for consensus. If there was no unanimous affirmation for the proposal, the state delegation would abstain. To make things worse, the affirmative vote of 9 states was required to pass any measure. The Continental Congress had no power to make laws binding individuals.

As anticipated, many disputes among the states arose, and there was no federal judicial or legislative branch to solve it. Not that it really mattered anyway, because Congress had no way to mediate disagreements. Nor did it have the right to punish offenders. In fact, Congress had very little power under the Confederation. For example, it could not tax anyone so it had no funds. Therefore, there was no army or federal police force to enforce laws.

Things went from bad to worse. In fact, some people were calling for a return to a monarchy — much like the British system from which they had departed.

Public Speaking: The Great Oratory

Have you ever heard a speech/sermon that changed your life? An oratory is a speech that communicates a truth or information to the listener. It persuades the reader to accept a particular view of reality. One of the best oratories is the "Gettysburg Address" by Abraham Lincoln, given at the dedication of the National Cemetery at Gettysburg, November 19, 1863.

Four score and seven years ago our fathers brought forth on this continent, a new nation, conceived in Liberty, and dedicated to the proposition that all men are created equal.

Now we are engaged in a great civil war, testing whether that nation, or any nation so conceived and so dedicated, can long endure. We are met here on a great battlefield of that war. We have come to dedicate a portion of it as a final resting place for those who here gave their lives that that nation might live. It is altogether fitting and proper that we should do this.

But in a larger sense we can not dedicate — we can not consecrate — we can not hallow this ground. The brave men, living and dead, who struggled here, have consecrated it far above our poor power to add or detract. The world will little note, nor long remember, what we say here, but can never forget what they did here. It is for us, the living, rather to be dedicated here to the unfinished work which they have, thus far, so nobly carried on. It is rather for us to be here dedicated to the great task remaining before us — that from these honored dead we take increased devotion to that cause for which they here gave the last full measure of devotion — that we here highly resolve that these dead shall not have died in vain; that this nation shall have a new birth of freedom; and that this government of the people, by the people, for the people, shall not perish from the earth.[1]

---

1   www.britannica.com/EBchecked/topic/232225/Gettysburg-Address.

Daily Assignment

- Warm-up: Write a paragraph on this topics as if it is the first paragraph of a research paper. Topic: Curfew: Should it be negotiated?

- Students will complete Concept Builder 24-D.

- Prayer journal

- Review the assigned text. Keep vocabulary cards.

- This is the day that students should write, and then rewrite the final drafts of their assigned essay and speech.

A Thesis Statement and Supporting Facts

Using the essay from Concept Builder 24-C, complete the following chart.

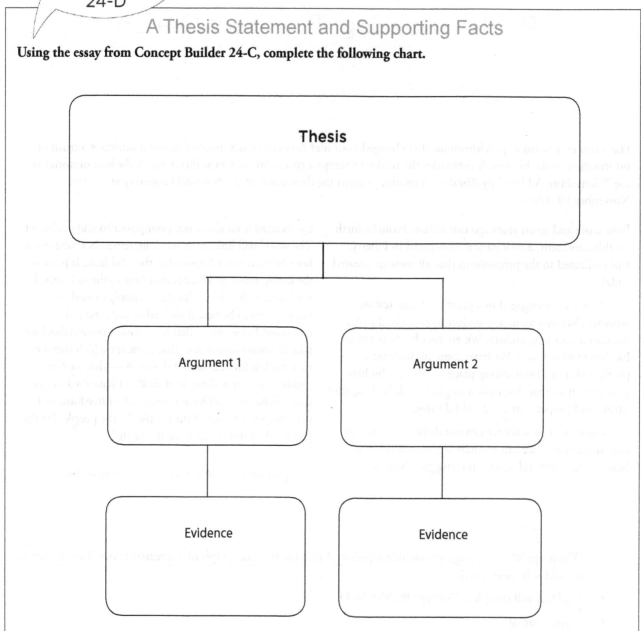

Thesis

Argument 1

Argument 2

Evidence

Evidence

Research Paper:
Preliminary Bibliography and Works Cited Page

Chapter 25

Style (Writing and Speaking): Usage

Public Speaking Skill: Oratory

First Thoughts

The pre-writing part of writing a research paper includes the following: selecting an interesting topic, gathering information, and limiting a subject. Presumably, your paper topic and thesis statement have already been established. Your job now is to continue the process of gathering information and taking notes. At this point, even if you create computer-generated files later, it would be advantageous to create a physical file or computer file where you can keep evidence such as magazine articles and pictures.

Chapter Learning Objectives

In chapter 25 we will continue the process of designing a working plan for a research paper by compiling a Preliminary Bibliography and begin your Works Cited Page.

Look Ahead for Friday

- Turn in a final copy of essay and speech
- Take Weekly Essay/Test

Prepare a preliminary bibliography of at least ten sources of information. At least one of these sources must be a primary source and at least one must be a journal article. While you may use encyclopedias and indexes in preparing this bibliography, they will not count as sources. Each bibliographic entry should be typed and contain all the necessary bibliographic information: author's name, title, translator's name, editor's name, place of publication, publisher's name, date of publication, and page numbers. At this point, format is not important. Create bibliography cards on note cards, or you may use files created on your computer's word-processing software.

Read the following biblical passage to an audience: Isaiah 6:1–8

Research Paper Benchmark

So far you have determined and narrowed your topic and written your thesis statement. During this lesson you will write your research paper preliminary bibliography.

Background

Now that you know where you are going, and why, and you have a fairly good idea of what problem you are going to address, the next step is to find the sources you will need to answer the question you have asked in your Thinking Game and your thesis statement. This means developing a preliminary bibliography. It is the "preliminary" bibliography, but since it will become a works cited page at the end of the research paper, be thorough.

What is the difference between a preliminary bibliography and a works cited page? A preliminary bibliography will not be submitted with the final project and lists all the sources you anticipate using. The preliminary bibliography is the whole salad bar; the works cited page is what you actually put on your plate. The works cited page is included with the final research paper and lists all the sources that you actually used in your paper. So you can see how the preliminary bibliography naturally evolves into the works cited page. What makes this so nice is that the punctuation and style of the preliminary bibliography is exactly the same as the works cited page.

Where does one begin? Most contemporary research begins with an online search engine. There are hundreds, but one of the best is www.dogpile.com. Next, visit your local library. Typically, many of you might prefer to skip the library visit and merely use internet resources. Don't. The library may have a video, book tape, or rare manuscript that you will not find online. Additionally, online sources must be carefully evaluated for validity.

Use the card catalog and *Reader's Guide for Periodical Literature*. Also, you may find several computer collections that will be beneficial (e.g., ERIC). Ask the librarian to help you. A public library is a good beginning, but a university library, if available, is better.

Daily Assignment

- Warm-up: Describe: You are in the library and you knock over the potted plant next to the reference librarian.
- Students will complete Concept Builder 25-A.
- Prayer journal: Students are encouraged to write in their prayer journal every day.
- Students should systematically review their vocabulary words daily.

CONCEPT
BUILDER
25-A

The Preliminary Bibliography

What sort of library resources should you use to research the following topics?

	Resource
The assassination of Abraham Lincoln.	
How to create a web page.	
Different kinds of spaghetti sauce.	

Style (Writing and Speaking): Usage — Further Vs. Farther; Than Vs. As

Farther refers to physical distance; *further* refers to quantity or degree.

After *than* and *as* introducing an incomplete construction, the student should use the form of the pronoun he would use if the sentence construction were actually completed.

John is a better soccer player than him is incorrect.

John is a better soccer player than he is correct. Think of the sentence this way: *John is a better soccer player than he (is).*

Daily Assignment

- Warm-up: Describe: You are in the library and as you stand in line to check out your library books, you happen to notice that an absolutely crucial resource is being checked out by another classmate.
- Students will complete Concept Builder 25-B.
- Prayer journal.
- Students should outline all assigned essays and speeches for the week.

CONCEPT
BUILDER
25-B

Locating Material in the Library

The following is the Dewey Decimal system employed by American libraries.

000-009	General Works
100-199	Philosophy
200-299	Religion
300-399	Social Science
400-499	Language
500-599	Science
600-699	Technology
700-799	Fine Arts
800-899	Literature
900-999	History

Write the Dewey Decimal category in which you will find books on the following subjects.

1. _____ The history of rugby.

2. _____ Is Pluto a planet?

3. _____ Literary criticism of Goethe's *Faust*.

4. _____ Causes of lung cancer.

Public Speaking: Dramatic Readings

Reading is a more difficult chore than may be supposed. In fact, reading effectively is extremely difficult. Familiarize yourself with the material, or even better, memorize the piece. Observe the places that require accents, pauses, and other punctuation. Finally, you must be careful to speak slowly and clearly. Narration is simply the verbal telling of a story, as opposed to telling it in other ways — through the media for instance. Dramatic readings tell the audience things that are not obvious from the acting alone.

Daily Assignment

- Warm-up: Describe: You are in the library and an important video (priceless) borrowed from the rare archives section is chewed up by your beagle dog. What do you tell the librarian?

- Students will complete Concept Builder 25-C.

- Prayer journal.

- Students should write rough drafts of all assigned essays and speeches.

Using the Library Catalogue

You should learn how to use the public library computer catalogue.

For the computer catalogue entry below, answer the questions that follow.

Search: Keyword	Classic Literature

1 **Christian Reading Companion for 50 Classics**

Save ☐

Stobaugh, James, 2013, Green Forest, AR: Master Books, 2013.

xiv, 304 p. ill; 24 cm.

Circulation Availability: **1 copy available at the Kansas City Public Library for checkout. Click on title to see status of all copies.**

Christian Reading Companion for 50 Classics
JAMES P. STOBAUGH

✓ Request

🔍 More Info

1. What is the keyword search?

2. Is this resource available, and if it is, where is it?

3. Who is the publisher?

4. Why is this book listed under the keyword "Classic Literature?"

Student Sample

Can you guess what the topic of this research paper is?

Preliminary Bibliography

1. "Roman Catholic Church," Microsoft® Encarta® Online Encyclopedia 2004 au.encarta.msn.com, © 1997–2004 Microsoft Corporation. All Rights Reserved.

2. Bingham, Jane. *Medieval World*. London: Usborne Publishing Ltd, 1999.

3. Boyd, Anne. *Life in a 15th Century Monastery*. Minneapolis, MN: Lerner Publications Company, 1979.

4. Coulton, G.G. *Medieval Panorama: The English Scene from Conquest to Reformation*. London: Cambridge University Press, 1939.

5. Eerdman. *The History of Christianity*. Michigan: WM. B. Eerdmans Publishing Co., 1985.

6. Fisher, David A. *World History*. Greenville, SC: Bob Jones University Press, 1999.

7. Hindley, Geoffrey. *The Medieval Establishment*. New York: G.P. Putnam's Sons, 1970.

8. Houghton, S.M. *Sketches from Church History: An Illustrated Account of 20 Centuries of Christ's Power*. Great Britain: Bath Press, 2001.

9. Howarth, Sarah. *Medieval People*. Connecticut: Millbrook Press, 1992.

10. MacDonald, Fiona. *How Would You Survive in the Middle Ages?* New York: Grolier Publishing, 1994.

11. Morgan, Gwyneth. *Life in a Medieval Village*. Minneapolis: Lerner Publications Company, 1982.

12. George Thompson and Jerry Combee. *World History and Cultures*. Pensicola, FL: A Beka Book, 1997. (Julia)

Daily Assignment

- Warm-up: Describe: You are in the library and you mistakenly get your ham and cheese sandwich caught in the copy machine. Your mother happens to walk by . . .
- Students will complete Concept Builder 25-D.
- Prayer journal.
- Review the assigned text. Keep vocabulary cards.
- This is the day that students should write, and then rewrite, the final drafts of their assigned essay and speech.

CONCEPT BUILDER 25-D

Using Internal Organizers of a Book

Once you find a book in the library, you need to know how to utilize the different components of the book.

Most books have a glossary or an alphabetical list of words and phrases and their definitions. Usually this is found at the end of the book. This would be next to the Appendix, which is also at the end of the book. The Appendix offers additional information on the information presented in the book. Likewise, the Index will alphabetically list all relevant information in the book. Finally, most books begin with a Table of Contents that lists the contents of the book and the order in which the content is presented in the book.

If you were using this resource, *American Civil War reports as recorded in Harper's Weekly.* **Verplanck, N.Y. : Historical Briefs, Inc., 1994. 314 p. : ill. ; 34 cm, what internal organizer(s) will you use to find the following information?**

1. How many chapters?

2. On what page is the Battle of Antietam?

3. How many soldiers were killed in the war?

4. How many Matthew Brady pictures are in the book?

Chapter 26

Style (Writing and Speaking): Usage - *There, And/Nor/Or, There/Their/They're*
Public Speaking Skill: Poetry Reading

First Thoughts

Your job this week will be to begin gathering information. Place this information in sentence form into your computer files or other organizational modes. If you take notes efficiently, you can read with more understanding and thereby gather information more efficiently. This technique will also save time and frustration when you actually write your re-search paper. You can invest a lot of time now and things will run smoother and more efficiently later — that is, you will have less difficulty writing your first draft — or you can fudge references, skimp on note taking, and not bother to keep note files now, but eventually you will spend more time finding your sources than you do now.

Chapter Learning Objectives

In chapter 26 we will begin to take notes on information to be used in the research paper.

Look Ahead for Friday

- Turn in a final copy of essay and speech

- Take Weekly Essay/Test

For the next two lessons you will be taking notes on your topic. You will create 3 x 5 note cards, or you may create files on your computer's word-processing software.

In front of an audience, read the last ten stanzas of "The Rime of the Ancient Mariner" by the British poet Samuel Taylor Coleridge.[1]

---

1   www.classicreader.com/read.php/sid.1/bookid.143/sec.7/.

Research Paper Benchmark

You should have your topic, thesis statement, and preliminary bibliography. During this lesson you will begin to take notes on your research paper topic.

Taking Notes

First, focus your approach to the topic before you start detailed research. Familiarize yourself with public facts about your topic. Determine the breadth of controversy surrounding your topic and, if possible, decide on which side you stand on an issue. It is helpful to begin with an encyclopedia. How does the encyclopedia divide the subject? You could use a similar organizing principle. Again, use the Thinking Game as a resource. List the subtopics you would expect to find in your readings. These may become handy as labels for notes.

At this point, resist recording a great deal of information until you are ready to structure your arguments. This is an important step on the way to making your research paper an expression of your own thinking, not merely a grid of other theories. Therefore, first summarize rather than quote. Write a paraphrase of the information in your notes. Whether you use standard note cards or employ a computer program, you should take notes in a way that you will be able to use. Save yourself some time later by recording bibliographic information in multiple locations: on a master list and on the note card. No matter how much extra time and material it requires, you should put notes on separate cards, files, or sheets. This will allow for synthesizing and ordering the material later. Finally, as you gather material, cross-reference related material.

Daily Assignment

- Warm-up: Solve this problem: You can find no books on your topic.
- Students will complete Concept Builder 26-A.
- Prayer journal: Students are encouraged to write in their prayer journal every day.
- Students should systematically review their vocabulary words daily.

Organizing Your Research Paper on the Computer

Virtually all college papers will be written on computers. You will need to create folders and sub-folders on your computer. Here is a typical organizational folders for a research paper entitled "Causes of the American Civil War."

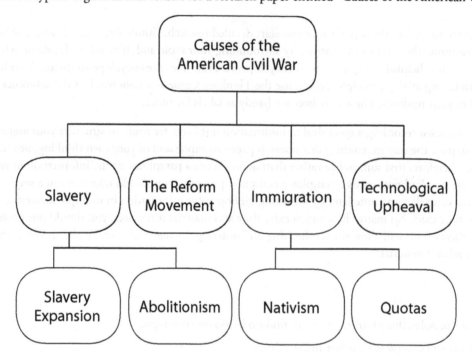

Now, create your own computer organizational chart.

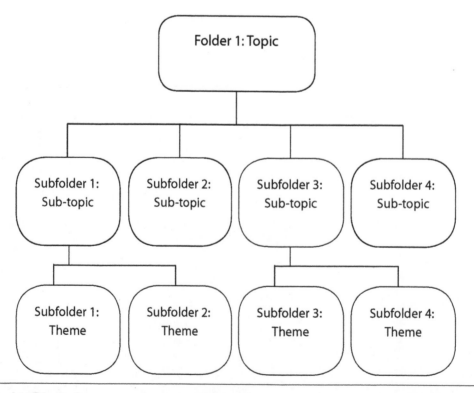

Lesson 2

Writing Your Paper On The Computer

Virtually all college papers will need to be typed. Follow these simple steps to help organize your information.

Create a folder (not a file) with the title of your paper.

Include a thesis statement in the title or on top of the outline.

Create a preliminary bibliography.

Organize your paper into several relevant topics. Make computer files on each topic in your folder. These topics will become outline headings.

Create an outline based on file headings.

Take notes on relevant topics from the preliminary bibliography. Type these notes in sentence form in the files you have created. If they are written well, you will be ready to import the material into your document at a later time. Be sure to record page numbers and references for future footnoting (or endnoting). When you finish, most of the paper should already have been written.

When you are ready, write your rough draft. "Writing the rough draft" basically should mean importing in-formation from your files.

Write and rewrite as often as necessary.

Daily Assignment

- Warm-up: Solve this problem: Your topic is too narrow.
- Students will complete Concept Builder 26-B.
- Prayer journal.
- Students should outline all assigned essays and speech for the week.

Note-taking

Taking notes is a way to keep a record of relevant information for your research paper. If you are thorough and careful, you will be able, at the end, to cut and paste this information into your paper itself. Take notes on all-important information. Look for key words and concepts. Use your thesis to drive your note taking. What notes would you draw from the following passage?

In less than six weeks after Lincoln actually became president, in the spring of 1861, a terrible war broke out between the North and the South. The people of South Carolina fired the first gun in that war. They, together with a great part of the people of ten other southern states, resolved to leave the Union. They set up an independent government called the Confederate States of America, and made Jefferson Davis its president.

The main reason why so many of the people of the South wished to withdraw from the United States was that little by little the North and the South had become like two different countries.

At the time of the Revolution, when we broke away from the rule of England, every one of the states held slaves; but in the course of eighty years a great change had taken place. Slaves in the North had become free, but those of the South still remained slaves. Now this difference in the way of doing work made it impossible for the North and the South to agree about many things.

They had come to be like two boys in a boat who want to go in opposite directions. One pulls one way with his oars, the other pulls another way, and so the boat does not get ahead.

At the South most of the people thought that slavery was right, and that it helped the whole country; at the North the greater part of the people were convinced that it was wrong, and that it did harm to the whole country.

But this was not all. The people who held slaves at the South wanted to add to the number. They hoped to get more of the new country west of the Mississippi River for slave states, so that there might always be at least as many slave states in the Union as there were free states. But Abraham Lincoln like most of the people at the North believed that slavery did no good to anyone. He and his party were fully determined that no slaves whatever should be taken into the territories west of the Mississippi River, and that every new state which should be added should be entirely free.

For this reason it happened that when Lincoln became president most of the slave states resolved to leave the Union, and, if necessary, to make war rather than be compelled to stay in it.

Causes: Divergent Elements of American Life.	
Results: the American Civil War	

Taking Notes (Cont.)

If a student takes notes efficiently, he can read with more understanding and thereby gather information more efficiently. This will also save time and frustration when he actually writes his research paper. He should first focus his approach to the topic before he starts detailed research.

Plan to invest your research time in understanding your sources and integrating them into your own thinking. Your note cards or note sheets will record only ideas that are relevant to your focus on the topic; and they will mostly summarize rather than quote.

Copy out exact words only when the ideas are memorably phrased or surprisingly expressed — when you might use them as actual quotations in your essay.

Otherwise, compress ideas in your own words. Paraphrasing word by word is a waste of time. Choose the most important ideas and write them down as labels or headings. Then fill in with a few subpoints that explain or exemplify.

Don't depend on underlining and highlighting. Find your own words for notes in the margin (or on "sticky" notes).

Label your notes intelligently. Whether you use cards or pages for note taking, take notes in a way that allows for later use.

Save bother later by developing the habit of recording bibliographic information in a master list when you begin looking at each source (don't forget to notebook and journal information on photocopies). Then you can quickly identify each note by the author's name and page number; when you refer to sources in the essay you can fill in details of publication easily from your master list. Keep a format guide handy (see Documentation Formats).

As far as possible, try to put notes on separate cards or sheets. This will let you label the topic of each note. Not only will that keep your note taking focused, but it will also allow for grouping and synthesizing of ideas later. It is especially satisfying to shuffle notes and see how the conjunctions create new ideas — yours. Leave lots of space in your notes for comments of your own — questions and reactions as you read, second thoughts and cross-references when you look back at what you've written. These comments can become a virtual first draft of your paper.

Daily Assignment

- Warm-up: Solve this problem: Your topic is too broad.
- Students will complete Concept Builder 26-C.
- Prayer journal.
- Students should write rough drafts of all assigned essays and speech.

Paraphrasing and Summarizing

As you take notes from important sources, you will want to paraphrase (restate a passage in your own words) and/or summarize (distill the passage to its basic ideas). Paraphrase and summarize the article from 25-B.

Causes: Divergent Elements of American Life.	
Results: the American Civil War	

Style (Writing and Speaking): Usage— There, And/Nor/Or, There/Their/They're

Rarely, if ever, should you use the expression there is in your paper. It is a weak, uneconomical expression.

Two subjects connected by and require a plural form of the verb. When two or more subjects are connected by or or nor, the subject closest to the verb determines the number/form of the verb.

He and I is ready to depart. (incorrect)

He and I are ready to depart. (correct)

Avoid using *would have* in "if" clauses that express the earlier of two past actions:

If he would have done what his parents asked him to do, he would have finished the work sooner (incorrect).

If he had done what his parents asked him to do, he would have finished the work sooner (correct).

Their is a possessive pronoun. *There* is an adverb. *They're* is a contraction for *they are.*

Daily Assignment

- Warm-up: Solve this problem: You lost your preliminary bibliography two days before the paper is due.
- Students will complete Concept Builder 26-D.
- Prayer journal.
- Review the assigned text. Keep vocabulary cards.
- This is the day that students should write, and then rewrite, the final drafts of their assigned essay and speech.

Evaluating Credibility of Information Resources

How reliable are the sources you are using for your research paper? Here are some questions you should ask:

- **Who is the author? Is he credentialed?**

- **Is the source unbiased?**

- **Is the source up-to-date?**

How reliable is the following source by clothing designer Emily Burbank? She was perceived as being very competent in her field in 1917.

There are a few rules with regard to the costuming of woman which if understood put one a long way on the road toward that desirable goal — decorativeness, and have economic value as well. They are simple rules deduced by those who have made a study of woman's lines and coloring, and how to emphasize or modify them by dress.

Temperaments are seriously considered by experts in this art, for the carriage of a woman and her manner of wearing her clothes depends in part upon her temperament. Some women instinctively feel line and are graceful in consequence, as we have said, but where one is not born with this instinct, it is possible to become so thoroughly schooled in the technique of controlling the physique — poise of the body, carriage of the head, movement of the limbs, use of feet and hands, that a sense of line is acquired. Study portraits by great masters, the movements of those on the stage, the carriage and positions natural to graceful women. A graceful woman is invariably a woman highly sensitized, but remember that "alive to the finger tips" — or toe tips, may be true of the woman with few gestures, a quiet voice and measured words, as well as the intensely active type.

The highly sensitized woman is the one who will wear her clothes with individuality, whether she is rounded or slender. To dress well is an art, and requires concentration as any other art does. You know the old story of the boy, who when asked why his necktie was always more neatly tied than those of his companions, answered: "I put my whole mind on it." There you have it! The woman who puts her whole mind on the costuming of herself is naturally going to look better than the woman who does not, and having carefully studied her type, she will know her strong points and her weak ones, and by accentuating the former, draw attention from the latter. There is a great difference, however, between concentrating on dress until an effect is achieved, and then turning the mind to other subjects, and that tiresome dawdling, indefinite, fruitless way, to arrive at no convictions. This variety of woman never gets dress off her chest.

The catechism of good dressing might be given in some such form as this: Are you fat? If so, never try to look thin by compressing your figure or confining your clothes in such a way as to clearly outline the figure. Take a chance from your size. Aim at long lines, and what dressmakers call an "easy fit," and the use of solid colors. Stripes, checks, plaids, spots, and figures of any kind draw attention to dimensions; a very fat woman looks larger if her surface is marked off into many spaces. Likewise a very thin woman looks thinner if her body on the imagination of the public subtracting is marked off into spaces absurdly few in number. A beautifully proportioned and rounded figure is the one to indulge in striped, checked, spotted or flowered materials or any parti-colored costumes.

Answer these questions:

1. Is the source unbiased?

2. Is the source up-to-date?

Emily Burbank, *Woman as Decoration*, 1917, chapter 1; www.gutenberg.org/files/18901/18901-h/18901-h.htm

Research Paper:
Taking Notes (Part Two) and Preliminary Outline

Chapter 27

Style (Writing and Speaking): Usage - Comparisons and Superlatives

Public Speaking Skill: Debate

First Thoughts

You started taking notes during your last lesson. You should continue to do the same during this lesson. In summary: start taking notes as soon as you receive your topic. Be careful to record all pertinent information — author, title, publication information, and page numbers. Follow the same format of note taking throughout the project.

An important part of note taking is the preliminary outline. A preliminary outline will help you focus in note taking. It is the rubric of your note taking. It is the skeleton on which you build your paper. The notes, as they are placed on the preliminary outline, become the research paper itself.

Chapter Learning Objectives

In chapter 27 we will continue to take notes on information to be used in the research paper and from those notes create a preliminary outline.

Look Ahead for Friday

- Turn in a final copy of essay and speech
- Take Weekly Essay/Test

Create a preliminary outline and continue to take notes on your research topic. Create note cards or use files created on your computer word-processing software.

Conduct some research and argue affirmatively about the following resolution: Resolved, whereas, in a time of national crisis, for the sake of national security, in the face of overwhelming danger, profiling of possible terrorists should be legal.

Research Paper Benchmark

You should have your topic, thesis statement, preliminary bibliography, and some notes. During this lesson you will create a preliminary outline and continue to take notes on your research paper topic.

Background

An important step for all writers is to create a preliminary outline. While this outline is only preliminary and probably will be expanded or be replaced later, it is an important resource to reference when you take notes. "Why didn't I need to create a preliminary outline before I started taking notes (during last lesson)?" you might ask. The answer is that you needed to enter the stream of research unprejudiced by any agenda. You have a thesis to guide you into the evidence but you did not need to make a writing strategy at that point. If you had, it would have been like creating a map to Toledo, Ohio, from Pittsburgh, Pennsylvania, without knowing exactly where Toledo was or how you were going to get there. A preliminary outline may be discarded later, and it most certainly will be revised, but for now it serves an important purpose: it guides your note-taking journey.

A typical preliminary outline might look like this:

I. What I know.

    A. Source 1

    B. Source 2

II. What I wish to prove.

    A. Source 1

    B. Source 2

    C. Source 3

III. What I need to know to support what I wish to prove.

    A. Source 1

    B. Source 2

    C. Source 3

    D. Source 4

IV. What I will conclude.

Again, this is merely a preliminary outline to guide you as you organize your thoughts. You will know more about the subject and be ready for a permanent outline next lesson.

Daily Assignment

- Warm-up: Discuss this concept in 75 words or less. Happiness

- Students will complete Concept Builder 27-A.

- Prayer journal: Students are encouraged to write in their prayer journal every day.

- Students should systematically review their vocabulary words daily.

CONCEPT BUILDER 27-A

Argumentation

You learned in Concept Builder 7-D that argumentation is the technique of choice to persuade the reader to accept a position. As you begin your research paper, it is very important that you understand the art of argumentation.

In the following argument, identify these three things.

1. **The Thesis: the purpose of the argument.**

2. **The Counter Argument: what the other side believes.**

3. **The Conclusion: a summary or restatement of the thesis.**

The Great Depression

President Herbert Hoover had been in office only seven months when the stock market crashed. This great crash ended the Roaring 20s. The Great Depression followed. The American dream seemed to have gone sour. Most Americans blamed themselves for the Depression. Americans believed that if they worked hard enough they would prosper. This was no longer possible for millions of Americans. The Great Depression destroyed America's confidence in the future. There had been recessions and depressions in American history but nothing close to what Americans experience in the 1930s.

In spite of President Hoover's innovative efforts, the Great Depression only worsened. When Franklin D.

Roosevelt became president in 1932, Americans were ready for a change. The Great Depression lasted from 1929 to the beginning of America's involvement in World War II (1941). Roosevelt attacked the Great Depression forcefully and with innovative tactics. His politics of intervention can be divided into two phases. He promised a "new deal" for the American people. The first was from 1933 to 1935 and focused mainly on helping the poor and unemployed. Roosevelt authorized, with Congressional support, massive spending to employ

millions of people. These projects included the Civilian Conservation Corps (CCC) and the Tennessee Valley Authority (TVA). While Roosevelt did not implement socialism, he did superimpose a welfare state on a capitalistic society with controversial results.

The so-called second new deal occurred from 1935 to 1937. During this period, Roosevelt emphasized social reform and social justice. To accomplish his goals, he established the Works Progress Administration (WPA), which helped many poor people and built massive projects (like the Blue Ridge Parkway in Virginia). Next, he enacted the Social Security Act, which provided a safety net and retirement income for workers.

Finally, in 1937–1938, Roosevelt implemented a third new deal. He did this primarily to help homeless farmers and agricultural workers. The New Deal failed to stop the Great Depression. Only World War II could end the Depression. However, the New Deal convinced most Americans that their government had a moral and legal right to intervene in public and private affairs if the general good of the public demanded it. America, for better or for worse, was never to be the same.

www.classicreader.com/read.php/sid.6/bookid.454/.

The thesis: **The purpose of the argument.**	
The counter argument: **What the other side believes.**	
The conclusion: **A summary or restatement of the thesis.**	

Lesson 2

Style (Writing and Speaking): Usage — Comparatives and Superlatives

Use the comparative degree when you compare two things. Use the superlative degree when you compare more than two.

Comparison of two things

Although Robert E. Lee was the **more talented** general, Ulysses S. Grant had the **stronger** army.

Comparison of more than two things

In spite of the commanding popularity of soccer in Europe and the widespread popularity of football in the United States, baseball is by far the **most popular** sport in the United States.

Daily Assignment

- Warm-up: Discuss this concept in 75 words or less. Warmth
- Students will complete Concept Builder 27-B.
- Prayer journal.
- Students should outline all assigned essays and speeches for the week.

CONCEPT BUILDER 27-B

Sequencing I

In Concept Builder 3-B you practiced sequencing. Now, at this point, it is important that you are able to employ some sort of time-committed order on your data.

First Event	
Event 2	
Event 3	
Event 4	

Public Speaking: Debate

Debate is the practice of comparing and contrasting ideas. At the beginning of the 21st century when our nation is in such turmoil and discord, when we have come so far from our Christian roots, this generation will be called to take a stand for Christ. In a nation increasingly confused about what truth is, it will be asked to state the truth clearly. Formal debate will equip this generation to argue the truth effectively in real life. A commitment to debate is a commitment to work two to three hours per week to research a topic. To the Christian, debate is not simply another speech-making or educational activity. Debate can become a life-changing entity that empowers critical advocacy for change. Akin to debate is apologetics, the tool Christians use to authenticate the claims of Christ in a hostile world. By nature, debate is about change.

How does formalized debate occur?

Two people form a "debate team." Sometimes the team will have to be for the issue (the affirmative) and sometimes it will have to be against the issue (negative).

Debaters deliver speeches in a format that is unique to debate. The speeches are called constructives and rebuttals. Each person on each team will speak twice. There are affirmative constructives and negative constructives. There are affirmative rebuttals and negative rebuttals.

All speeches are presented to the judges, who will determine who wins the debate.

Debaters argue the same resolution throughout the course of the debate.

Daily Assignment

- Warm-up: Discuss this concept in 75 words or less. Trepidation
- Students will complete Concept Builder 27-C.
- Prayer journal.
- Students should write rough drafts of all assigned essays and speeches.

Sequencing II

Use the chart below to organize the sequence of your research paper. This time, organize your essay according to points you will be making.

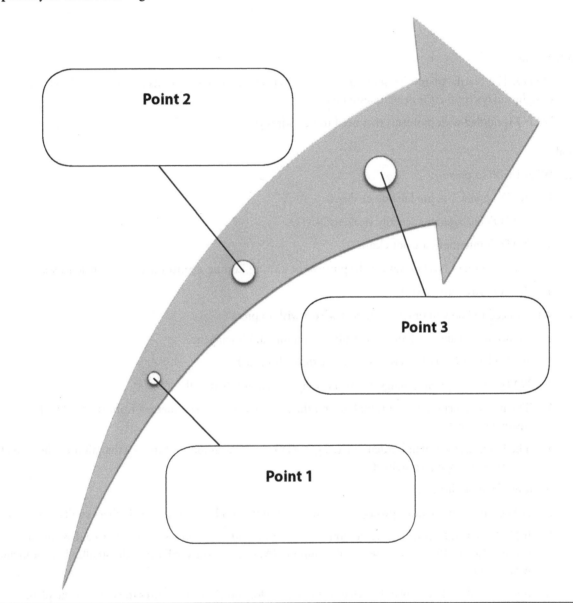

Point 2

Point 3

Point 1

Student Example

I. What I know

  A. NATO, The North Atlantic Treaty Organization has been questioned as to its effectiveness. NATO's ability to fight today's conflicts is being questioned.

  B. NATO is riddled with problems that need to be addressed.

II. Body

  A. What I wish to prove

    1. NATO operations are hurting civilians.

    2. NATO's enlargement actually weakens NATO.

    3. NATO's intentions are not clear.

    4. The creation of NATO was for the purpose of uniting Europe against the communistic Russia.

    5. NATO's structure is weak.

  B. What I need to know in order to support what I wish to prove

    1. Innocent civilians are dying as a result of weapons and intelligence.

    2. With a larger NATO, decisions are more difficult to make.

    3. NATO does too many things so that nothing is accomplished well.

    4. The new democratic Russia is no longer a threat. A new threat has emerged from the Middle East involving terrorists.

    5. The USA has the unfair burden of paying NATO twice the amount of money that all the other NATO countries are paying combined.

  C. What needs to be changed

    1. NATO needs to use more precise weaponry like bombs and be more aware of where civilians are.

    2. If NATO enlarges, it will be harder to reach decisions and act upon votes. If NATO enlargement involves Russia, Russia may use membership in NATO to press its will upon the smaller European and Asian countries.

    3. NATO needs to have a plan for what it is going to do, and clear procedures to act upon the plan. NATO should provide security in places like Iraq and Afghanistan.

    4. NATO must refocus and adapt to today's threats.

    5. The members of NATO need to finance NATO equally.

  D. The results of these changes

    1. There will be less civilian casualties in NATO operations

    2. NATO will be able to reach a consensus on anything.

    3. NATO will adapt to today's style of fighting and new threats.

III. Conclusion

    A. If these changes come, NATO will be able to fight and adapt to today's situations more easily. NATO will also be able to reach agreement on a problem quickly.

    B. Also, each member country should financially support NATO equally. Those who do not provide support will not benefit from NATO's security. (Chris)

Daily Assignment

- Warm-up: Discuss this concept in 75 words or less. Coldness
- Students will complete Concept Builder 27-D.
- Prayer journal.
- Review the assigned text. Keep vocabulary cards.
- This is the day that students should write, and then rewrite, the final drafts of their assigned essay and speech.

Using Note Cards

When I started my dissertation in 1978, I used hard note cards. By the time I finished it in 1995, I had all my files on my computer. Still, there are some advantages to using hard note cards. Use the following suggestions.

1. Start with a fresh pack of research note cards. Large, lined cards are probably best, especially if you want to make your own detailed personal notes. Also consider color coding your cards by topic to keep your paper organized from the start.

2. Devote an entire note card to each idea or note. Don't try to fit two sources (quotes and notes) on one card. Don't share space!

3. Narrow down your sources. As you read your potential sources, you will find that some are helpful, others are not, and some will repeat information you already have. This is how you narrow your list down to include the most solid sources.

4. Record as you go. From each source, write down any notes or quotes that could be useful in your paper. As you take notes, try to paraphrase all information. This reduces the chance of committing accidental plagiarism.

5. Include everything. For each note you will need to record:
    Author's name
    Title of reference (book, article, interview, etc.)
    Reference publication information, to include publisher, date, place, year, issue, volume
    Page number
    Your own personal comments

6. Create your own system and stick to it. For instance, you may want to pre-mark each card with spaces for each category, just to make sure you don't leave anything out.

7. If you think it might be useful, write it down. Don't ever, ever pass over information because you're just not sure whether it will be useful! This is a very common and costly mistake in research. More often than not, you find that the passed-over tidbit is critical to your paper, and then you won't be able to find it again.

8. Avoid using abbreviations and code words as you record notes — especially if you plan to quote. Your own writing can look completely foreign to you later. It's true! You may not be able to understand your own clever codes after a day or two, either.

Take notes on two resources

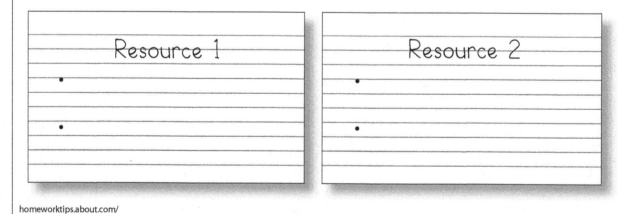

Research Paper: Designing a Working Plan

Chapter 28

Style (Writing and Speaking): Punctuation - Quotation Marks
Public Speaking Skill: Debate

First Thoughts

This week you will write a working outline, continue developing your research, and revise your outline. The research paper outline is also a plan for the research. In other words, it is an organized description of your research. Don't even think about skipping this step.

Chapter Learning Objectives

In chapter 28 we will write an outline (working plan) for our research plan.

Look Ahead for Friday

- Turn in a final copy of essay and speech
- Take Weekly Essay/Test

Write your outline for your research paper. The student should outline and present an affirmative speech and then a negative speech for the following resolution: Resolved, capital punishment should be banned.

Research Paper Benchmark

You should have your topic, thesis statement, preliminary bibliography, a preliminary outline to guide you in your note taking, and many notes. During this lesson you will create an outline.

Background

The following is an example of an outline for a research paper entitled "Racial Anger."

Outline

I. Introduction: unexplored lands

II. Body

  A. Paradox of pluralism

  B. Race mixing

  C. The promised land, or Babylon revisited

  D. So much time, so little change

  E. Positive liberal state

III. Conclusion

  A. Patterns of racial accommodation

  B. Power of forgiveness

An outline is a tool that organizes your material. It is nothing more and nothing less. It shapes information into a pattern you can follow as you write your research paper. It is a road map that guides you to your goal. Once your thoughts are organized, it will be easy for you to write your first draft. More detail in the outline makes it easier to write the first draft.

Daily Assignment

- Warm-up: Compare a research paper with a cold shower.
- Students will complete Concept Builder 28-A.
- Prayer journal: Students are encouraged to write in their prayer journal every day.
- Students should systematically review their vocabulary words daily.

How to Work with Notes

After you take notes, re-read them. Then re-organize them by putting similar information together. Working with your notes involves re-grouping them by topic instead of by source. Re-group your notes by re-shuffling your index cards or by color coding or using symbols to code notes in a notebook. Review the topics of your newly grouped notes. If the topics do not answer your research question or support your working thesis directly, you may need to do additional research or re-think your original research. During this process you may find that you have taken notes that do not answer your research question or support your working thesis directly. Don't be afraid to throw them away.

Organize the following notes.

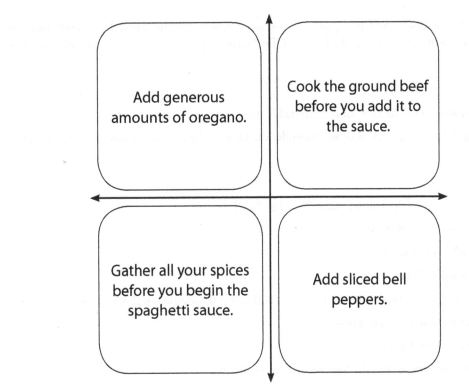

Outline Example

Each heading in the outline is tied to several note cards. The following is the outline of a paper on the causes of the American Civil War.

Outline

Thesis Statement: The combination of an expanding economy, a flood of immigrants, the Second Great Awakening, Manifest Destiny, the rise of nativism, and the failure of the American political system doomed the young republic to a Civil War.

I.   Introduction

    A.   Sectionalism assured by the U.S. Constitutional Convention

    B.   "Slavery was the sleeping serpent coiled up under the table at the Constitutional Convention." (Abraham Lincoln)

II. Body

    A.   Economic explosion in the United States from 1812 to 1860

        1.   Invention of the cotton gin

        2.   Industrial revolution in the North

        3.   Problem with tariffs

    B.   Immigrant explosion in the United States from 1800 to 1860 (population doubled every 20 years)

        1.   Immigrants from northern Europe

        2.   Immigrants from Ireland

        3.   Very few immigrants into the South (stagnant economy)

        4.   Rise of nativism

    C.   The Second Great Awakening

        1.   Cane Ridge Revival, 1800

        2.   Finney Revival

    D.   The Manifest Destiny: Mexican War

    E.   Failure of American political system

        1.   Jacksonian democracy

        2.   Rise of Republican Party

    F.   Slavery and slavery expansion

III. Conclusion

Daily Assignment

- Warm-up: Compare a research paper with your favorite CD.
- Students will complete Concept Builder 28-B.
- Prayer journal.
- Students should outline all assigned essays and speeches for the week.

CONCEPT BUILDER 28-B

Preliminary Outline

An important part of note taking is the preliminary outline, as detailed in lesson 1 of chapter 27.. A preliminary outline will help you focus in note taking. It is the rubric of your note taking. It is the skeleton on which you build your paper. The notes, as they are placed on the preliminary outline, become the research paper itself.

Complete the following preliminary outline for your research paper.

Title: "The Setting in Jack London's *Call of the Wild*"

Thesis Statement: Using Buck as a prototype, London uses the setting to show the reader that all species will revert to their "call of the wild."

Heading in the research essay: I. Buck the dog is a domesticated, "soft" pet.

Subtopic: A. The setting matches his character.

Heading in the research essay: II. Buck, the dog, becomes an aggressive, "wild" sled dog.

Subtopic: The setting matches his character.

Title: _____

Thesis Statement: _____

Heading in the research essay: _____

Subtopic: _____

Heading in the research essay: _____

Subtopic: _____

Style (Writing and Speaking): Punctuation — Quotation Marks

Introduce a quotation either by indicating what it is intended to show, by naming its source, or both. For poetry that is not narrative, it is customary to attribute quotations to "the speaker"; for a story with a narrator, to "the narrator." For plays, novels, and other works with characters, identify characters as they are quoted.

For example, "The speaker in Robert Frost's 'Death of a Hired Hand' guides the reader through the intricacies of growing old." Another example is "The reader has serious questions about the saneness of the narrator in Edgar Allan Poe's 'Tell-Tale Heart.' "

Daily Assignment

- Warm-up: Compare a footnote and an endnote. Which do you prefer? Why?

- Students will complete Concept Builder 28-C.

- Prayer journal.

- Students should write rough drafts of all assigned essays and speeches.

CONCEPT BUILDER 28-C

Writer Self-Reflection

The following are questions you will need to answer before you begin writing your research paper (owl.english. purdue.edu/owl/resource).

Who is the audience for your writing?	
Do you think your audience is interested in the topic? Why or why not?	
Why should your audience be interested in this topic?	
What does your audience already know about this topic?	
What does your audience need to know about this topic?	
What experiences has your audience had that would influence them on this topic?	
What do you hope the audience will gain from your text?	

Lesson 4

Public Speaking: Debate (B)

At the heart of debate is argument. Argument is communication in which logic is used to influence others. Normally, argument is used to change attitudes or to establish new ones. Much that is called argument is not that; it is merely the expression of opinion over and against another's opinion. The real process of argument is the demonstration of conclusions from facts or premises that the debater has established as truths. (It is beyond the scope of this course to teach students everything they need to know about debate. Interested students can find ample information online.)

Daily Assignment

- Warm-up: Compare a question mark with a colon.

- Students will complete Concept Builder 28-D.

- Prayer journal.

- Review the assigned text. Keep vocabulary cards.

- This is the day that students should write, and then rewrite, the final drafts of their assigned essay and speech.

CONCEPT BUILDER 28-D

Focus Review: Choosing the Best Thesis

Circle the best working thesis for the proposed research paper.

Thesis A: The American Revolution has many causes.

Thesis B: The Stamp Act was a major cause.

Thesis C: Upheaval at the end of the French and Indian War, the growing influence of rationalism, and the affects of mercantilism all conspire to cause the American Revolution.

Chapter 29

Style (Writing and Speaking): Introductory Words and Phrases
Public Speaking Skill: The Spoken Introduction

First Thoughts

The introduction is one of the most important parts of a research paper. It invites the reader into the paper; it can also warn the reader that he is in for a difficult, if not boring, reading! Every essay creates a new world in a new universe. The new world has a tone, theme, prejudice, and, above all, an argument(s). The reader can choose whether or not to go into the world, staying in this universe for a while. It is the reader's choice. You can help readers decide to enter your world if you have an effective introduction. What in this paper is going to change the reader's life? What new revelation will be discovered? Let readers know that it is well worth their time to proceed. If your 3-paragraph introduction is boring, then do you really think readers will want to read your 15-page main body? The introduction, in other words, is a hook to the rest of the paper.

Chapter Learning Objectives

In chapter 29 we will create an introduction for our research paper.

Look Ahead for Friday

- Turn in a final copy of essay and speech
- Take Weekly Essay/Test

Write and then present a persuasive speech pro or con on this resolution: Resolved: homeschoolers should be allowed to participate in local school athletic events.

Research Paper Benchmark

You should have your topic, thesis statement, preliminary bibliography, a preliminary outline to guide you in your note taking, many notes, and an outline. During this lesson, you will begin the introduction to your research paper.

Background

An introduction can begin with a quote or a rhetorical question. Don't be trite by beginning your essay with "Webster defines so and so as . . ." and don't be redundant and shy by beginning with "I think so and so is true. . . ." Of course you think it, or you wouldn't write it!

Then, you should state precisely, with no equivocation, or fanfare, your thesis statement. We have already talked about a thesis. If I am reading your paper, for better or for worse, I want to know within 25 words what I am reading and why I am reading it. Finally, state your arguments. There are no surprises in academic writing. Surprises belong to cheap fiction, like that written by O. Henry, for instance, who loved to trick his reader. His cheap tricks were a camouflage for mediocre rhetoric. Good story; bad writing.

Anyway, your introduction should state your arguments. You don't have to evidence them yet, but state all your arguments. I can't say this enough: in your introduction, state all the arguments that will be argued in your research paper.

Then, end the introduction with a catchy summary or even provocative statement.

A fairly typical introduction then would look something like this:

A. Rhetorical question or quote or some other catchy beginning sentence

B. Thesis

C. Evidence

D. Catchy summary statement

Daily Assignment

- Warm-up: Discuss what profound significance a research paper has to a high school student.
- Students will complete Concept Builder 29-A.
- Prayer journal: Students are encouraged to write in their prayer journal every day.
- Students should systematically review their vocabulary words daily.

Organizing Your Research Paper on the Computer

In the next few weeks you will use the following essay to answer a series of questions. Today I want you to identify the thesis statement for this essay.

Civilization in its onward march has produced only three important non-alcoholic beverages — the extract of the tea plant, the extract of the cocoa bean, and the extract of the coffee bean.

Leaves and beans — these are the vegetable sources of the world's favorite non-alcoholic table-beverages. Of the two, the tea leaves lead in total amount consumed; the coffee beans are second; and the cocoa beans are a distant third, although advancing steadily. But in international commerce the coffee beans occupy a far more important position than either of the others, being imported into non-producing countries to twice the extent of the tea leaves. All three enjoy a worldwide consumption, although not to the same extent in every nation; but where either the coffee bean or the tea leaf has established itself in a given country, the other gets comparatively little attention, and usually has great difficulty in making any advance. The cocoa bean, on the other hand, has not risen to the position of popular favorite in any important consuming country, and so has not aroused the serious opposition of its two rivals.

Coffee is universal in its appeal. All nations do it homage. It has become recognized as a human necessity. It is no longer a luxury or an indulgence; it is a corollary of human energy and human efficiency. People love coffee because of its two-fold effect — the pleasurable sensation and the increased efficiency it produces.

Coffee has an important place in the rational dietary of all the civilized peoples of earth. It is a democratic beverage. Not only is it the drink of fashionable society, but it is also a favorite beverage of the men and women who do the world's work, whether they toil with brain or brawn. It has been acclaimed "the most grateful lubricant known to the human machine," and "the most delightful taste in all nature."

No "food drink" has ever encountered so much opposition as coffee. Given to the world by the church and dignified by the medical profession, nevertheless it has had to suffer from religious superstition and medical prejudice. During the thousand years of its development it has experienced fierce political opposition, stupid fiscal restrictions, unjust taxes, irksome duties; but, surviving all of these, it has triumphantly moved on to a foremost place in the catalog of popular beverages.

But coffee is something more than a beverage. It is one of the world's greatest adjuvant foods. There are other auxiliary foods, but none that excels it for palatability and comforting effects, the psychology of which is to be found in its unique flavor and aroma.

Men and women drink coffee because it adds to their sense of well being. It not only smells good and tastes good to all mankind, heathen or civilized, but all respond to its wonderful stimulating properties. The chief factors in coffee goodness are the caffeine content and the caffeol. Caffeine supplies the principal stimulant. It increases the capacity for muscular and mental work without harmful reaction. The caffeol supplies the flavor and the aroma — that indescribable Oriental fragrance that woos us through the nostrils, forming one of the principal elements that make up the lure of coffee. There are several other constituents, including certain innocuous so-called caffetannic acids, that, in combination with the caffeol, give the beverage its rare gustatory appeal.

The year 1919 awarded coffee one of its brightest honors. An American general said that coffee shared with bread and bacon the distinction of being one of the three nutritive essentials that helped win the World War for the Allies. So this symbol of human brotherhood has played a not inconspicuous part in "making the world safe for democracy." The new age, ushered in by the Peace of Versailles and the Washington Conference, has for its hand-maidens temperance and self-control. It is to be a world democracy of right-living and clear thinking; and among its most precious adjuncts are coffee, tea, and cocoa — because these beverages must always be associated with rational living, with greater comfort, and with better cheer.

Like all good things in life, the drinking of coffee may be abused. Indeed, those having an idiosyncratic susceptibility to alkaloids should be temperate in the use of tea, coffee, or cocoa. In every high-tensioned country there is likely to be a small number of people who, because of certain individual characteristics, cannot drink coffee at all. These belong to the abnormal minority of the human family. Some people cannot eat strawberries; but that would not be a valid reason for a general condemnation of strawberries. One may be poisoned, says Thomas A. Edison, from too much food. Horace Fletcher was certain that over-feeding causes all our ills. Over-indulgence in meat is likely to spell trouble for the strongest of us. Coffee is, perhaps, less often abused than wrongly accused. It all depends. A little more tolerance! Trading upon the credulity of the hypochondriac and the caffeine-sensitive, in recent years there has appeared in America and abroad a curious collection of so-called coffee substitutes. They are "neither fish nor flesh, nor good red herring." Most of them have been shown by official government analyses to be sadly deficient in food value — their only alleged virtue. One of our contemporary attackers of the national beverage bewails the fact that no palatable hot drink has been found to take the place of coffee. The reason is not hard to find. There can be no substitute for coffee. Dr. Harvey W.

Wiley has ably summed up the matter by saying, "A substitute should be able to perform the functions of its principal. A substitute to a war must be able to fight. A bounty-jumper is not a substitute."

It has been the aim of the author to tell the whole coffee story for the general reader, yet with the technical accuracy that will make it valuable to the trade. The book is designed to be a work of useful reference covering all the salient points of coffee's origin, cultivation, preparation, and development, its place in the world's commerce and in a rational dietary.

Good coffee, carefully roasted and properly brewed, produces a natural beverage that, for tonic effect, cannot be surpassed, even by its rivals, tea and cocoa. Here is a drink that ninety-seven percent of individuals find harmless and wholesome, and without which life would be drab indeed—a pure, safe, and helpful stimulant compounded in nature's own laboratory, and one of the chief joys of life!

Thesis Statement:

William H. Ukers, *All About Coffee* (New York: The Tea and Coffee Trade Journal Co., 1922), foreword; www.gutenberg.org/files/28500/28500-h/28500-h.htm

Sample Introduction

How effective is the following introduction?

I. Introduction: A Tragedy That Could Have Been Avoided

For years the question "What caused the Civil War?" has puzzled historians. They suggest many reasons, but what is the main cause? Slavery was the chief irritant, but it did not cause the conflict. Both Rachel and Samuel Cormany, Civil War contemporaries, supported their government's efforts to quell the Southern rebel-lion, but neither of them was irritated by slavery. In fact, there were many things that contributed to the Civil War — some more than others. Certainly slavery was a cause but not *the* cause.

The Civil War was caused because Southern and Northern Americans chose not to live together. Again, the operative word is *chose*. They chose to fight a war. The North and the South were always two nations, and by 1860 it was difficult to live together in the same house. But not impossible. They had solved their problems be-fore — in 1820 and 1850, for instances. But suddenly in 1860, the political system failed.

The Civil War was the fault of neither the North nor the South. Or rather, it was the fault of both! Ultimately, though, the failure of nerve manifested by American political leaders thrust the nation into its bloodiest war in American history.

I agree with historians who in their assessment of the causes of the Civil War wrote:

> When the Union was originally formed, the United States embraced too many degrees of latitude and longitude, and too many varieties of climate and production, to make it practi-cable to establish and ad-minister justly one common government which should take charge of all the interests of society. To the wise men who were entrusted with the formation of that union and common government, it was obvious enough that each separate society should be entrusted with the management of its own peculiar interests, and that the united govern-ment should take charge only of those interests which were common and general (Hunter 1, 7–8).

What is ironic is that, in a way, the North and the South were fighting for the same thing. Both saw them-selves preserving what was vitally important to America. The Confederacy was really fighting for the American dream as much as the Union! They saw themselves as the new patriots. The South had some justification; many Founding Fathers owned slaves (Hunter 1, 9–10).

In summary, the Civil War was a struggle between conflicting worldviews. Each section held to a belief system that increasingly felt alienated from the other. They disagreed over the power of the federal government; they disagreed over tariffs; and they especially disagreed over slavery and its expansion westward (Williams 203). These disagreements were nothing new and did not bring a civil war. The war was avoidable. However, by the middle of the 19th century, these differing viewpoints — coupled with the almost violent change inflicted on America, and the collapse of compromise as a viable option in the political arena — brought the young republic into a horrendous Civil War. Americans chose to fight because they were unwilling to choose an alternative.

The first American to observe that the Civil War was avoidable, not inevitable, was former President Buchanan. He argued that the cause of the Civil War was to be found in "the long, active, and persistent hostility of the Northern Abolitionists, both in and out of Congress, against Southern slavery, until the final triumph of President Lincoln; and on the other hand, the corresponding antagonism and violence with which the advocates of slavery resisted efforts, and vindicated its preservation and extension up till the period of secession." Buchanan's assumption that the war need not have taken place had it not been for Northern fanatics and, to a lesser extent, Southern extremists, was a correct one. To put it another way, there was no substantive issue important enough in 1861 to necessitate a resort to arms; the war had been brought on by extremists on both sides. The moderate political center refused to solve the problem and left the solution to extremists. The extremists brought on a civil war.

The remainder of this paper will examine several issues whose accumulated effect made the Civil War seem necessary to a generation of Americans. (Jessica)

In the introduction you must make no presumptions about the reader. You need to notify the reader about what your arguments will be. You don't have to explain everything, but after the introduction, the reader must know where you are going with your paper. Once the introduction is completed there can be no more surprises in the paper.

The introduction accomplishes six purposes. It piques the reader's interest. It presents contextual material. It defines any necessary terms. It focuses the paper and reveals the plan of attack. The student should never surprise the reader. Most of all, the thesis must be stated in the introduction.

Daily Assignment

- Warm-up: Analyze why you choose a particular CD to compare to a research paper.
- Students will complete Concept Builder 29-B.
- Prayer journal.
- Students should outline all assigned essays and speech for the week.

CONCEPT
BUILDER
29-B

Outline

This week you will write a working outline, continue developing your research, and revise your outline. The research paper outline is also a plan for the research. In other words, it is an organized description of your research. Create an outline for the above essay.

I. Introduction

Thesis: _____

I. Body

A. Argument 1: _____

Evidence 1: _____

B. Argument 2: _____

Evidence 2: _____

II. Conclusion

_____

Style (Writing and Speaking): Introductory Words and Phrases

The introduction in a research paper may be 1 to 5 paragraphs in length. You need to give careful attention to the way you begin these critical paragraphs that will make or break your paper.

The first sentence of an introductory paragraph(s) must make clear the purpose of the research paper. Using a rhetorical question or a quote from a well-known, respected authority is one way to clarify the purpose. The second paragraph of the introduction, of course, must include a transition. It too, pulls the reader into the story that you are telling. An effective way to begin introduction paragraphs is to repeat a key word from the previous paragraphs. One final word: avoid the overused expression, "Webster's Dictionary defines. . . ."

Daily Assignment

- Warm-up: Discuss why a footnote is superior to an endnote.

- Students will complete Concept Builder 29-C.

- Prayer journal.

- Students should write rough drafts of all assigned essays and speech.

CONCEPT
BUILDER
29-C

Paraphrasing and Summarizing

As you take notes from important sources, you will want to paraphrase (restate a passage in your own words) and/or summarize (distill the passage to its basic ideas). Paraphrase and summarize the article from 25-B.

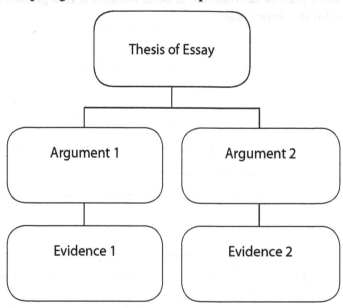

Lesson 4

Public Speaking: Arguing a Point

As we discovered in a previous lesson, a persuasive speech is effective when it causes the listener to accept a viewpoint or course of action that he does not presently hold. The following is the famous eulogy of Julius Caesar by Mark Antony:

Friends, Romans, countrymen, lend me your ears!
I come to bury Caesar, not to praise him.
The evil that men do lives after them,
The good is oft interred with their bones;
So let it be with Caesar. The noble Brutus
Hath told you Caesar was ambitious;
If it were so, it was a grievous fault,
And grievously hath Caesar answer'd it.
Here, under leave of Brutus and the rest-
For Brutus is an honorable man;
So are they all, all honorable men-
Come I to speak in Caesar's funeral.
He was my friend, faithful and just to me;
But Brutus says he was ambitious,
And Brutus is an honorable man.
He hath brought many captives home to Rome,
Whose ransoms did the general coffers fill.
Did this in Caesar seem ambitious?
When that the poor have cried, Caesar hath wept;

Ambition should be made of sterner stuff:
Yet Brutus says he was ambitious,
And Brutus is an honorable man.
You all did see that on the Lupercal
I thrice presented him a kingly crown,
Which he did thrice refuse. Was this ambition?
Yet Brutus says he was ambitious,
And sure he is an honorable man.
I speak not to disprove what Brutus spoke,
But here I am to speak what I do know.
You all did love him once, not without cause;
What cause withholds you then to mourn for him?
O judgement, thou art fled to brutish beasts,
And men have lost their reason. Bear with me;
My heart is in the coffin there with Caesar,
And I must pause till it come back to me.
(William Shakespeare, *Julius Caesar*).

Daily Assignment

- Warm-up: Analyze why you like question marks more than a semi-colon.
- Students will complete Concept Builder 29-D.
- Prayer journal.
- Review the assigned text. Keep vocabulary cards.
- This is the day that students should write, and then rewrite, the final drafts of their assigned essay and speech.

---

1. www.classicreader.com/read.php/sid.1/bookid.155/sec.10/

Outline

Now create an outline for your research paper.

I. Introduction

Thesis: _____

I. Body

    A. Argument 1: _____

    Evidence 1: _____

    B. Argument 2: _____

    Evidence 2: _____

II. Conclusion

_____

_____

_____

Research Paper: The Introduction (Part Two)

Chapter 30

Style (Writing and Speaking): Using the Right Word - Being Specific

Public Speaking Skill: Impromptu Speech

First Thoughts

In summary, all information discussed in the essay is presented in the introduction. No new arguments may be added after the introduction is created. Don't surprise your reader! Presume nothing. Explain everything.

Chapter Learning Objectives

In chapter 30 we begin the body, the heart of the research paper.

Look Ahead for Friday

- Turn in a final copy of essay and speech
- Take Weekly Essay/Test

Finish your introduction.

Deliver a 2- to 3-minute impromptu speech on the following topic: In a three-point argumentative speech, persuade a friend of yours that he/she should not date but should practice *courtship*.

Research Paper Benchmark

You should have your topic, thesis statement, preliminary bibliography, a preliminary outline to guide you in your note taking, many notes, and an outline. During this lesson you will finish the introduction to your research paper.

Introduction

The introduction is the broad beginning of the essay that asks three important questions:

1. What is this?

2. Why am I reading it?

3. What argument/position do you want me to accept?

You should ask these questions by doing the following:

1. **Set the context** — provide general information about the main idea, explaining the situation so the grader can make sense of the topic and the claims you make and support. Restate the question and ask it.

2. **State why the main idea is important** — tell the grader why she/he should care and keep reading. Your goal is to create a compelling, clear, and convincing essay the grader will want to read and act upon.

3. **State your thesis/claim** — compose a sentence or two stating the position you will support with logos (sound reasoning: induction, deduction), pathos (balanced emotional appeal), and ethos (author credibility).

Daily Assignment

- Warm-up: Write an introduction for a paper describing the dangers of eating stale popcorn.

- Students will complete Concept Builder 30-A.

- Prayer journal: Students are encouraged to write in their prayer journal every day.

- Students should systematically review their vocabulary words daily.

Introduction: The Beginning

You never get a second chance to make a first impression. The opening paragraph of your paper will provide your readers with their initial impressions of your argument, your writing style, and the overall quality of your work. A vague, disorganized, error-filled, off-the-wall, or boring introduction will probably create a negative impression. On the other hand, a concise, engaging, and well-written introduction will start your readers off thinking highly of you, your analytical skills, your writing, and your paper. This impression is especially important when the audience you are trying to reach (your instructor) will be grading your work.

Which introduction is better? Why?

A. "The Trial and Death of Socrates," written by Plato, contains four scenes of Socrates' trial and death. In the first one, Euthyphro, Socrates questions Euthyphro on what the pious is. Throughout this discussion, Socrates cannot come up with a clear definition of piety because Euthyphro's answers are always contradicting his previous answers.

B. During the last quarter of the 19th century, the United States emerged as a world power. Its industrial and agricultural productivity, large size, growing population, and modern navy gave it a prominence that could not be ignored. In 25 years, American became a dominant power in both the Caribbean (Cuba and Puerto Rico) and the Pacific (the Philippines). At the same time, America was to fight and to lose its first Vietnam-type war.

(writingcenter.unc.edu/handouts/introductions/)

Background

Evaluate the effectiveness of the following introduction and determine where the author should have placed footnotes in order to cite sources of the information given:

The year 1989 marked the 200th anniversary of the French Revolution. To celebrate, the French government threw its biggest party in at least 100 years, scheduled to last all year. In the United States, an American Committee on the French Revolution was set up to coordinate programs on this side of the Atlantic, emphasizing the theme "France and America: Partners in Liberty." The French should be uneasy about their Revolution, for whereas the American Revolution brought forth a relatively free economy and limited government, the French Revolution brought forth anarchy, then dictatorship. The French Revolution brought forth Napoléon Bonaparte.

However, were the French and American Revolutions really similar? On the surface, there were parallels. Yet over the past two centuries, many observers have likened the American Revolution to the bloodless Glorious Revolution of 1688 while the French Revolution has been considered the forerunner of many modern violent revolutions that have ended in totalitarianism. Because the French Revolution ended so violently, many Frenchmen were troubled about celebrating its 200th anniversary. An Anti-89 Movement actually sold mementos including Royalist black arm bands and calendars that mocked the sacred dates of the French Revolution, reminding today's Frenchmen of the excesses of the Revolution.

July 14, 1789, marked a day that France will not soon forget. The mobs flocked to the Bastille Prison to free their friends and neighbors. Screaming, threatening, they did whatever they could to inflict fear on the poor soldiers guarding this prison. At first, the officer in charge, Monsieur de Launay, refused to negotiate, refused to surrender. Soon, though, Luanay saw he had no choice but to surrender. He did so but only after the mob promised to let his troops go free.

However, the mob could not be stopped, could not be controlled, could not be satisfied until they had their revenge on the nobility. They stormed the Bastille, killing, looting, and destroying. Launay and his troops were slaughtered. Their heads were carried on pikes in the streets of Paris.

The French Revolution had begun. It began as an aristocratic revolution — a revolt of the nobility against the king when he was forced to call a meeting of the Estates-General in 1789. In 1789–91, a comparatively peaceful period, the National Assembly did much to modernize France. Despite the Declaration of Rights, the reformed franchise which promoted free trade still excluded the poor; but the public maintained its faith in freedom and unity, as shown in the first Festival of Federation, a celebration of national unity on July 14, 1790. However, the groundwork was laid for the secularization and tragedy that was to fall on France in later years. Power and special interests had joined together in the bloodbath called the French Revolution, and they were not going to step apart easily. Already French leadership was turning its back on centuries of Judeo-Christian morality and tradition.

By 1791, radical Jacobins had taken over the government. Louis XVI was beheaded because he had escaped and invited foreign intervention. A few years later his wife, the infamous Marie Antoinette, joined him at the guillotine. In the bloodbath that was called the Reign of Terror, forty thousand Frenchman lost their lives. The young 30-year-old Napoléon was a member of the Jacobins. It is at this point that the young soon-to-be dictator enters the story.

Napoléon Bonaparte, who is also known as the "little Corsican," was born on August 15, 1769, in Ajaccio, Corsica. His original name was Napoléon. He had seven brothers and sisters. His original nationality was Corsican-Italian, and he despised the French. He thought they were oppressors of his native land. His father was a lawyer and was also anti-French. One reason Napoléon may have been such a conqueror was that he was reared in a family of radicals. When Napoléon was nine, his father sent him to a French military government school. He attended Brienne in Paris. While there, he was constantly teased by the French students. Because of this, Napoléon started having dreams of personal glory and triumph.

In 1784 and 1785 Napoléon attended the E´cole Militaire in Paris. That was the place where he received his military training. He studied to be an artillery man and an officer. He finished his training and joined the French army when he was 16 years old. Soon after that his father died, and he was left with the responsibility of taking care of the huge Bonaparte family. Napoléon was stationed in Paris in 1792. After the French monarchy was overthrown on August 10, 1792, Napoléon decided to make his move up in the ranks. After this, Napoléon started becoming a recognized officer. Through hard work, bravery, political connections, and being born in a turbulent age, Napoléon rose to the rank of general. In 1799, Bonaparte was elected First Consul of France and Her Dependencies for Life and began his astonishing political career. Later he proclaimed himself France's emperor.

Among Napoléon's enduring legacies to France were his innovations in government. Napoléon drew up a new constitution and submitted it to the people in a plebiscite. Of course the people accepted it. The constitution established a phony parliamentary system, but everyone knew that the real power lay with the Council of State, whose leader was Napoléon. From the beginning then, the so-called "Republic" was really a paper government whose real leadership lay in one man: Napoléon Bonaparte. Napoléon was in control and meant to stay there.

Napoléon's views of religion were even more radical. It appeared that Napoléon was trying to work with the Church. In fact, Napoléon intended — and succeeded to a certain degree — to control the Church. To Napoléon, religion was a tool. It was his practice to claim to be a follower of the religion of whomever he was dealing with at a given time. Gone were the days where a leader like Robiesperre in the Festival of the Supreme Being, June 8, 1794, held a ceremony where he set fire to a statue of Atheism, and it burned down to reveal an incorruptible statue of wisdom. Napoléon's religion was not open atheism; in some ways it was more dangerous to Christianity. His view of atheism, as his views of government, was manipulative and cynical. He used the Church and religion to gain whatever ends he could. In that sense, Napoléon Bonaparte was truly a modern European. He represents what all European secular leaders will one day be.

Napoléon had it all — fame, money, authority, and respect, but there was one very important element he left out: God. His government brought order and peace and his religion brought control, but at what cost?

Napoléon saw no one but himself as the ultimate ruler and so his dictatorship was brought to an unhappy closure in 1815. Hitler, Stalin, King Saul, and Napoléon left God out of their decisions; their rules, leadership, and dictatorships did not prevail. (Jessica)

Daily Assignment

- Warm-up: Write an introduction for a paper discussing the advantages of having no television.
- Students will complete Concept Builder 30-B.
- Prayer journal.
- Students should outline all assigned essays and speeches for the week.

The Introduction: A Road Map

Your introduction is an important road map for the rest of your paper. Your introduction conveys a lot of information to your readers. You can let them know what your topic is, why it is important, and how you plan to proceed with your discussion. It should contain a thesis that will assert your main argument. It will also, ideally, give the reader a sense of the kinds of information you will use to make that argument and the general organization of the paragraphs and pages that will follow. After reading your introduction, your readers should not have any major surprises in store when they read the main body of your paper.

Read this introduction. Next, state at least three reasons America expanded its influence in the 19th century.

During the last quarter of the 19th century, the United States emerged as a world power. Its industrial and agricultural productivity, large size, growing population, and modern navy gave it a prominence that could not be ignored. In 25 years, American became a dominant power in both the Caribbean (Cuba and Puerto Rico) and the Pacific (the Philippines). At the same time, America was to fight and to lose its first Vietnam-type war.

Several times in the last part of the 19th century Americans had to decide whether or not to participate in global expansion. There were some major concerns. For one thing, some Americans still felt antipathy toward Europe. The American Revolution was scarcely a century away from their memory. Americans felt natural affinity with colonized people groups since they themselves were once a colony. Besides, America has always taken the side of the underdog. Were Americans ready to assume the role of colonizer instead of colonist?

Next, some even wondered if America's democratic institutions were compatible with an overseas empire and the large military establishment that would be required to maintain it. Did America really want, for instance, a standing, large navy that was necessary for overseas possessions?

Finally, curiously, others rejected the concept of empire because they opposed bringing under the American flag racial and ethnic groups they deemed inferior.

At the same time, Americans wanted a piece of the imperialist pie. European competitors were grabbing the best seaports and market locations and some Americans felt that they needed to be in the action.

Reason 1	
Reason 2	
Reason 3	

Billias, et al., p. 173 Interpretations of American History, 6th Ed, Vol. (Interpretations of American History; Patterns and Perspectives) NY: Simon & Schuster, 2010, p. 173

Style (Writing and Speaking): Using the Right Word: Being Specific

You should be as specific as possible in your writing. Metaphors should be concrete and drawn from ordinary experience. Adjectives should be specific in type and description. Technically correct, *The ocean is pretty* is too general. *The emerald-green ocean with its frothy waves and shimmering tide is breathtakingly beautiful* is more descriptive and specific.

Daily Assignment

- Warm-up: Write an introduction for a paper discussing the advantages of having a television.

- Students will complete Concept Builder 30-C.

- Prayer journal.

- Students should write rough drafts of all assigned essays and speeches.

CONCEPT BUILDER 30-C

The Introduction: The Power of the Story

Ideally, your introduction will capture your readers' interest and make them want to read the rest of your paper. Opening with a compelling story, a fascinating quotation, an interesting question, or a stirring example can get your readers to see why this topic matters and serve as an invitation for them to join you for an interesting intellectual conversation.

What story does this author use to invite the reader into his essay?

WAKING UP

If there is anything that we all enjoy, it is waking up on a bright spring morning and seeing the sunlight pouring into the room.

You all know the poem beginning — "I remember, I remember / The house where I was born; The little window where the sun / Came peeping in at morn."

You are feeling fresh and rested and happy after your good night's sleep and you are eager to be up and out among the birds and the flowers. You are perfectly right in being glad to say "Good morning" to the sun, for he is one of the best friends you have. Doesn't he make the flowers blossom, and the trees grow? And he makes the apples redden, too, and the wheat-ears fill out, and the potatoes grow under the ground, and the peas and beans and melons and strawberries and raspberries above it. All these things that feed you and keep you healthy are grown by the heat of the sun.

So if it were not for the sunlight we should all starve to death. While sunlight is pouring down from the sun to the earth, it is warming and cleaning the air, burning up any poisonous gases, or germs, that may be in it. By heating the air, it starts it to rising. If you will watch, you can see the air shimmering and rising from an open field on a broiling summer day, or wavering and rushing upward from a hot stove or an open register in winter. Hold a little feather fluff or blow a puff of flour above a hot stove, and it will go sailing up toward the ceiling. As the heated air rises, the cooler air around rushes in to fill the place that it has left, and the outdoor "drafts" are made that we call "winds (Hutchinson, *The Child's Day*).

Story_____

writingcenter.unc.edu/handouts/introductions/

Public Speaking:
Didactic Speech

The most frightening speech to many believers is the witness, which is a version of the impromptu speech. Like all speeches, the witness requires speakers to know their material, to know their audience, and to present the material in an organized and respectful way. The impromptu speech is the same as the extemporaneous speech. In both speeches, the speaker is presented a topic and given three to five minutes to prepare a speech in response to the topic. The following are strategies for presenting the impromptu speech.

- While it is impossible to anticipate all possible impromptu speech topics, it is helpful if the presenter invests some time reflecting upon what is occurring in current events. For instance, if one is presenting an impromptu speech on September 18, 2001, it is obvious that one topic could be on the World Trade Center catastrophe.

- The presenter should not try to write an entire speech. An outline is all that will be possible. The presenter should only make one or two good points.

- The introduction is critical in an impromptu speech. It basically should include the thesis statement and a rhetorical question and almost nothing else.

- Though time is an issue, the presenter should be careful to have an effective conclusion.

Daily Assignment

- Warm-up: Write an introduction for a paper arguing that anchovies should be a required ingredient on a pizza.

- Students will complete Concept Builder 30-D.

- Prayer journal.

- Review the assigned text. Keep vocabulary cards.

- This is the day that students should write, and then rewrite, the final drafts of their assigned essay and speech.

CONCEPT BUILDER 30-D

Introduction: Answering a Question

Start by thinking about the question. Your entire essay will be a response to the assigned question, and your introduction is the first step toward that end. Your direct answer to the assigned question will be your thesis, and your thesis will be included in your introduction, so it is a good idea to use the question as a jumping off point. Imagine that you are assigned the following question:

Some people believe that there is only one foolproof plan, perfect solution, or correct interpretation. But nothing is ever that simple. For better or worse, for every so-called final answer there is another way of seeing things. There is always a "however." Is there always another explanation or another point of view? Is there another way to look at things?

Answer the above question(s) and you will have the start of a great introduction!

Research Paper: The Body (Part One)

Chapter 31

Style (Writing and Speaking): Avoid Sexist Language

Public Speaking Skill: Didactic Speech

First Thoughts

Finally! The day has arrived that you write the major part of your research paper. Gather your notes, preliminary bibliography, and, most importantly, your outline. Write from your outline, not your notes, not your memory. Write from the road map of your paper — the outline. You already have your introduction; now let's begin the main part of your paper.

Chapter Learning Objectives

In chapter 31 we finally begin the main part of the paper — the body!

Look Ahead for Friday

- Turn in a final copy of essay and speech
- Take Weekly Essay/Test

Write the first-draft body of your research paper.

Write a 2- or 3-minute didactic speech highlighting the main points of your research paper. Typically, the didactic speech is greatly informed by the outline and thesis statement.

Research Paper Benchmark

You should have your topic, thesis statement, preliminary bibliography, a preliminary outline to guide you in your note taking, many notes, the outline, and the introduction to your research paper. Congratulations! During the next lesson you will begin the main body of your research paper.

Background

If you have created computer files, insert or cut and place them into your document. If you have hard-copy file cards, you will need to type your notes in your paper. Add transitions between paragraphs to pull the paper together. Be careful to reference every thought or quote from a source. Typically, 80 percent of a research paper is footnoted and/or endnoted.

Once the reader is invited into the paper via the introduction, it is time to defend your thesis. In other words, restate your arguments and defend them. Evidence your arguments — with much evidence. The more controversial your argument, the more evidence you will need. Again, don't worry if you have a lot of endnotes/footnotes. Most valid research uses multiple footnotes. It demonstrates a well-researched topic.

Move the reader slowly, but methodically, through your arguments. Use transitions and constantly restate the thesis. Keep your readers focused. Remind them often about where they are going, how they will get there, and what they will find when they get there. Tell them what they are learning and why it is important. Don't patronize them. Don't say, "Any educated person knows my argument is correct." Instead, say: "The evidence clearly proves that my arguments are correct." It also helps to remind readers why they are investing so much time reading your paper. Say something like, "The reader now understands why my topic is so important to so and so."

Daily Assignment

- Warm-up: Write a body (middle) for a paper describing the dangers of eating stale popcorn.
- Students will complete Concept Builder 31-A.
- Prayer journal: Students are encouraged to write in their prayer journal every day.
- Students should systematically review their vocabulary words daily.

Introduction: Another Visit to the Beginning

Pay special attention to your first sentence. Start off on the right foot with your readers by making sure that the first sentence actually says something useful and that it does so in an interesting and error-free way. Be straightforward and confident. Avoid statements like "In this paper, I will argue that Frederick Douglass valued education." While this sentence points toward your main argument, it isn't especially interesting. It might be more effective to say what you mean in a declarative sentence. It is much more convincing to tell us that "Frederick Douglass valued education" than to tell us that you are going to say that he did. Assert your main argument confidently. After all, you can't expect your reader to believe it if it doesn't sound like you believe it!

Rewrite the following introduction in a better way:

Everyone knows that revival movements have their historical roots in Protestant, Puritan, pietistic reactions to the rationalism of the Enlightenment. Every single time their mode of attack has always been the revivalist (not necessarily didactic) sermon. Millions of revivalist leaders discovered a more experiential element in Reformation faith which emphasized personal commitment and obedience to Christ and a life regenerated by the indwelling Holy Spirit. They also emphasized witness and missions as a primary responsibility of the individual Christian and the Church. Subjective religious experience and the importance of the individual became a new force in renewing and expanding the Church.

American revivalism has always been marked by an appeal for a personal, public response to the gospel. A key component of this response is called the conversion.

writingcenter.unc.edu/handouts/introductions/

Student Essay

The following example represents a pretty good main body of a research paper. Does she effectively argue her points? Remember: a research paper is all about what *other scholars* know. It is not about what you know! Caution: Don't have one quote immediately after another — paraphrase your sources. Remember, you must reference paraphrases just like you reference quotes. Your job is to locate, to analyze, and then to offer the best information you can find to the reader.

One final point, keep the thesis in front of you and your reader. As I write my research paper, I like to put the thesis on large bold letters and tape it on the edge of my computer screen. At least every other paragraph, refer the paper to your thesis. The thesis runs like a thread through the main body. Never let the reader forget why he is reading this paper and what he should learn from it. Make your case time and time again. Build your case on one evidence argument after another.

The following is the body of a paper on the origins of the American Civil War.

Two Nations, Two Economies

"I heard much of the extreme difficulty of ginning cotton, that is, separating it from its seeds. . . . I involuntarily happened to be thinking on the subject and struck out a plan of a machine in my mind."[1] The machine was the cotton gin, and the author of this letter was Eli Whitney. More than anything else, the cotton gin made cotton a profitable business and assured its future in Southern economy.

Originally, cotton had been a minor crop because of the difficulty of separating the fiber from the seeds. In 1793, Eli Whitney's cotton gin solved this problem. In 1800, only about 70,000 bales of cotton were produced in the South. By 1825 cotton production increased 700 percent. Demand for cotton of all sorts was growing, especially in England, where new textile factories, with their weaving and spinning machines, created an insatiable appetite. Demand and supply came together when Eli Whitney set his mind to the problem of short-staple cotton and its seeds.[2] Eli Whitney supplied the technology for cotton to be king, and the industrial revolution supplied the market. By the early 19th century, British and American factories demanded more cotton. The expanding Southern plantation system was ready to meet that demand.

In 1813, Boston Manufacturing Company opened the first textile factory to perform all cloth-making operations by power in Waltham, Massachusetts. Financed with large capital, the company recruited New England farm girls as operatives, boarded them in dormitories, and produced a standard coarse cotton cloth requiring minimum labor skill. By 1826, in Lowell, Massachusetts, one plant turned out two million yards of cloth annually.[3] Their production grew more and more over the next few years.

In 1828, a new sore spot appeared in North-South relations. That year Congress raised the tariff on imports in order to protect native industry struggling to compete with European manufacturers. On the grounds that it favored the North at her expense, the South protested loudly over the tariff. She was dependent almost wholly on the North and on Europe for manufactured goods. While an increase in prices would enrich the North, it would mean a rise in the cost of living for the Southerners, with no compensating increase in wealth. In their view, all the benefits of protection were going to Northern manufacturers. Though the country as a whole grew richer, South Carolina grew poorer, with its planters bearing the burden of higher prices. South Carolina planters, and Southern planters in general, sold their products to British industrials, who sold manufactured

---

1   Charles Van Doren and Robert McHenry, *Webster's Guide to American History* (Springfield, MS: G. & C. Merriam Co., 1971), p. 89.

2   Gary B. Nash et al., editor. *The American People: Creating a Nation and a Society* (New York: Harper Collins, 1990), p. 309.

3   Van Doren and McHenry, *Webster's Guide to American History*, p. 128.

good to Southerners. When Northern tariffs raised the price of industrial goods, the price of cotton consequently fell. If one British table was worth 30 pounds of cotton, after tariffs increased British prices the same table would then be worth 50 pounds of cotton.

Ironically, it was the Southern planter President Andrew Jackson who insisted that tariffs be increased. The protective tariff passed by Congress and signed into law by Jackson in 1832 was milder than that of 1828, but it further embittered many in the state of South Carolina. In response, a number of South Carolina citizens endorsed the states'-rights principle of "nullification," which was enunciated by John C. Calhoun, Jackson's vice president until 1832 in his *South Carolina Exposition and Protest*.[4]

South Carolina dealt with the tariff by adopting the Ordinance of Nullification, which declared both the tariffs of 1828 and 1832 null and void within state borders. The legislature also passed laws to enforce the ordinance, including authorization for raising a military force and appropriations for arms.

Resentment reached its highest pitch in South Carolina, which at this time was experiencing a depression because of the drop in cotton prices. The state legislative body met and threatened to nullify the act of Congress because it favored one section of the country at the expense of another. If carried out, this proposal would have placed the authority of a state over that of the federal government and would have made the Constitution useless.

The Nullification proceeding threw the country into turmoil. Abuse was heaped on South Carolina, which, as a result, threatened to withdraw from the Union.[5] "We, therefore, the people of the state of South Carolina, in Convention assembled, do declare . . . that several acts of the Congress . . . are null, void, and no law, nor binding upon this state, its officers, or citizens."[6] This was not the first attempt at secession. New England states first suggested it as a possibility with the Hartford Convention Resolutions of 1815. However, this attempt was more serious, and only the vigorous intervention of President Andrew Jackson stopped civil war from occurring.

Until the invention of the cotton gin, the North and the South were primarily farming communities, but the cotton gin put new value on slaves, profit, and demand in the South. The industrial revolution demanded workers and economic growth.

By the time of the Civil War, America was two nations. Eli Whitney's inspiring ingenuity gave a tragic guarantee that the North would welcome the industrial revolution, and the South would reject it. The North would go one way, and the South another; sooner or later they would collide. (Jessica)

---

4   www.sewanee.edu/faculty/willis/Civil_War/.../SCExposition.html

5   Eric Wollencott Barnes, *The War Between the States* (New York: Whittlesey House, 1959), p. 13.

6   Van Doren and McHenry, *Webster's Guide to American History*, p. 146.

Daily Assignment

- Warm-up: Write a body (middle) for a paper discussing the advantages of having no television.
- Students will complete Concept Builder 31-B.
- Prayer journal.
- Students should outline all assigned essays and speeches for the week.

Five Ineffective Introductions

The University of North Carolina Writing Center lists five ineffective introductions:

1. The placeholder introduction. When you don't have much to say on a given topic, it is easy to create this kind of introduction. Essentially, this kind of weaker introduction contains several sentences that are vague and don't really say much. They exist just to take up the "introduction space" in your paper. If you had something more effective to say, you would probably say it, but in the meantime this paragraph is just a placeholder.

2. The restated question introduction. Restating the question can be an effective strategy, but it can be easy to stop at JUST restating the question instead of offering a more effective, interesting introduction to your paper.

Match the ineffective introduction with the example. (Other three are in Concept Builder 31-C.)

Example	Example #
Indeed, education has long been considered a major force for American social change, righting the wrongs of our society. *The Narrative of the Life of Frederick Douglass* discusses the relationship between education and slavery in 19th-century America, showing how white control of education reinforced slavery and how Douglass and other enslaved African Americans viewed education while they endured. Moreover, the book discusses the role that education played in the acquisition of freedom. Education was a major force for social change with regard to slavery.	
Slavery was one of the greatest tragedies in American history. There were many different aspects of slavery. Each created different kinds of problems for enslaved people.	

Lesson 3

Writing Style:
Avoid Sexist Language

When writing, use the plural form of pronouns. "They" refers to all genders. *They finished their assignment* is better than the exclusivist sexist language of *Everyone has finished his assignment.*

Daily Assignment

- Warm-up: Write a body (middle) for a paper discussing the advantages of having a television.

- Students will complete Concept Builder 31-C.

- Prayer journal.

- Students should write rough drafts of all assigned essays and speeches.

CONCEPT BUILDER 31-C

Five Ineffective Introductions (cont.)

3. The Webster's Dictionary introduction. This introduction begins by giving the dictionary definition of one or more of the words in the assigned question. This introduction strategy is on the right track — if you write one of these, you may be trying to establish the important terms of the discussion, and this move builds a bridge to the reader by offering a common, agreed-upon definition for a key idea. You may also be looking for an authority that will lend credibility to your paper. However, anyone can look a word up in the dictionary and copy down what Webster says — it may be far more interesting for you (and your reader) if you develop your own definition of the term in the specific context of your class and assignment. Also recognize that the dictionary is not a particularly authoritative work — it doesn't take into account the context of your course and doesn't offer particularly detailed information. If you feel that you must seek out an authority, try to find one that is very relevant and specific. Perhaps a quotation from a source reading might prove better. Dictionary introductions are also ineffective simply because they are so overused. Many graders will see 20 or more papers that begin in this way, greatly decreasing the dramatic impact that any one of those papers will have.

4. The "dawn of man" introduction. This kind of introduction generally makes broad, sweeping statements about the relevance of this topic since the beginning of time. It is usually very general (similar to the placeholder introduction) and fails to connect to the thesis. You may write this kind of introduction when you don't have much to say — which is precisely why it is ineffective.

5. The book report introduction. This introduction is what you had to do for your fifth-grade book reports. It gives the name and author of the book you are writing about, tells what the book is about, and offers other basic facts about the book. You might resort to this sort of introduction when you are trying to fill space because it's a familiar, comfortable format. It is ineffective because it offers details that your reader already knows and that are irrelevant to the thesis.

Example	Example #
Since the dawn of man, slavery has been a problem in human history.	
Webster's dictionary defines slavery as "the state of being a slave," as "the practice of owning slaves," and as "a condition of hard work and subjection."	
Frederick Douglass wrote his autobiography, *Narrative of the Life of Frederick Douglass, An American Slave*, in the 1840s. It was published in 1986 by Penguin Books. He tells the story of his life.	

Public Speaking: Didactic Speech

A didactic speech informs the audience about an issue with which they may be unfamiliar. Didactic speakers share revelation about a subject about which they know much and feel that what they know is important. The speaker must be almost dogmatic in his application of his new-found truth to a problem. Webster's Dictionary defines *didactic* as "Excessively prone to instruct, even those who do not wish to be instructed." Didactic speakers who are sensitive, enthusiastic, and informative can be effective teachers. However, their topic must have present and future implications, or it will not interest their audience.

Daily Assignment

- Warm-up: Write a body (middle) for a paper arguing that anchovies should be a required ingredient on a pizza.
- Students will complete Concept Builder 31-D.
- Prayer journal.
- Review the assigned text. Keep vocabulary cards.
- This is the day that students should write, and then rewrite, the final drafts of their assigned essay and speech.

CONCEPT BUILDER 31-D

Write Your Introduction

Now is the time for you to write the first draft of the introduction based on the topic assigned to you by your teacher.

Research Paper: The Body (Part Two)

Chapter 32

Style (Writing and Speaking): Avoid Pretentious Language, Evasive Language, Euphemisms; Footnote or Endnotes

Public Speaking Skill: Summary

First Thoughts

You are now ready to finish the core, the body, of your paper. Again, remember: the thesis is the controlling idea of your research paper. It should appear in one form or another in almost every section, if not paragraph, of the research paper. The paper should include both supportive and opposing arguments. By presenting both sides of the issue, the paper will reflect a much clearer perspective of the research topic. Notes gathered in files and organized in the outline become the skeleton of the paper. By using your notes to provide good quotes, paraphrases, and summaries, you are well on your way to writing an effective research paper.

Chapter Learning Objectives

In chapter 32 we finish the body of the research paper.

Look Ahead for Friday

- Turn in a final copy of essay and speech
- Take Weekly Essay/Test

Write the first draft body of your research paper.

Present a 2- or 3-minute speech on your research paper topic. Memorize the introduction and give particular attention to your main body.

Research Paper Benchmark

You should have your topic, thesis statement, preliminary bibliography, a preliminary outline to guide you in your note taking, many notes, the outline, the introduction, and you should have begun the main body of your research paper. During this lesson you will finish the main body to your research paper.

Background

The following sample is part of a chapter of a doctoral dissertation that is much like a research paper topic. The Turabian-style (*Chicago Manual of Style*) for footnotes has been used. The student should observe several things about this paper:

Text boxes are an effective way to highlight important points.

Topic headings are a helpful way to direct the reader in the right direction but are not typically used in the high school research paper.

Copious footnotes make the paper more effective.

Sample From Chapter III: The Promised Land Or Babylon Revisited? Slavery To The End Of The Great Migration

A. Introduction

The most grievous historical metaphor for the African-American community is chattel slavery. It is the quintessential image of the apparent triumph of white racism in American civilization. This unhappy time captures the African heart as strongly as the Egyptian bondage motif captures the Old Testament community. Slavery presented African-American Americans with a disconcerting contradiction: legally, they were defined as property; but at the same time, they were called upon to act in sentient, articulate, and human ways.

Within the context of chattel slavery, the African-American community created patterns of resistance that remain today. Resistance — not accommodation, not abdication — was the behavioral outcome of three hundred years of white American prejudice. This resistance was usually passive but occasionally violent. This pattern was repeated in one form or another throughout American history.

The dominant white community did not allow the African-American community overtly to express their frustration. Therefore, the African-American slave community used the folk tale to express hostility toward their masters, impart wisdom to the young, and teach survival skills. In the folk tale "The Tar Baby Tricks Br'er Rabbit," Br'er Rabbit slyly convinced his arch enemies, Fox and Bear, to throw him into the brier patch rather than into the well. Of course, that was exactly what Bear and Fox did and exactly what Br'er Rabbit wanted them to do. For now, Br'er Rabbit escaped through the brier patch! The African-American slave community resisted slavery in every possible way. From the beginning, the African community saw itself in an adversarial role to the white community and has sought to escape into its own culture as a way to defend itself against white domination.

Angry resistance was not inherent to most West African experiences. The ultimate goal of many African peoples was preservation and promotion of community, not retribution and revenge. This community spirit of beneficence, forbearance, practical wisdom, improvisation, forgiveness, and justice was nurtured, preserved, and celebrated in the African-American community — but only at great personal sacrifice. Therefore, African-American resistance was a uniquely American phenomenon. This resulted from three hundred years of historical oppression.

B. Slave Resistance Patterns

There are two of them, . . . Uncle Buck and Uncle Buddy. . . . They lived in a two-room log house with about a dozen dogs, and they kept the n****** in the manor house. It don't have any windows now and a child with a hairpin could unlock any lock in it, but every night when the n******s come up from the fields Uncle Buck or Uncle Buddy would drive them into the house and lock the door with a key al-most as big as a horse pistol; probably they would still be locking the front door long after the last n****** has escaped out the back. And folks said that Uncle Buck and Uncle Buddy knew this and that the n*******s knew that they knew it.

Most white masters — like William Faulkner's Uncle Buck and Uncle Buddy — knew that slaves were resisting their enslavement. Therefore, slaves had to be controlled, to be managed. White masters created slave dependence upon their owners. The demon of white privilege lodged itself well into the institution of slavery.

A basic step toward successful slave management was to implant in the slaves an identity of personal inferiority. They had to keep their places, to understand that bondage was their natural status. Thus, from the beginning, African Americans understood that their resistance to white domination was a question of identity survival. Indeed, resistance seemed to be the only way to survive in the face of profound white systemic racism. It was from this root that later separatism ideology sprang.

Daily Assignment

- Warm-up: Write a conclusion for a paper describing the dangers of eating stale popcorn.

- Students will complete Concept Builder 32-A.

- Prayer journal: Students are encouraged to write in their prayer journal every day.

- Students should systematically review their vocabulary words daily.

The Body: A New Beginning

Finally! The day has arrived that you write the major part of research paper. Gather your notes, preliminary bibliography, and, most importantly, your outline. Write from your outline, not your notes or your memory. Write from the roadmap of your paper — the outline. You already have your introduction; now let's begin the main part of your paper. You will use this essay for exercises during the coming week. Today, though, circle the Body.

Preface 1

Jamestown, a name of first rank among historic names, saw the birth of English America. Here on an island in the James River in the heart of tidewater Virginia the English carved a settlement out of the wilderness. It grew from a rude palisaded fort into a busy community and then into a small town that enjoyed many of the comforts of daily living. For 13 years (until 1620) Virginia was the only English colony on the American mainland. Jamestown served this colony as its place of origin and as its capital for 92 years — from 1607 to 1699.

After its first century of prominence and leadership, "James Towne" entered a long decline, precipitated in 1700 by the removal of the seat of government to Williamsburg. Its residents drifted away, its streets grew silent, its buildings decayed, and even its lots and former public places became cultivated fields. Time passed and much was forgotten or obscured. So it was when it became a historic area, in part, in 1893, and when the whole island became devoted to historical purposes in 1934.

Since these dates, the Association for the Preservation of Virginia Antiquities and the National Park Service have worked toward the preservation of all that still exists of old Jamestown, and are dedicated to learning its story more completely. Thus, the American people can more fully understand and enjoy their historic heritage of Jamestown. A great deal of study along many lines has been required and much more is still needed to fill the many gaps. Libraries have been searched for pictures, documents, and plans. Land records have been carefully scrutinized and old existing landmarks studied. Seventeenth-century buildings and objects still surviving in England, America, and elsewhere have been viewed as well as museum collections...

These valuable objects are a priceless part of the Jamestown that exists today. Collectively, they form one of the finest groups of such early material that has been assembled anywhere. Although most are broken and few are intact, they would not be traded for better preserved and more perfect examples that do exist elsewhere. These things were the property and the possessions of the men and women who lived, worked, and died at Jamestown. It was because of these people, who handled and used them in their daily living, and because of what they accomplished, that Jamestown is one of our best-remembered historic places.

John L. Cotter and J. Paul Hudson, *New Discoveries at Jamestown* (Washington, DC: U.S. Department of the Interior, National Park Service, 1957), preface

Lesson 2

Style (Writing and Speaking): Avoid Pretentious Language, Evasive Language, and Euphemisms

Do not show off in your speech and writing. Speak clearly and precisely what you mean to say. *The perfunctory reply caused the fecund friend to flinch* is ostentatious; *The dispassionate reply hurt the loyal friend* is better. Avoid pretentious language. Do not use evasive language. *The soldier experienced an awful dose of reality* should be *The soldier was shocked by all the violence around him*. Say what you mean clearly. Finally, euphemisms are words that camouflage harsh expressions. It is permissible to use a few euphemisms — *The man passed away* — is certainly a proper way to talk about death. If you do this too often, however, it makes your essay and speech trite.

Daily Assignment

- Warm-up: Write a conclusion for a paper discussing the advantages of having no television.
- Students will complete Concept Builder 32-B.
- Prayer journal.
- Students should outline all assigned essays and speeches for the week.

CONCEPT
BUILDER
32-B

The Body: Transitions

Transitions establish logical connections between sentences, paragraphs, and sections of your papers. Whether single words or quick phrases, they function as signs for readers that tell them how to think about your material as they read through what you have written. There are two ways one can create a transition: repeat a concluding thought from a previous paragraph or use these transition words:

- For example
- For instance
- In fact
- In addition
- In other words
- Clearly
- Furthermore
- However
- Nonetheless

- In regard to
- Thus
- Hence
- Finally
- Overall
- Lastly
- In the end
- Clearly

Underline three transitions (repeated thoughts or words) in the essay in 32-A.

Lesson 3

Public Speaking: Summary

The basic speech outline includes:

    Introduction: memorize the introduction

    Exciting beginning

    Importance of topic

    Summary of argument

    Thesis

    Body

    First point: evidence

    Second point: evidence

    Conclusion

    Review

    Restatement of argument

    Final statement

Daily Assignment

- Warm-up: Write a conclusion for a paper discussing the advantages of having a television.

- Students will complete Concept Builder 32-C.

- Prayer journal.

- Students should write rough drafts of all assigned essays and speeches.

CONCEPT BUILDER 32-C

Body: The Argument

Complete the following chart.

The Jamestown Settlement	
Argument 1	
Argument 2	
Argument 3	

Student Sample

Even though many people now think that the North Atlantic Treaty Organization, (NATO), is no longer needed, I believe it still can serve a purpose if its problems are fixed. NATO has played a major role in protecting North America and Europe and I believe it still can.

NATO, or the North Atlantic Treaty Organization, is a group of countries that work together to ensure the security and prosperity of each other. NATO was founded in 1949 and is composed of 28 countries. As NATO is 58 years old, the necessity of NATO has been questioned by modern leaders. One of their main arguments questions the effectiveness of this organization to properly fight the enemy, primarily terrorists. NATO's importance started to fade from many of the citizens and leaders in Europe and North America. However, NATO remains a valuable asset to protect the United States and other European countries. *I hereby stand resolved: that the North Atlantic Treaty Organization (NATO) should be significantly reformed or abolished.*

NATO needs to be reformed because it is riddled with many problems that weaken the organization. Once these weaknesses are eliminated, NATO will be better able to fight today's threats. I believe that NATO will be a stronger and more united organization if its problems are dealt with.

Five major problems demonstrate NATO's need for structural change. First, as seen and confirmed in Yugoslavia and Kosovo in 1999 and in Afghanistan in 2003, military operations carried out by NATO are hurting innocent civilians. Second, NATO was created to fight communistic Russia in the mid-1900s, by uniting North America and Europe. NATO needs to change its focus because communistic Russia no longer exists. Third, NATO needs to be reformed because its current structure allows for enlargement. Logically, when organizations get bigger, it gets more difficult to reach a decision on an issue. If NATO includes more countries, it will be harder to reach decisions. Lastly, NATO's internal structure needs better organization to be more effective. This is seen in the unfair structure of funding.

Despite these problems, I believe that since NATO has proven that it has been united against a threat in the past, it should prove that NATO will be better able to unite if its problems are eliminated. By doing so, NATO will be better able to fight today's threats and protect North America and Europe.

First, NATO needs to be reformed because its operations are hurting innocent civilians in Afghanistan and a region in Yugoslavia called Kosovo. "A joint NATO/Afghan investigation has found that a nighttime NATO attack killed 31 civilians in southern Afghanistan last month, the highest civilian death toll since NATO took over security in the south in August." (Rohde, 2006) This is the highest death toll caused by NATO since they took over security in the southern region of Afghanistan. In Kosovo, "UK Foreign Secretary Robin Cook has refuted reports that NATO deliberately bombed the Chinese embassy in Yugoslavia during the Kosovo conflict. The attack on 7 May, which killed three Chinese journalists and injured 20 diplomats, was condemned by China at the time as a "war crime." NATO and the Allies have always maintained the bombing was a mistake." (BBC, 1999) In Kosovo, NATO's faulty intelligence led to the accidental attack on the Chinese Embassy. Such civilian casualties may be preventable. In a testimony before the Armed Services Committee by Douglas Feith, Under Secretary of Defense, he stressed that success against terrorists depends on an army's intelligence and weaponry. "Success in dissuading, deterring, and defeating our enemies in the war on terrorism requires strategies, capabilities and command structures that allow for flexibility and quick action. We need a set of diverse tools for the job. As for the military tools, we need rapidly usable, long-range and lethal strike capabilities in response to good intelligence about unexpected events. In the war on terrorism, it is useful for the United States to have allies. NATO has contributed valuably to the war effort." (Feith, 2003)

So, in order for NATO to be successful in defeating

our enemies, NATO needs good strategies, capabilities, and command structures. Regarding capabilities, NATO needs better weaponry that allows them to strike an enemy target while leaving surrounding civilian targets unscathed. Mr. Feith may have the solution to increasing NATO's precision. NATO's strategies, capabilities, and command structures must include current and accurate intelligence as well as leaders who can interpret the information with good judgment. Weak intelligence can lead to a strike hitting a civilian target thought to be military as may have been the case in the August 2006 attack. NATO must use its precise weaponry, strategy, and leadership to fight today's threat to world peace: jihadism.

Secondly, NATO was created to fight communistic Russia in the mid 1900s, by uniting North America and Europe. "During the cold war, military and geopolitical considerations mainly determined NATO's decisions. Promoting democracy within NATO states and good relations among them was only complementary — desirable but not the primary motive for bringing new members. Today, with the end of the cold war, other, nonmilitary goals can and should help shape the new NATO." (Gangale, 2001) Today, communism is no longer as great of a threat as it was. Instead, communism has been replaced by jihadism. "Jihadism has replaced Communism, as Communism replaced Nazism, as an existential threat to the liberal democracies." (Aznar, 2006) Jihadism is the Islamic idea that non-Muslims should be killed. As a result, NATO should try to combat jihadism in a similar way it combated communism. NATO should strive to unite countries against this ideology. However, during the Cold War, NATO was focused on arming united countries in the event of a communistic attack. Jihadism is not a visible threat like a large army is. Instead, Jihadists consist of small cells that strike from inside enemy countries. In order to fight jihadism, NATO needs to use a different method of defense. Now, NATO needs to promote freedom, democracy, and human rights so that jihadism cannot take root. NATO needs to consist of countries that accept its ideas of freedom, human rights, and democracy for all.

Third, enlargement of NATO in the future must take ideology into consideration. Some countries that have been trying to join do not accept all these ideas. One example is Russia. If Russia joins NATO, it may at-tempt to use and twist NATO to fit its agenda. Part of Russia's agenda is providing terrorist countries with nu-clear and advanced weapon capabilities. If NATO includes more countries and countries that do not accept

its ideas, it may be harder for NATO to reach decisions on topics. "Enlargement weakens NATO because the more members it has, the more difficult it will be to reach decisions. As NATO includes more states, it will become increasingly difficult to reach consensus, especially on the conduct of peacekeeping and out-of-area operations." (Gangale, 2001) In my opinion, NATO must enlarge cautiously so that decision making can be quick. With potentially divided members, decision making will most likely take longer. The president of the NATO Assembly noted that enlargement can be successful if ideas are taken into consideration. "It must be stressed that the Alliance remains extremely attractive; there have been several waves of enlargement, in 1999 and 2004, which have helped to eliminate divisions in Europe by bringing in former adversaries form the Warsaw Pact. However, there are still other candidate countries, such as Georgia or Ukraine, which have clearly shown their willingness to join the Euro-Atlantic community of values and have embarked upon the necessary reforms with determination." (Lellouche, 2006)

The fourth reason that NATO should be reformed, is because NATO was created to unite Europe militarily against the USSR. NATO did not try to spread democracy; instead its goal was to unite Europe and North America against Russia. "During the Cold War, NATO was focused more on maintaining allied unity in the face of the Soviet threat rather than on democratizing its members, arguably reducing the significance of the Cold War period in evaluation of the claim that NATO spreads democracy." (Gangale, 2001) Because NATO was created to fight against communist Russia, and communist Russia no longer exists, NATO needs a new purpose. The organization should not only focus on democratizing nations and fighting against the ideology of Islam and jihadism, it also must unite Europe and North America to fight against terrorists who attack from inside countries. This should be the basis of the new NATO. NATO is still a valuable asset despite the end of the Cold War. "The Cold War may be over, but NATO's role is just as important today as it was at its founding in 1949. The scourge of global terrorism poses as great a threat to the world's security as communism and fascism once did." (Gardiner, 2004) Now, NATO needs to fight terrorists more with ideas rather than armies.

The last reason NATO should be reformed is that its structure is weak. One of the areas where NATO's structure is failing is evident in funding. Funding, with its problems, is an area that does not receive much attention. In the chart below, from the CRS

(Congressional Research Service) report of defense spending, the funding of NATO was evaluated. (Camberlin, 2004)

The USA is currently contributing nearly twice the amount of money to NATO as all the other members combined. This is placing the unfair burden on the USA. In addition, the smaller countries are having to pay a tiny amount, yet they get the same benefits as the USA does. Faults like these will cause division, tiffs, and weakness in NATO, resulting in an ineffective, money-eating organization.

So why should NATO be reformed and ameliorated? The alliance overall is meager. The first of five reasons that NATO should be reformed is because NATO's operations are hurting innocent civilians as seen in Kosovo and Afghanistan. NATO requires better intelligence prior to an attack and more precise weaponry to carry out the attack. The second reason for reforming NATO is because NATO was created to fight communist Russia. Now, NATO must combat jihadism which has replaced communism. Third, NATO must be reformed because its current structure allows for enlargement which will weaken the organization. With more members, decision-making will be more difficult. The fourth reason that shows NATO's need for reformation is that NATO was created to unite Europe and North America against communistic Russia militarily. Today, one of NATO's primary goals should be to unite Europe and North America by using ideas. NATO must keep the mindset that democracy is good. The fifth and final reason NATO needs to be reformed is because NATO's structure is weak. This is evident when the complicated structure of funding is evaluated. The USA has the unfair burden of paying twice the amount of money as all the members combined. Yet countries barely contributing to NATO receive the same protection as the USA does.

Consequently, faults like these will strain relations between member countries. If these five main controversial issues are attended to, I believe NATO will be more effective, closer united, and a stronger protector of democracy and freedom.

Bibliography

BBC News. "NATO Embassy Attack 'Not Deliberate.'" 1999. http://news.bbc.co.uk/2/hi/477374.stm.

Camberlin, Jeffrey, analyst in National Defense Foreign Affairs, Defense, and Trade Division. CRS Report For Congress, Comparisons of U.S. and Foreign Military Spending: Data From Selected Public Sources. January 28, 2004. p. 22, figure 8. U.S. Defense Expenditures as a Percentage of NATO Defense Expenditures, 2002. http://fpc.state.gov/documents/organization/30046.pdf.

Gangale, Thomas. OPS-Alaska/San Francisco State University, International Relations, 305 p. 3, section 2.2 paragraph 2. 2001. http://pweb.jps.net/~gangale/opsa/ir/NATO_Expansion.htm.

Gardiner, Nile, Ph. D., Fellow, Anglo-American Security Policy, and John Hulsman, Ph. D., Research Fellow in European Affairs, the Heritage Foundation, "An Historic Moment for NATO." (April 1, 2004).

Rohde, David, Foreign Desk of the *The New York Times*. "The Reach of War." 2006. The New York Times Times Online. http://select.nytimes.com/gst/abstract.html?res=F50716FC3C5A0C778DPPA80994DE4

Daily Assignment

- Warm-up: Write a conclusion for a paper arguing that anchovies should be a required ingredient on a pizza.
- Students will complete Concept Builder 32-D.
- Prayer journal.
- Review the assigned text. Keep vocabulary cards.
- This is the day that students should write, and then rewrite, the final drafts of their assigned essay and speech.

Body: The Evidence

Complete the following chart.

The Reform Movement	
Evidence 1	
Evidence 2	
Evidence 3	
Evidence 4	
Evidence 5	
Evidence 6	
Evidence 7	

Research Paper: The Conclusion

Chapter 33

Style (Writing and Speaking): Mixed Metaphors

Public Speaking Skill: Enunciation

First Thoughts

You are now ready to finish your paper. In a general way, your conclusion will:

- restate your topic and why it is important
- restate your thesis/claim

Remember that once you accomplish these tasks you are finished. Done. Don't try to bring in new points or end with a sermon or polemic. Stay focused! Stay on task! Finish with confident humility.

Chapter Learning Objectives

In chapter 33 we will add a conclusion to the research paper.

Look Ahead for Friday

- Turn in a final copy of essay and speech
- Take Weekly Essay/Test

Finish your paper with an inspiring conclusion. You are now ready to correct your paper, wait a few days, and then rewrite the paper.

Compose a speech that includes the following words: *tongue, fang, harangue, prong, anger, hunger, bungle,* and *jungle,* then present it to an audience.

Research Paper Benchmark

You should have your topic, thesis statement, preliminary bibliography, a preliminary outline to guide you in your note taking, many notes, the outline, the introduction, and now you have even finished the main body of your research paper. During this lesson you will write a conclusion to your research paper.

Before the Essay Ends . . .

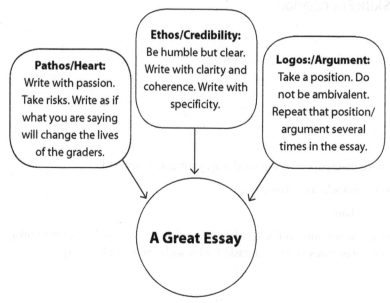

Pathos/Heart: Write with passion. Take risks. Write as if what you are saying will change the lives of the graders.

Ethos/Credibility: Be humble but clear. Write with clarity and coherence. Write with specificity.

Logos:/Argument: Take a position. Do not be ambivalent. Repeat that position/argument several times in the essay.

A Great Essay

Daily Assignment

- Warm-up: How do you end a bad research paper?

- Students will complete Concept Builder 33-A.

- Prayer journal: Students are encouraged to write in their prayer journal every day.

- Students should systematically review their vocabulary words daily.

CONCEPT BUILDER 33-A

Proofreading the Essay

Carefully edit this essay.

French Revolution

France on the eve of the French Revolution was an absolute monarchy whose economy was approaching bankruptcy.

This was not always the case. France was once the richest and most powerful nations in Europe. Louis XIV (1643-1715) was the envy of all other rulers in Europe. During his reign he had centralized the civil service and had stimulated trade and industry. He took his country into the industrial revolution.

His, and his successor's undoing were the long list of costly wars that they had fought. His successors, Louis XV (1715-74) and Louis XVI (1774-93), all fought in wars that gained little but cost a great deal in men and material. In fact, France had suffered defeat in the Seven Years War against Britain (1756-63). At the same time, her army, once feared in all the western hemisphere was crushed by the Germans. Even victories were defeats. The involvement in the American Revolution was for revenge against Britain after the Seven Years War but it brought little gain while costing a great deal. Besides, most of the monarchs were self-indulgent, wimpish kings who did not have the backbone of a Henry VIII or the vision of an Elizabeth I. Louise XVI was a particularly poor choice of a king.

On the eve of revolution all sections of French society had reason to be unhappy: The nobles wanted more power, the growing middle class needed tax relief, and the peasants needed almost everything.

France in 1789 had three classes, or estates. The so-called Third Estate was made up of the lower middle class store owners, day workers, and the country peasantry. The Third Estate was the majority.

The Second Estate was the nobility and was much smaller. It numbered one-half million with most of the nobility is of unimportant rank. The First Estate comprised the clergy. The Upper Clergy is very wealthy and powerful and therefore they related to the First Estate. The other priests lived among the poor. The First Estate numbered around 90-100,000.

The First Estate enjoyed all the privileges of patronage. They were the top of the feeding chain. Woe to the Third Estate! The first two states enjoyed privileges over the Third Estate. Most galling of all, especially to the growing middle class, was the fact that the First Estate–the richest of the best — were exempt from paying taxes. By virtue of their rank, whether they were competent or not, they were also the only members in society who could hold positions of importance.

The extravagant waste of the monarchs, the failure of numerous foreign wars, forcing the government into bankrupt. This meant that basic services, however paltry, were withheld from the group that needed it the most–the poor. To add injury to harm, the ruling class — the First Estate — merely placed more taxes on the Third Estate.

New and revolutionary ideas was entering the picture too. Revolutionary thinkers such as Voltaire and Rousseau offered a new path to walk. They saw their American allies overcome tyranny. Why couldn't they? Voltaire and Rousseau challenged the absolute right to rule and presented ideas of equal rights and the abolition of the class system. All of this appealed to middle class and peasant grievances. If only things could change, they could see a different way of life.

Voltaire and Rousseau advanced the notion that reason was a higher power than the monarch's claim to divine right. The brotherhood of men, equal rights and responsibilities should replace privileges. Men should develop through opportunity and education and not because of birth. The allure of this viewpoint to the middle class was obvious.

King Louis XVI's wife, Marie Antoinette, exacerbated the problem even more. Her extravagant spending seemed to represent all that was wrong with the French aristocracy

1788 was a very bad year. All classes were discontent at Louis XVI's reign–called the Ancien Regime. Louis XVI did not take advantage of this situation to introduce reforms and gain the support of the people. He could have taxed the nobility and released the pressure on the middle class. At the same time, France did not experience anything like the Wesleyan Revival sweeping England. Revivalism often brings upheaval but it also causes the participant to take stock of their relationship to God and to man.

Under pressure Louis agreed to summon the Estates General (a sort of French Parliament). Again, A few reforms would have prevented Louis from summoning the Estates General. Instead this encouraged further criticism of the Ancient regime and provided further evidence against absolutism in France. He did not know it, but this was the beginning of the end for Louis XVI. On the 17th of June the Third Estate decided to break the deadlock in the voting issue. They decided to declare themselves the representative body of France (the National Assembly) and to disregard the King's opinion. Louis was alarmed at this and decided to close down their assembly hall. This did not deter them in fact it led them to the infamous Tennis Court Oath. They vowed to continue protesting until they had a constitution. On that fateful day Absolutism ended and a Constitutional Monarchy began (much like the British model). Louis XVI had to recognize the National Assembly. Overnight, the middle class had control of the government. It was not enough.

Virtually no one knew it, but the French Revolution had begun. This was called the National Assembly phase.

A nasty beginning of National Assembly rule was the storming of the Bastille on July 14th , 1789. This proved to be a significant event in the revolution. The Bastille Prison was regarded as a symbol of political oppression. Here people were sent when they had opposed the Ancien Regime. A huge crowd stormed the bastion. Then, aristocrats, government officials and army officers were indiscriminately hanged from lampposts. A new phase of the French Revolution began: the rise of violence.

In the countryside, peasants then stormed and looted country estates and church monasteries. French aristocrats fled the country in wholesale fashion. Foreign nations were alarmed. The Austrian Emperor and Prussian King threatened war if Louis XVI was harmed.

On July 13th 1789 the Paris Commune (Municipal council) and the National Guard were formed. They were "mob" with a chip on their shoulders. They indiscriminately served justice on the guilty and innocent alike. Ultimately they calmed down and began to restore order. The units of the National Guard were responsible to the municipal councils.

Meanwhile, the National Assembly met and all forms of feudalism were abolished. At least the peasants were satisfied. City dwellers would get their satisfaction later.

On the 26th of August 1789 the National Assembly issued the Declaration of the Rights of Men. This document proclaimed the sovereignty of the people.

In October, 1789, the King and his family were taken hostage. Two years later they tried to escape to Austria. They were captured and returned to Paris. The King lived to see all his power disappear with the Constitution of 1791.

Again, though, war brought another national crisis. Austria led a coalition to punish the new revolutionary government. To meet the threat a small group called The Committee of Public Safety began to rule. It had nine members. They had unlimited power to do anything to save the Republic from internal and external perils. They exercised control over every aspect of French life.

Within the Committee of Public Safety a revolutionary tribunal was also set up. The Revolutionary tribunal tried "enemies of the state" and literally murdered thousands of citizens. It was lead by the infamous Robespierre.

With the passing of military danger, Robespierre himself was executed. The Convention then abolished the Committee of Public Safety after the fall of Robespierre and also the Revolutionary Tribunals. As almost an afterthought, King Louis XVI and his wife Marie Antoinette were beheaded in 1793.

A group of 5 men — called the Directory ruled from 1795-1799.

The Convention then formed the Constitution of Year III (Year III of the Revolutionary Calendar).

The period of 1795 to 1799 was marked with attempted coups. However the Directory was able to continue in Government as it had the backing of the military. A final successful rebellion was led by Napoleon Bonaparte. He joined with three of the Directors in a conspiracy to take control.

Now began a series of Napoleon instigated wars until Napoleon ultimately became Emperor. France had traded one dictator — Louis XVI — for another — Napoleon.

Napoleon gave France what it wanted: A "friendly dictator." He insisted on human rights–witness the Napoleon Code — but he would force them on people at sword point.

By winning the battles at Austerlitz (2 December 1805), Jena, Averstadt and Friedland (June 1807), Napoleon made France a super power again. Napoleon then failed in his campaign in Spain. Austria encouraged by Spanish success rose in revolt in 1809. In 1811 Napoleon suffered a humiliating defeat in Russia. On April 14th 1814 Napoleon abdicated and was banished to the Island of Elba. Ten months later he returned but was defeated by British Prussian forces on the June 18th at Waterloo.

The French Revolution put an end to feudalism. The middle class benefitted significantly. France now had a Republic and had spread republican ideas all over Europe. The Revolution spread new political ideas such as Nationalism. Napoleon introduced the citizen army and introduced the world to modern, total warfare.

Analyze this essay using the checklist below.

Composition Evaluation Technique 1

Based on 100 points: _____

I. **Grammar and Syntax:** Is the composition grammatically correct? (25 points)

II. **Organization:** Does this composition exhibit well-considered organization? Does it flow? Transitions? Introduction and a conclusion? (25 points)

III. **Content:** Does this composition answer the question, argue the point well, and/or persuade the reader? (50 points)

Sample Conclusion

Conclusion: No Way To Compromise

So what caused the Civil War? Why did Americans fight one another for four long years at the cost of 600,000 lives? The American Civil War occurred because Americans allowed it. They let their differences be more important than their similarities. The government was no help.

Before the Civil War, Americans had done a lot of compromising. In 1820, there was the Missouri Compromise, when Congress took charge of the question of slavery in the territories by declaring it illegal in the huge region acquired by the Louisiana Purchase.

When Andrew Jackson was president (1829–37), a sharp division arose between Northerners and Southerners over the tariff issue. The South favored free trade; the industrial North needed protection. Jackson confronted South Carolina, and it backed down.

Next, President Polk's war with Mexico opened the slavery issue again. Should slavery be allowed in the new territories? The Wilmot Proviso (1846), which was supposed to have excluded slavery, became an irritating subject for both the North and the South. It was also being voted on again and again in Congress and successfully held off by Southerners. Abolitionists, led by William Lloyd Garrison and others, became strong in many Northern circles and called for the immediate emancipation of slaves, with no compensation to slave owners. However, the majority of Northern whites disliked blacks and refused to support abolition; they did not want to allow slavery in the territories so that they would be preserved for white settlement based on Northern expectations: free labor, dignity of work, and economic progress.

In 1848, Northern impatience with the existing parties helped form the Free-Soil party. By polling 300,000 votes for their candidate, Martin Van Buren, victory was denied to the Democrats, and the Whig Zachary Taylor was put in the White House. No one was happy, and the nation was ill-suited to handle the next crisis.

The Compromise of 1850 appeared to have settled the issue of slavery expansion by the principle of popular sovereignty, which said that the people who lived in the Mexican secession territories were to decide for themselves. A new Fugitive Slave Law, passed in 1850, enraged Northerners because it let slave owners cross into Northern states to claim their runaway slaves.

As the 1850s began, it seemed for a time that the issue of slavery and other sectional differences between North and South might eventually be reconciled. However, with the westward expansion of the American nation, all attempts to compromise disappeared, and contrasting economic, political, and philosophical endeavors became more evident. The resulting Civil War altered the American nation.

In 1860, the political system became dysfunctional. All consensus was lost. The American political system no longer functioned.

Southerners considered the rise of the Yankee-dominated Republican Party with great apprehension. They were convinced that the party was secretly controlled by abolitionists (although most Northerners loathed the abolitionists) and that Yankees believed in using government to administer their moralistic campaigns. Their fears were confirmed in 1859 when John Brown led a raid on the federal arsenal at Harpers Ferry, Virginia, hoping to encourage a slave uprising. His action — and his subsequent adoration by some Northerners — helped convince Southerners that if Northerners attained authority in the country, the emancipation of the slaves was inevitable, sooner or later. They then fought a war to protect their rights and property.

Again, all the different causes that led up to the American Civil War — the expanding of the economy, a flood of immigrants, the Second Great Awakening, Manifest Destiny, and the rise of nativism — all these doomed the Republic to a civil war. The war was essentially fought because the American political system failed to present a compromise that suited the North's demands as well as the South's. At the same time, massive immigration and Western expansion conspired to bring division in the nation. With no political consensus and cultural unanimity, the nation crumbled. The 1850s generation blundered into a needless war because they played on emotions to gain votes rather than facing the issues. Agitation over slavery led to mistaken and false sectional images and fanaticism. Therefore, they fought it out in the great and awful Civil War. (Jessica)

Daily Assignment

- Warm-up: How do you end an awkward conversation?
- Students will complete Concept Builder 33-B.
- Prayer journal.
- Students should outline all assigned essays and speeches for the week.

CONCEPT BUILDER 33-B

Composition Evaluation Technique 2

Evaluate the essay in 32-A using the checklist below.

I. Organization

____ Is the writer's purpose stated clearly in the introduction? Is there a thesis sentence? What is it?

____ Does the writer answer the assignment?

____ Does the introduction grab the reader's attention?

____ Is the purpose advanced by each sentence and paragraph?

____ Does the body (middle) of the paper advance the purpose?

____ Does the conclusion accomplish its purpose?

II. Mechanics

____ Does the writer use active voice?

____ Does the writer use the appropriate verb tense throughout the paper?

____ Is there agreement between all pronouns and antecedents?

____ Is there appropriate subject/verb agreement?

____ Are the transitions effective and appropriate?

III. Argument

____ Are you persuaded by the arguments?

Style (Writing and Speaking): Mixed Metaphors

From previous lessons you know that precision is much desired in writing and speaking. Avoid mixed metaphors that combine two or more incompatible objects. *He runs like a deer but stops like a bad dream* is mixing metaphors. *He runs like a deer but stops like an elephant* is much better.

Daily Assignment

- Warm-up: How do you tastefully excuse yourself from a boring dinner conversation?

- Students will complete Concept Builder 33-C.

- Prayer journal.

- Students should write rough drafts of all assigned essays and speeches.

CONCEPT BUILDER 33-C

Composition Evaluation Technique 3

Evaluate the same essay with this evaluation technique.

I. Organization

____ Is the writer's purpose clearly introduced? What is it?

____ Does the organization of the paper coincide with the outline?

____ Does the writer answer the assignment?

____ Does the introduction grab the reader's attention?

____ Is the purpose advanced by each sentence and paragraph? (Are there sentences that don't seem to belong in the paragraphs?)

____ Does the body (middle) of the paper advance the purpose?

____ Does the conclusion solve the purpose of the paper?

II. Mechanics

____ Does the writer use active voice?

____ Does the writer use the appropriate verb tense throughout the paper?

____ Is there agreement between all pronouns and antecedents?

____ Are there effective and appropriately used transitions?

III. Argument

____ Are you persuaded by the arguments?

____ Does the author need stronger arguments? More arguments?

Public Speaking: Enunciation

No matter how well organized or written a speech may be, it will not be effective if it is not presented well. It is beyond the scope of this introductory course to mention every speech challenge. However, know that in most speeches the pronunciation of *ng* causes problems. In general, all words ending in *ng* are pronounced like the final sound in *ring*. A combination like *nge* at the end of a word is pronounced *nj*, as in *mange* or *range*. In all other words, *ng* is pronounced as in *zinger* or *ringer*.

Daily Assignment

- Warm-up: How do you leave an embarrassing movie without offending your friends?
- Students will complete Concept Builder 33-D.
- Prayer journal.
- Review the assigned text. Keep vocabulary cards.
- This is the day that students should write, and then rewrite, the final drafts of their assigned essay and speech.

CONCEPT BUILDER 33-D

Composition Evaluation

Complete the following chart.

Who Are The Scouts?

In the early days of this great country of ours, before telephones and telegrams, railroads and automobiles made communications of all sorts so easy, and help of all kinds so quickly secured, men and women — yes, and boys and girls, too! — had to depend very much on themselves and be very handy and resourceful, if they expected to keep safe and well, and even alive.

Our pioneer grandmothers might have been frightened by the sight of one of our big touring cars, for instance, or puzzled as to how to send a telegram, but they knew an immense number of practical things that have been entirely left out of our town-bred lives, and for pluck and resourcefulness in a tight place, it is to be doubted if we could equal them today.

"You press a button and we do the rest" is the slogan of a famous camera firm, and really it seems as if this might almost be called the slogan of modern times; we have only to press a button nowadays, and someone will do the rest.

But in those early pioneer days there was no button to press, as we all know, and nobody to "do the rest": everybody had to know a little about everything and be able to do that little pretty quickly, as safety and even life might depend upon it.

The men who stood for all this kind of thing in the highest degree were probably the old "Scouts," of whom Natty Bumpo, in Cooper's famous old Indian tales is the great example. They were explorers, hunters, campers, builders, fighters, settlers, and in an emergency, nurses and doctors combined. They could cook, they could sew, they could make and sail a canoe, they could support themselves indefinitely in the trackless woods, they knew all the animals and the plants for miles around, they could guide themselves by the sun, and stars, and finally, they were husky and hard as nails and always in the best of health and condition. Their adventurous life, always on the edge of danger and new, unsuspected things, made them as quick as lightning and very clever at reading character and adapting themselves to people.

In a way, too, they had to act as rough and ready police (for there were no men in brass buttons in the woods!) and be ready to support the right, and deal out justice, just as our "cowboys" of later ranch days had to prevent horse-stealing.

Now, the tales of their exploits have gone all over the world, and healthy, active people, and especially young people, have always delighted in just this sort of life and character. So, when you add the fact that the word "scout" has always been used, too, to describe the men sent out ahead of an army to gain information in the quickest, cleverest way, it is no wonder that the great organizations of Boy and Girl Scouts which are spreading all over the world today should have chosen the name we are so proud of, to describe the kind of thing they want to stand for.

Our British Scout-sisters call themselves "Girl Guides," and here is the thrilling reason for this title given by the Chief Scout and Founder of the whole big band that is spreading round the world today, as so many of Old England's great ideas have spread.

I. Organization

___ Is the writer's purpose stated clearly in the introduction? Is there a thesis sentence? What is it?

___ Does the writer answer the assignment?

___ Does the introduction grab the reader's attention?

___ Is the purpose advanced by each sentence and paragraph?

___ Does the body (middle) of the paper advance the purpose?

___ Does the conclusion accomplish its purpose?

II. Mechanics

___ Does the writer use active voice?

___ Does the writer use the appropriate verb tense throughout the paper?

___ Is there agreement between all pronouns and antecedents?

___ Is there appropriately subject/verb agreement?

___ Are the transitions effective and appropriate?

III. Argument

___ Are you persuaded by the arguments?

Scouting for Girls: Official Handbook of the Girl Scouts (New York: Girl Scouts, Inc., 1920), p. 17–18

Research Paper: Rewriting and Submission

Style (Writing and Speaking): Summary
Public Speaking Skill: Summary

First Thoughts

You are almost finished with your research paper! You have finished the first draft. Now, you will need to write one to three more drafts.

Chapter Learning Objectives

In chapter 34 we will finish our research paper.

Look Ahead for Friday

- Turn in a final copy of essay and speech
- Take Weekly Essay/Test

Rewrite your entire paper.

Students should practice saying the following phrases aloud in a speech.

Loose lips sink ships.

The sixth soldier sold his soul to the shepherd.

The big black bug bit the bitter bright burglar.

Round and round the rugged rocks the ragged rascals ran.

Research Paper Benchmark

You should have your topic, thesis statement, preliminary bibliography, a preliminary outline to guide you in your note taking, many notes, and an outline. During this lesson, you will begin the introduction to your research paper.

Assignment Cover Sheet

Can You Create A Sample Cover Sheet Or Two Or Three Types?

An assignment cover sheet is a paper used by students when completing assignments. In this case, the assignment is a research paper. These coversheets generally contain metadata about the assignment (such as the name of the student and the course number). This aids the efficient handling of assignments. Other types of data may be included, depending on the needs of the course and requirements of the instructor.

Title of Project
Name of Student
(Do not use "by")

School
Date

Title of Project
Name of Student
(Do not use "by")
School
Date

Daily Assignment

- Warm-up: Are you glad you took this course?
- Students will complete Concept Builder 34-A.
- Prayer journal: Students are encouraged to write in their prayer journal every day.
- Students should systematically review their vocabulary words daily.

Conclusion

Identify the conclusion in the previous essay, "Who are the Scouts?"

Find the conclusion below.

Of all man's great achievements none is, perhaps, more full of human interest than are those concerned with flight. We regard ourselves as remarkable beings, and our wonderful discoveries in science and invention induce us to believe we are far and away the cleverest of all the living creatures in the great scheme of Creation. And yet in the matter of flight the birds beat us; what has taken us years of education, and vast efforts of intelligence, foresight, and daring to accomplish, is known by the tiny fledglings almost as soon as they come into the world. . . .

One of the mysteries of Nature is known as the FORCE OF GRAVITY. It is not our purpose in this book to go deeply into a study of gravitation; we may content ourselves with the statement, first proved by Sir Isaac Newton, that there is an invisible force which the Earth exerts on all bodies, by which it attracts or draws them towards itself. This property does not belong to the Earth alone, but to all matter — all matter attracts all other matter. In discussing the problems of aviation we are concerned mainly with the mutual attraction of The Earth and the bodies on or near its surface; this is usually called TERRESTRIAL gravity.

It has been found that everybody attracts very other body with a force directly proportionate to its mass. Thus we see that, if every particle in a mass exerts its attractive influence, the more particles a body contains the greater will be the attraction. If a mass of iron be dropped to the ground from the roof of a building at the same time as a cork of similar size, the iron and the cork would, but for the retarding effect of the air, fall to the ground together, but the iron would strike the ground with much greater force than the cork. Briefly stated, a body which contains twice as much matter as another is attracted or drawn towards the centre of the Earth with twice the force of that other; if the mass be five times as great, then it will be attracted with five times the force, and so on.

It is thus evident that the Earth must exert an overwhelming attractive force on all bodies on or near its surface. Now, when man rises from the ground in an airplane he is counteracting this force by other forces.

A short time ago the writer saw a picture which illustrated in a very striking manner man's struggle with Nature. Nature was represented as a giant of immense stature and strength, standing on a globe with outstretched arms, and in his hands were shackles of great size. Rising gracefully from the earth, immediately in front of the giant, was an airman seated in a modern flying-machine, and on his face was a happy-go-lucky look as though he were delighting in the duel between him and the giant. . . .

No doubt many of those who saw that picture were reminded of the great sacrifices made by man in the past. In the wake of the aviator there are many memorial stones of mournful significance.

It says much for the pluck and perseverance of aviators that they have been willing to run the great risks which ever accompany their efforts. Four years of the Great War have shown how splendidly airmen have risen to the great demands made upon them. In dispatch after dispatch from the front, tribute has been paid to the gallant and devoted work of the Royal Flying Corps and the Royal Naval Air Service. In a long and bitter struggle British airmen have gradually asserted their supremacy in the air. In all parts of the globe, in Egypt, in Mesopotamia, in Palestine, in Africa, the airman has been an indispensable adjunct of the fighting forces. Truly it may be said that mastery of the air is the indispensable factor of final victory.

William J. Claxton, *The Mastery of the Air*, 1919, chapter 1

Sample Final Copy

CAUSES OF THE CIVIL WAR
Jessica Stobaugh

I. Introduction: A Tragedy That Could Have Been Avoided

As the Civil War was beginning to unfold, the Southerner Mary Chestnut wrote, "We [the North and the South] are divorced because we have hated each other so!" This hatred led to a bloody and horrible civil war.

For years the question "What caused the Civil War?" has puzzled historians. They have suggested many reasons, but what is the real cause? Slavery was the chief irritant but did not cause the conflict. Both Rachel and Samuel Cormany, typical Civil War contemporaries, supported their government's efforts to quell the Southern rebellion. But neither of them was irritated by slavery. In fact, there were many things that contributed to the Civil War — some more than others. Certainly slavery was a cause but not *the* cause.

The Civil War was caused because Southern and Northern Americans chose not to live together. Again, the operative word is *chose*. They chose to fight a war. The North and the South were always two nations, and by 1860 it was difficult to live together in the same house. It was not impossible, though. They chose to live apart. They had solved their problems before — in 1820 and 1850, for instance. But suddenly in 1860, the political system failed.

The Civil War was the fault of neither the North nor the South. Or rather, it was the fault of both! An expanding economy, a flood of immigrants, the Second Great Awakening, Manifest Destiny, and the failure of the American political system — the combination of these events brought the young republic to the brink of the Civil War. Ultimately, though, the failure of nerve manifested by American political leaders thrust the nation into its bloodiest war in American history.

I agree with a historian's assessment of the causes of the Civil War:

When the Union was originally formed, the United States embraced too many degrees of latitude and longitude, and too many varieties of climate and production, to make it practicable to establish and administer justly one common government which should take charge of all the interests of society. To the wise men who were entrusted with the formation of that union and common government, it was obvious enough that each separate society should be entrusted with the management of its own peculiar interests, and that the united government should take charge only of those interests which were common and general. (Hunter, 1)

What is ironic is that, in a way, the North and the South were fighting for the same thing. They both saw themselves preserving what was vitally important to America. The Confederacy was really fighting for the American dream as much as the Union! They saw themselves as the new patriots. The South had some justification. Many of the Founding Fathers owned slaves (Hunter 1, 9–10). George Washington, Thomas Jefferson, and James Madison were all slave-holding presidents.

In summary, the Civil War was a struggle between conflicting worldviews. Each section held to a belief system that increasingly felt alienated from the other. They disagreed over the power of the federal government; they disagreed over tariffs; and they especially disagreed over slavery and its expansion westward (Williams, 203). However, these disagreements were nothing new and did not bring a civil war. The War was not inevitable. By the middle of the 19th century, these differing viewpoints — coupled with the almost violent change inflicted on America, and the collapse of compromise as a viable option in the political arena — brought the young republic into a horrendous civil war. Americans chose to fight because they were unwilling to choose an alternative.

The first American to observe that the Civil War was avoidable, not inevitable, was former President Buchanan. He argued that the cause of the Civil War was to be found in

> the long, active, and persistent hostility of the Northern Abolitionists, both in and out of Congress, against Southern slavery, until the final triumph of President Lincoln; and on the other hand, the corresponding antagonism and violence with which the advocates of slavery resisted efforts, and vindicated its preservation and extension up till the period of secession.

Buchanan's assumption that the war need not have taken place had it not been for Northern fanatics and, to a lesser extent, Southern extremists, was essentially correct. To put it another way, there was no substantive is-sue important enough in 1861 to necessitate a resort to arms; the war had been brought on by extremists on both sides. The moderate political center refused to solve the problem and left the solution to extremists. The extremists brought on a civil war.

The remainder of this paper will examine several issues whose accumulated effect made the Civil War seem necessary to a generation of Americans.

II. Two Nations, Two Economies

"I heard much of the extreme difficulty of ginning cotton, that is separating it from its seeds . . . I involuntarily happened to be thinking on the subject and struck out a plan of a machine in my mind" (Van Doren and McHenry, 89). The machine was the cotton gin, and the author of this letter was Eli Whitney. More than anything else, the cotton gin made cotton a profitable business and assured its future in the Southern economy.

Originally, cotton had been a minor crop because of the difficulty of separating the fiber from the seeds. In 1793, Eli Whitney's cotton gin solved this problem. In 1800, only about 70,000 bales of cotton were produced in the South. By 1825, cotton production increased 700 percent (Fenton, 185) Demand for cotton of all sorts was growing, especially in England, where new textile factories, with their weaving and spinning machines, created an insatiable appetite. Demand and supply came together when Eli Whitney set his mind to the problem of short-staple cotton and its seeds (Nash, et al., 309). Eli Whitney supplied the technology for cotton to be king, and the industrial revolution supplied the market. By the early 19th century, British and American factories demanded more cotton. The expanding Southern plantation system was ready to meet that demand.

In 1813, Boston Manufacturing Company opened the first textile factory to perform all cloth-making operations by power in Waltham, Massachusetts. Financed with large capital, the company recruited New England farm girls as operatives, boarded them in dormitories, and produced a standard coarse cotton cloth requiring minimum labor skill. By 1826, in Lowell, Massachusetts, one plant turned out two million yards of cloth annually (Van Doren and McHenry, 128). Their production grew more and more over the next few years.

In 1828, a new sore spot appeared in North-South relations. That year Congress raised the tariff on imports, in order to protect native industry struggling to compete with European manufacturers. The South protested loudly over the tariff on the grounds that it favored the North at her expense. She was dependent almost wholly on the North and on Europe for manufactured goods. While an increase in prices would enrich the North, it would mean a rise in the cost of living for the Southerners, with no compensating increase in wealth. In their view, all the benefits of protection were going to Northern manufacturers. Though the country as a whole grew richer, South Carolina grew poorer, with its planters bearing the burden of higher prices. South Carolina planters, and Southern planters in general, sold their products to British industrials, who sold manufactured good to Southerners. When Northern tariffs raised the price of industrial goods, the price of cotton consequently fell. If one British table was worth 30 pounds of cotton, the same table would be worth 50 pounds of cotton after tariffs increased British prices.

Ironically, it was the Southern planter president Andrew Jackson who insisted that tariffs be increased. The protective tariff passed by Congress and signed into law by Jackson in 1832 was milder than that of 1828, but it further embittered many in the state of South Carolina. In response, a number of South Carolina citizens endorsed the states'-rights principle of "nullification," which was enunciated by John C. Calhoun, Jackson's vice president until 1832, in his *South Carolina Exposition and Protest* (1828). South Carolina dealt with the tariff by adopting the Ordinance of Nullification, which declared both the tariffs of 1828 and 1832 null and void within state borders. The legislature also passed laws to enforce the ordinance, including authorization for raising a military force and appropriations for arms.

Resentment reached its highest pitch in South Carolina, which at this time was experiencing a depression because of a drop in cotton prices. The state legislative body both met and threatened to nullify the act of Congress because it favored one section of the country at the expense of another. If carried out, this proposal would have placed the authority of a state over that of the federal government and would have made the Constitution useless.

The Nullification proceeding threw the country into turmoil. Abuse was heaped on South Carolina which, as a result, threatened to withdraw from the Union (Barnes 13). "We, therefore, the people of the state of South Carolina, in Convention assembled, do declare . . . that several acts of the Congress . . . are null, void, and no law, nor binding upon this state, its officers, or citizens" (Van Doren, 146). This was not the first attempt at secession. New England states first suggested it as a possibility with the Hartford Convention Resolutions of 1815. But this was a more serious attempt, and only the vigorous intervention of President Andrew Jackson stopped civil war from occurring.

Until the invention of the cotton gin, the North and the South were primarily farming communities. But the cotton gin brought new value on slaves, profit, and demand in the South. The industrial revolution demanded workers and economic growth.

By the time of the Civil War, America was two nations. Eli Whitney's inspiring ingenuity gave a tragic guarantee that the North would welcome the industrial revolution and the South would reject it. The North would go one way and the South another, and sooner or later they would collide.

III. A Nation of Immigrants

Immigrants furnished much of the labor that made the productive explosion possible and many of the consumers who made it profitable. The industrializing processes that were at work opened job opportunity and uprooted millions in Europe whose occupations became unneeded or whose land was confiscated by the more "efficient." The immigrants moved the United States population up from 4 million to 32 million in just 90 years. American culture simply molded itself around their presence (Weisberger, 783).

Population growth can weaken the economy of a country that is limited in its natural and capital resources. The United States was not so limited and therefore the economy soared (Fenton, 280; Cooke, 273). This was good. What was bad was that bad feelings grew among some Americans toward immigrants. That was called nativism. At the same time, while millions of Americans flooded into Northern cities, very few came South. This only served to accentuate the growing differences between these two American sections. Foreign immigrants damaged an already enfeebled Whig party and created concern among many native-born Americans. To the average hard-working Protestant American, the foreigners pouring into the cities and following the railroads westward spoke unfamiliar languages, wore funny clothes, drank alcohol freely in the grogshops, and increased crime and pauperism. Worst of all, they attended Catholic churches, where the Latin mass and Eucharistic rituals offended those used to the Protestant worship. Furthermore, they sent their children to their own schools. They also seemed content with lower standards of living and would work for lower pay and worse conditions than any American laborers, thus endangering American jobs.

Massive immigration, then, like economic differences, was one of the causes of the Civil War. It brought instability to the North. At the same time, immigrants were flooding into the western territories. These new western immigrants had no wish to compete with black slaves.

IV. Slavery Expansion as a Cause But Not *the* Cause . . .

Rev. Abraham Essick, pastor of Chambersburg Lutheran Church, a moderate unionist, well-educated pastor, and a reliable witness, wrote a friend and admitted that slavery was an issue but not the most important issue of the coming crisis. "Conservative men, who did all in their power to avert the collision before our flag was dis-honored [the fall of Fort Sumter], are now burning with indignation. . . . The government must be sustained, rebellion suppressed and the honor of the nation vindicated. May God defend the right!" He expressed no outrage at slavery and was more concerned about the honor and dignity of his nation and the breaking away of the South from that nation than any other issue (Abraham Essick, May 8, 1861).

Other diarists concurred with Abraham Essick. James Lemuel Clark, a member of the Southern army, dis-cussed the reasons he went to war with "Yankees" but never mentioned slavery as a cause. In 1860, Cooke

County, Texas, where James Lemuel Clark lived, had a population of nearly 4,000 white people and only 65 slave owners! There were only 300 to 400 slaves and they were held by 10 slaveholders (Clark, 20). Another Texan, William A. Fletcher, was delighted when he heard he could fight the Yankees. He even entertained a thought of arming the slaves to fight Yankees, too! (Fletcher, 2). Fletcher and Clark did not fight on the South-ern side for slavery!

As one of the earliest attempts to make sense of this tragedy, the Southern Historical Society concluded in 1876:

> The late civil war which raged in the United States has been very generally attributed to the abolition of slavery as its cause. When we consider how deeply the institutions of Southern society and the operations of Southern industry were founded in slavery, we must admit that this was cause enough to have produced such a result. But great and wide as was that cause in its far-reaching effects, a close study of the history of the times will bring us to the conclusion that it was the fear of a mischief far more extensive and deeper even than this which drove cool and reflecting minds in the South to believe that it was better to make the death struggle at once than submit tamely to what was inevitable, unless its coming could be averted by force. Men, too old to be driven blindly by passion, women, whose gentle and kindly instincts were deeply impressed by the horrors of war, and young men, with fortune and position yet to be won in an open and inviting field, if peace could be maintained so as to secure the opportunities of liberty and fair treatment, united in the common cause and determined to make a holocaust of all that was dear to them on the altars of war sooner than submit without resistance to the loss of liberty, honor, and property by a cruel abuse of power and a breach of plighted faith on the part of those who had professed to enter with them into a union of justice and fraternal affection. (Hunter, 1)

Other evidence that slavery could not have been the cause of the Civil War was the issue of slavery in Brazil. Brazil and America were settled around the same time. Both had slavery. However, Brazil did not have a civil war in order to rid themselves of this injustice (Degler, xviii). Therefore, the presence of slavery, as controversial as it might be, as divisive as it may be, in no way assured that the United States would fight a civil war, just as it did not cause a civil war in Brazil.

What about slavery expansion? This issue is as heated as the issue of slavery. President Lincoln never intended to stop slavery; what he didn't want was slavery expansion. He stated this in his first Inaugural Address:

> Apprehension seems to exist among the people of the Southern states that, by accession of a Republican Administration, their property and their peace and personal security are to be endangered. There has never been any reason-able cause for such apprehension. Indeed, the most ample evidence to the contrary has all the while existed and been open to their inspection. It is found in nearly all the published speeches of him who now address you. (Lincoln, 1).

Lincoln said that there was no reason for the South to choose secession, for he by no means wanted the slaves free. We know that Lincoln changed later, but for now, this was his position. Lincoln, like the Republican Party, was opposed to slavery expansion, not to slavery (1860 Republican National Platform, 1).

If slavery expansion threatened Northerners, the cessation of slavery expansion infuriated Southerners.

> The gospel of prosperity and the defense of bondage were inseparable in the minds of most slave holders. But when they made explicit reference to slavery, masters drew also from an intellectual tradition that reaffirmed their faith in the destiny of the white man as the harbinger of global wealth. In the antebellum South, racism and the gospel of prosperity were joined in symbiotic relation. (Oakes, 130).

The end of no slavery expansion was tantamount to commercial poverty in the mind of most Southerners. The more slavery expansion, the more money for the slaveholders. Lincoln did not want slavery expansion because that meant less money for the paid workers; and what the South wanted was inflated slavery prices. Southerners also needed the ability to expand westward with their slaves, to find rich farmland. The whole controversy about slavery was further exacerbated by Harriet Beecher Stowe's *Uncle Tom's Cabin* (1852). Moderate Northerners thought that it was an exaggeration of slavery. Southerners thought that it was downright libelous! They hated Mrs. Stowe (McCullough, 337). Many Southerners, like my great-great-great uncle Howard, fought for the South even though they had no or few slaves (Stobaugh, 6).

Slavery, then, was an important cause of the Civil War. But it was not the most important cause. In fact, there was no substantive issue important enough in 1861 to fight a civil war. The war was brought on by extremism and misunderstandings on both sides (Grob and Billias, 392).

Another contributing factor was the Second Great Awakening that spread across antebellum America, creating instability and heightened expectations.

V. Fire Across the Land: The Second Great Awakening

While all this was occurring, the Second Great Awakening broke over the country. This was preceded by what was called the Cane Ridge Revival, started in 1800 by a Presbyterian minister named James McGready, who preached against formality and the darkness of the churches. Many people were touched — even the "boldest most daring sinners in the county covered their faces and wept bitterly," and "many fell to the ground, and lay powerless, groaning, praying and crying for mercy." This was the beginning of a great change (Weisberger, 24).

The Second Great Awakening represents the contradiction that was so much a part of American religious history. For one thing, the Awakening was a revival — a phenomenon which we will describe below. On the other hand, the Awakening grew in the fragile air of pluralism, which was both the greatest strength and greatest challenge of American religious life. For instance, the Second Great Awakening flourished in upstate New York, also the place where heretical Mormonism, the only indigenous American religion, originated.

In the 1820s, Charles Finney held a series of revivals in New York state. Finney was known as a "soul-winner" and a man who "made good" in his choice of work, which was to bring men to Christ (Weisberger, 95; Ahlstrom, 653). All this change made Americans more willing to follow their own wishes and not follow the government or other authority. By 1860, more Americans than ever had personal relationships with their God and wished to make personal decisions about where they lived and what they owned. In a real sense, then, when the North tried to take away the Southern slaves, or so they thought, the South saw it as a personal attack on their property and life. They were ready to do whatever was necessary to protect those rights — even if it was rebellion against the government. At the same time, Northern Christians were prepared to cause their Southern brothers to stay in the Union no matter what the cost. The religious revivals of the early and middle 19th century prepared them for this decision.

VI. Manifest Destiny: Will Western States Be Free or Slave?

On top of all the revivals, the issue of slavery expansion, and the tariffs, Americans also claimed a manifest destiny. The phrase "Manifest Destiny" was coined by John L. O'Sullivan, editor of the *Democratic Review*. It advanced the idea that America's superior culture and institutions gave us a God-given right to take over the entire continent (Nash, 448). Manifest Destiny allowed the expansion westward but did not cause it to happen. Occurrences in Texas triggered the government's determination to take possession of the territories west of the Mississippi River (Nash, et al. 448).

Many people in the North opposed the Mexican War. They thought that it was a Southern plot to extend slavery. In 1846, David Wilmot, a congressman from Pennsylvania, introduced an amendment to a bill designed to appropriate $2 million for negotiating an agreement with Mexico. Part of his amendment suggested that slavery should be kept away from any territory acquired from Mexico. A bitter and prolonged debate broke out between those who were for slavery and those who were not. Finally, the Wilmot Proviso, as the amendment was called, was passed in the House of Representatives. However, it failed to pass the Senate (Fenton, 282–83). This debate showed how fragile the unity of North and South was. They had fought a war together because they had no idea about how to live together in peace.

The impulse to expand ran into problems when the nation discussed whether new states would be slave or free. This then led to the failure of the American political system to keep as one these two nations, North and South. Now nothing was working to unify the nations. They could not seem to agree on any ground. In every issue, situation, and problem, they were disagreeing.

VII. Conclusion: No Way To Compromise

So what caused the Civil War? Why did Americans fight one another for four long years, at the cost of 600,000 lives? What did it all mean? The American Civil War occurred because Americans allowed it to happen. They let their differences be more important than their similarities. The government was no help.

Before the Civil War, Americans had done a lot of compromising. In 1820, there was the Missouri Compromise, when Congress took charge of the question of slavery in the territories by declaring it illegal in the huge region acquired by the Louisiana Purchase.

When Andrew Jackson was president (1829–37), a sharp division arose between Northerners and Southerners over the tariff issue. The South favored free trade; the industrial North needed protection. South Carolina asserted superior state's rights and tried to declare the tariff of 1828 null and void within its borders. Jackson confronted South Carolina, and it back down. Needless to say, Jackson was not a favorite in that state.

Next, President Polk's war with Mexico opened the slavery issue again. Should slavery be allowed in the new territories? The Wilmot Proviso (1846), which was supposed to have excluded slavery, became an irritating subject for both the North and the South. It was also being voted on again and again in Congress and successfully held off by Southerners. Abolitionists led by William Lloyd Garrison and others became strong in many Northern circles and called for the immediate emancipation of slaves, with no compensation to slave owners. The majority of Northern whites disliked blacks and refused to support abolition; they did not want to allow slavery in the territories so that they would be preserved for white settlement based on Northern expectations: free labor, dignity of work, and economic progress (Multimedia Encyclopedia Online).

In 1848 Northern impatience with the existing parties helped form the Free-Soil party, which endorsed Martin Van Buren, nominated by the Barnburners, a group of Northern Democrats opposed to extending slavery. The polls gave Martin Van Buren 300,000 votes; he ran a poor third but denied victory to the Democrats. The Whig Zachary Taylor was put in the White House, no one was happy, and the nation was ill-suited to handle the next crisis.

The Compromise of 1850 appeared to have settled the issue of slavery expansion by the principle of popular sovereignty, which said that the people who lived in the Mexican cession territories were to decide for themselves. A new Fugitive Slave Law was passed in 1850. This enraged Northerners because it let slave owners cross into Northern states to claim their runaway slaves.

As the 1850s began, it seemed for a time that the issue of slavery and other sectional differences between North and South might eventually be reconciled. But with the westward expansion of the American nation, all attempts to compromise disappeared, and contrasting economic, political, and philosophical endeavors became more evident. The resulting Civil War altered the American nation.

In 1860, the American political system became completely dysfunctional and began to shatter. The Democrats fractured into Northern and Southern wings, broaching two different candidates for the presidency; the bantam Constitutional Union party aspired to rally former Whigs behind a third. The Republicans, however, were able to assure the election of Abraham Lincoln to the White House.

With great apprehension Southerners had watched the rise of the Yankee-dominated Republican Party, organized in 1856 to be against slavery. They were convinced that the Republican Party was secretly controlled by abolitionists (although most Northerners loathed the abolitionists) and that Yankees believed in using government to administer their moralistic campaigns. In 1859, John Brown led a raid on the federal arsenal at Harpers Ferry, Virginia, hoping to encourage a slave uprising. His action — and his subsequent adoration by some Northerners — helped convince Southerners that emancipation of the slaves, if Northerners attained authority of the country, was inevitable, sooner or later. They then fought a war to protect their rights and property.

Because of slavery and constitutional compromises, America was never a real nation until after the Civil War. That war was essentially fought because the American political system failed to present a compromise that suited the North's demands as well as the South's. The 1850s generation blundered into a needless war because they played on emotions to gain votes rather than face the issues. Agitation over slavery led to mistaken and false sectional images and fanaticism (Crum, 93). Therefore, they fought it out in the great and awful Civil War.

Daily Assignment

- Warm-up: Recommend this course to someone else.
- Students will complete Concept Builder 34-B.
- Prayer journal.
- Students should outline all assigned essays and speech for the week.

CONCEPT
BUILDER
34-B

Conclusion

Identify the type of conclusion each is: SUMMARY or EXPOSITION.

_____When the war finally came to an end on November 11, 1918, and the Central Powers were defeated, the political order and geographical map of Europe had been radically transformed. The Versailles Treaty, the treaty that ended the war, changed the future of the world. The German, Austria-Hungarian, Russian, and Ottoman empires had collapsed and new countries (e.g., Poland) were created. World War I was also partially the cause of the Russian Revolution. The humiliating terms imposed by the Versailles Treaty on German became a rallying cry for the Nazis who rose to power in the 1920s and ultimately precipitated a Second World War.

_____By the end of the Second World War in 1945, the Nazi regime and its accomplices had physically annihilated about 11.5 million people: 6 million Jews, and 5.5 million non-Jews, undesirable "others" — mentally ill, disabled, political opponents, homosexuals, Slavs, Gypsies, Jehovah's Witnesses, "Blacks," and other "undesirables."

Identify the type of conclusion each is: SUMMARY or EXPOSITION.

_____Early 21st-century Chinese society has developed out of some 3,300 years of society. For these 3,000 years China progressed from dynasty to dynasty until it reached the present Communist Republic. The following factors more or less determined Chinese history: 1. The vastness of the land. China is a huge geographical area. 2. Aggressive neighbors. China has few natural, physical barriers to its neighbors. Thus, it had to build things like the Great Wall. 3. Large population. China's ready labor supply delayed the industrial revolution until the 20th century.

_____As Japan emerged as a world power it found new enemies. It fought a war with China and then with Russia. Japan handedly won both wars. Joining the allies to fight Germany in World War I, Japan was able to expand its empire into the Pacific. Increasingly, virulent, fanatical nationalistic leaders began to emerge in Japan. While maintaining a fervent dedication to the emperor, samurai leadership assumed control over the government and led Japan first into war against China (1930s) and against the allies (1941–45). Japan lost both wars. Japan lost World War II but emerged as one of the premier economic powers of the post-World War II world.

Style (Writing and Speaking): Summary

Make every word count. Speak/write precisely and clearly. Use commas and pronouns to cut down on words. Repeat words and phrases for emphasis, but do so carefully. Avoid problems in parallelism. Choose your figurative language carefully. Make sure that it is appropriate to your task and to your audience.

Daily Assignment

- Warm-up: Persuade your parents to let you write another research paper this summer.
- Students will complete Concept Builder 34-C.
- Prayer journal.
- Students should write rough drafts of all assigned essays and speeches.

CONCEPT BUILDER 34-C

Literary Review

Book

Author   Date of reading

I.   Briefly describe:

Protagonist —

Antagonist —

Other characters used to develop protagonist —

If applicable, state why any of the books' characters remind you of specific Bible characters.

II.   Setting:

III.   Point of view: (circle one) first-person, third-person, third-person omniscient

IV.   Brief summary of the plot:

V.   Theme (the quintessential meaning/purpose of the book in one or two sentences):

VI.   Why did you like/dislike this book?

VII. The next literary work I read will be. . . .

Rewrite

Rewrite the following material. All punctuation has been removed.

indian history begins 4,000 years ago india is a success story India's population recently exceeded 1 billion people yet a noted Indian historian said that " although it is difficult to accept, the indians totally lacked the historical sense" the ancient indians made great inroads into astronomy, physics, mathematics, all kinds of literature and arts but never seriously took to documenting their history and their indifference has cost their posterity very dearly civilization, when an agricultural economy gave rise to extensive urbanization and trade the second stage occurred around 1000 bc, when the ganga-yamuna river basin and several southern river deltas experienced extensive agricultural expansion and population growth

Proofreading: Using Your Grammar and Spell Check

One powerful tool you possess for proofreading is your computer software or apps. Microsoft Word and other programs have a feature that allows you to do grammar check. Do a grammar check and spell check of the following paragraph and correct many mistakes.

It has been said that the honor of making the first ascent in an balloon from British soil must be awarded to Mr. Tytler. This took place in Scotland. In this chapter we will relate the almost romantice story of the first ascent made in England. . . .

His craft was a "Charlier" — that is, it was modelled after the hydrogen-inflated balloon built by Professor Charles — and it resembled in shape an enormous pear. A wide hoop encircled the neck of the envelope, and from this hoop the car was suspended by stout cordage.

It is said that on the day announced for the ascent a crowd of nearly 200,000 had assembled, and that the Prince of Wales was an interested spectator. Farmers and laborers and, indeed, all classes of people from the prince down to the humblest subject, were represented, and seldom had London's citizens been more deeply excited.

Many of them, however, were incredulious, especially when an insufficiency of gas caused a long delay before the balloon could be liberated. Fate seemed to be thwarting the plucky Italian at every step. Even at the last minute. When all arrangements had been perfected as far as was humanly possible, and the crowd was agog with excitement, it appeared probable that he would have to postpone the ascent.

It was originally intended that Lunardi should be accompanied by a passenger; but as there was a shortage of gas the balloon's lifting power was considerably lessened, and he had to take the trip with a dog and cat for companions. A perfect ascent was made and in a few moments the huge balloon was sailing gracefully in a northerly direction over innumerable housetops.

Claxton, *The Mastery of the Air*, chapter 4;

Public Speaking: Enunciate Clearly

You should not be guilty of lazy lips; you must speak clearly and slowly. The following is a late 19th-century guide to enunciation.

Key To The Pronunciation Of Therespelling

The long sounds of a, e, i, o, u are represented by ā, ē, ī, ō, ū.

The short sounds of a, e, i, o, u are represented by ă, ĕ, ĭ, ŏ, ŭ.

a, as in air, pair, is represented by â

a, " far, arm, " ä or ah

a, " all, haul, " aw

a, " what, squat, " ŏ

e, " ere, where, " ê

e, " obey, weight, " ā

e, " her, term, " ë

i, " machine, " ē or ee

i, " dirk, whirl, " ï

o, " done, son, " ŭ

o, " woman, " ŏŏ

o, " do, move, " ōō

o, " for, storm, " ô or aw

oo, " soon, moon, " ōō

oo, " foot, good, " ŏŏ

u, " rude, rule, " ōō

u, " push, pull, " ŏŏ

u, " burn, turn, " ü

oi,} " oil, toy, " oi

oy,}

ou,} " found, owl, " ow

ow,}

c, as in city, cite, is represented by s or ç

c, " can, cut, " k

ch, " child, much, " ch

ch, " machine, " sh

ch, " chorus, " k

g, " ginger, " j

n, " think, uncle, " ñ

qu, " require, " kw

s, " these, ease, " z

Obscure vowel sounds, or those which are glided over in a word without any noticeable accent, are unmarked. In those cases where the pronunciation is so evident that mistakes seem improbable, the marks are also omitted.

Daily Assignment

- Warm-up: Describe a Sunday morning at your house?
- Students will complete Concept Builder 34-D.
- Prayer journal.
- Review the assigned text. Keep vocabulary cards.
- This is the day that students should write, and then rewrite, the final drafts of their assigned essay and speech.

Proofreading: Properties of Your Document

Most word-processing programs have a feature that will tell you the properties of your research paper. For instance, in Microsoft Word 2007 you would find that information on the left, bottom part of your screen.

Answer these questions:

How many pages are in your document?

How many words?

What are the margins on your document?

Do you have a header? Footer?

Think Critically.

Write Articulately.

Live Biblically.

	Teacher	Student
American LITERATURE	978-0-89051-672-0	978-0-89051-671-3
British LITERATURE	978-0-89051-674-4	978-0-89051-673-7
World LITERATURE	978-0-89051-676-8	978-0-89051-675-1
AMERICAN HISTORY	978-0-89051-643-0	978-0-89051-644-7
BRITISH HISTORY	978-0-89051-645-4	978-0-89051-646-1
WORLD HISTORY	978-0-89051-647-8	978-0-89051-648-5

Coursework designed by Dr. James Stobaugh: ordained pastor, certified secondary teacher, SAT coach, recognized homeschool leader and author.

Master Books®
A Division of New Leaf Publishing Group
www.masterbooks.net